Becoming *the* Woman
God Wants Me *to* Be

Becoming *the* Woman God Wants Me *to* Be

A 90-DAY GUIDE TO LIVING THE PROVERBS 31 LIFE

DONNA PARTOW

Revell

a division of Baker Publishing Group
Grand Rapids, Michigan

© 2008 by Donna Partow

Published by Revell
a division of Baker Publishing Group
P.O. Box 6287, Grand Rapids, MI 49516-6287
www.revellbooks.com

New paperback edition published 2017
ISBN 978-0-8007-2835-9

Printed in the United States of America

The Library of Congress has cataloged the previous edition as follows:
Partow, Donna.
       Becoming the woman God wants me to be : a 90-day guide to living the Proverbs 31 life / Donna Partow.
          p.   cm.
       Includes bibliographical references.
       ISBN 978-0-8007-3072-7 (pbk.)
       1. Bible. O.T. Proverbs XXXI—Criticism, interpretation, etc. 2. Christian women—Religious life—
   Biblical teaching. I. Title.
   BS1465.52.P37 2008
   248.8′43—dc22   2008007562

Disclaimer: The information provided herein should not be construed as a health care diagnosis, treatment regimen, or any other prescribed health care advice or instruction. The information is provided with the understanding that the publisher is not engaged in the practice of medicine or any other health care profession and does not enter into a health care practitioner/patient relationship with its readers. The publisher does not advise or recommend to its readers treatment or action with regard to matters relating to their health or well-being other than to suggest that readers consult appropriate health care professionals in such matters. No action should be taken based solely on the content of this publication. The information and opinions provided herein are believed to be accurate and sound at the time of publication, based on the best judgment available to the author. However, readers who rely on information in this publication to replace the advice of health care professionals, or who fail to consult with health care professionals, assume all risks of such conduct. The publisher is not responsible for errors or omissions.

      22   23   24   25   16   15   14

Contents

Introduction

Welcome to the next ninety days of your life. These days will unfold whether or not you live them with purpose and passion. You can just mark time, muddle through each day, and stumble closer to the end of your time on earth, or you can choose to "run with perseverance the race marked out for us" (Heb. 12:1). This book is your invitation to run with perseverance. But it's more than an invitation. It's your own personal jumpstart for living the Proverbs 31 life!

I've been following God and studying his Word for nearly thirty years, yet somehow I thought the Proverbs 31 woman was a mythological creature or worse—I thought she was a weapon spiritual leaders use to make all of us ordinary Christian women feel bad about ourselves.

But then I met her in person.

They say the wife of noble character is hard to find, and it's true. But I finally found her, tucked away in the mountains north of Bogotá, Colombia. And having met her, I became convinced that becoming the woman God wants me to be, the woman he describes in Proverbs 31, is not an impossible dream. It's the only goal worthy of my life's devotion.

I had been invited to Colombia to speak at a conference for Christian leaders from throughout Latin America. Afterward my host, Hector Torres of Hispanic International Ministries, invited me to spend a few days with his family at his aunt's home at the base of the Andes Mountains. I didn't know quite what to expect. The bookstore didn't have a travel guide on Colombia. The book they had on Latin America didn't even devote

a chapter to the country, which has been torn by civil war and drug traf-
ficking for the last three decades. It simply said: it's too dangerous; don't
go there. The mountains, in particular, are known for guerilla activity. I
was somewhat apprehensive, to say the least.

Imagine my surprise when I arrived at Hector's aunt's home and stepped
into the most peaceful paradise I'd ever experienced anywhere in the world.
Our hostess, Beatriz Duenas, was the picture of beauty, elegance, and ease
as she welcomed us, showed us to our rooms, and then gave us a tour of
the breathtaking grounds. We walked and talked amid trees bursting with
avocados, bananas, blackberries, guavas, oranges, papayas, plantains, and
tangerines. She showed us her chicken coops, trout pond, coffee crop, and
even her worm farm. Every inch of her property is productive; it's a reflection of a woman who embodies energy, creativity, and productivity.

Breakfast the next morning featured a variety of fresh-squeezed juices,
eggs scrambled with tomatoes, peppers, and onions, and freshly grown
coffee—and every item on the menu was produced right on the property. Our morning walk took us to her favorite place: a small stone and
wrought-iron chapel with wooden benches that looked centuries old.
Beatriz exuded quiet God-confidence as she explained that she has spent
many hours praying, reading, and meditating in this open-air sanctuary.
I knew I was standing on holy ground.

In the early afternoon, following our three-hour horseback ride through
lightly tamed jungle that featured every conceivable shade of green, we sat
by an open-fire woodstove, eating steak from a nearby cattle ranch along
with freshly grown and grilled vegetables. I marveled at the self-sufficiency
of this beautiful place and the beautiful woman who oversaw it all.

But Beatriz's story doesn't begin in this beautiful paradise. Later that
night her story unfolded. In 1950, at the age of sixteen, Beatriz married a
handsome nineteen-year-old, Jose, whom she had met at a relative's wedding two years earlier. A year later she had their first child and three more
daughters followed in fairly quick succession. She worked side by side with
her husband in an auto parts store they began together with borrowed
money. Although still a teenager, Beatriz had a knack for business. The
couple began to prosper. Soon they had a successful corporation, complete
with employees and multiple store locations. They were business partners
and best friends. They were inseparable.

Then on January 23, 1984, at 6:30 p.m., Jose was driving home from work when his car was surrounded by six kidnappers who seized him and, *two months later*, demanded the outrageous sum of thirty million dollars for his release. On March 19 Beatriz paid her husband's captors one million dollars.

She never saw her beloved husband again.

Through the pain of that ordeal, Beatriz began seeking God and learned to walk by faith. She started attending a little church where she found Christians who comforted, encouraged, and sustained her. The believers gave her the strength she needed to make one of the most difficult decisions of her life: to remain in the mountain home her husband loved so much and to continue tending the gardens that brought him such joy. Slowly she began planting money-producing fruit trees, using funds that came in from rental properties in which her husband had wisely invested. She was learning to make it on her own.

Her first major business venture was building four massive chicken coops, which now house forty-eight thousand chickens. She has no regrets about taking out a second mortgage on the house to start this business, because it now generates a very steady income for her and will continue doing so for many years to come.

Then Beatriz began taking classes to learn how the coffee industry operated. Today her coffee harvest fills in the income gap when fruit is out of season and there are no chickens ready to send to market. Somewhere along the line, she started a worm farm—she's quite proud of it, although I bypassed that part of the tour! About six years ago, she added a grouper pond. "It hasn't succeeded yet," she admits, "but time will tell." Given her track record, it's bound to become another success. At age seventy-three, Beatriz still works three to four days a week, energetically managing her business affairs.

But what I will always remember about Beatriz is not her thriving enterprises and the wisdom God gave her to develop multiple streams of income. What I will always remember is the overwhelming peace that permeated her countenance, her home, and her entire surroundings. I'll always remember her as one of the most capable, dignified women I've ever met. In a word, she is altogether *lovely*. There was not an ounce of bitterness or self-pity in her voice as she recounted her losses. There was only

11

gratitude for the goodness of God. I asked her for her secret. *"Forgiveness,"* she answered immediately. "It took me a long time to completely forgive the people who kidnapped my husband and robbed me of all that could have been. But the moment I did, the peace of God overcame me and it has never left."

Beatriz Duenas personifies the peace that passes understanding. It's a peace that's returning to these mountains. "The guerillas used to be active in this area, raiding farms and cattle ranches, destroying people's livelihoods, and trying to intimidate everyone," she recalls. "But I refused to live controlled by fear. I refused to be intimidated and driven out of my own home. Now there are cattle on the hills again." There were tears of both pride and joy in her eyes as she spoke that last miraculous sentence. She knew she had outlasted the guerillas. Even the developer who decided to build a discotheque in her peaceful mountain town didn't stand a chance against her prayers. Day after day she sat in her small chapel, praying for God to intervene. And he did. The disco never opened. The developer did all the work, then sold it to a group of Christians who turned it into a church instead.

Beatriz can laugh at the days to come, not because the days before were so easy, but because she knows her God. Her parting words to me were, "Tell the women they must come to full confidence and assurance that what God has done for me, he can do for them also." Just two short days in the presence of a genuine Proverbs 31 woman gave me that assurance. It's the assurance I pray you'll find in the pages of this book.

There's something else I want to assure you about, too. And this is important. God has been working on Beatriz's life and character for seventy-three years. Do not expect to be entirely transformed into her clone in the next ninety days. Not only is that impossible, it's not even desirable. God has a completely customized plan for your life. Trust him. He has brought this book into your life at this particular time because there are certain things he wants to show you, lessons you need to learn. This book is intended to encourage and educate you; if at any moment you are discouraged, stop and focus on what you are *learning*. You won't be able to apply every lesson or implement every strategy. That's okay. Let the Holy Spirit be your guide as he instructs you day by day.

This journey will be different for every woman who travels it. What will be the same is our final destination of becoming the woman God wants each of us to be. To support you along the way, I encourage you to find at least one partner to work through this material with you, and preferably, join with a group. Of course that's not always possible. You can also visit www.donnapartow.com to find out about the 90-Day Jumpstart online support program.

Program Overview

Here's what you can hope to accomplish on this 90-Day Jumpstart:[1]

Faith

- Complete a comprehensive study of Proverbs 31:10–31.
- Memorize the entire passage, one manageable portion at a time.
- Discover practical, contemporary applications for this ancient biblical wisdom.
- Establish a routine of spiritual disciplines you can follow for the rest of your life.
- Develop the habit of daily Bible reading and time alone with God.
- Pray ninety Scripture-based prayers, which will have both immediate and eternal impact.
- Practice the learned skill of positive prayer journaling.
- Cultivate an awareness of the constant presence of God.
- Increase your biblical knowledge in a broad range of subjects.

Family

- Gain practical insight and advice to improve the quality of your most important relationships.

Fitness

- Begin the habit of a daily prayer walk.
- Learn about the powerful impact of diet on your total well-being.

- Follow a simple cleansing diet, designed to promote greater vitality and weight loss.

Personal Appearance and Fashion

- Develop a well-balanced approach to personal appearance.
- Determine the colors that look best on you.
- Streamline your wardrobe to save time and money.
- Discover when less is more, and when more is more!
- Learn the keys to age-appropriate dress.

Finances and Retirement Planning

- Get your finances in order.
- Start an automatic savings and investment plan.
- Implement a debt-reduction strategy.
- Create a retirement strategy.
- Study basic financial principles from God's Word.

Household Management

- Discover the simple, proven method for keeping yourself and your family on track.
- Get your home in order by de-junking, de-cluttering, and creating a realistic, personalized household routine.
- Discipline yourself to fulfill your obligations and to do so on time.

Ministry

- Turn your home into a center of life and ministry.
- Make your home a mission sending station.
- Incorporate ministry into your life naturally.
- Live your life on mission to fulfill God's purposes for you and the world at large.

Business

- Study what the Bible says about self-employment.
- Discover the importance of developing multiple streams of income.
- Get an overview of real estate investments.
- Consider various business opportunities.

Self-Management

- Learn powerful self-management tools guaranteed to increase your personal effectiveness.
- Maintain a positive attitude by changing your focus.
- Fill your mind with ninety Scripture-based affirmations (personalized statements of God's promises).
- Restore strength and stability to your soul (your inner life of thoughts, decisions, and emotions).

Do these sound like worthwhile goals to you? The best part is that we'll accomplish them together, little by little, using God's Word and relying on the power of the Holy Spirit. Our motto will be "Little bits with consistency." Each day will include spiritual actions and practical actions.

Spiritual

Becoming the woman God wants you to be means, first and foremost, becoming spiritually healthy. To strengthen your spirit, you'll devote time each day to the spiritual disciplines of Scripture memory, Bible reading, praying Scripture-based prayers, and prayer journaling. All four are described below.

SCRIPTURE TO MEMORIZE

The first item on your daily journey is your Scripture to memorize. Every week you will be assigned a new portion of the Proverbs 31 passage to commit to memory. At the end of the ninety days, you will have mastered all of Proverbs 31:10–31. (At the back of the book, you'll find cut-out cards to carry in your purse to help you memorize the verse assignments on the go.)

Passage to Read

Each day you will have a Bible passage to read. For your convenience, I've printed out the entire text right here on these pages.

Guided Prayer

Next, you'll find a Scripture-based prayer derived from the daily passage. Please, don't rush past these. Instead, slowly pray through each one. I would strongly encourage you to pray them aloud. That way, the words become more than just marks on a page; they become the prayer of your own heart. When you not only base your prayer requests on Scripture but actually turn Scripture into a prayer, you don't have to worry whether or not you are praying according to God's will—you are.

Affirmation

Next, you'll have a positive statement, or affirmation, to recite. Most of the affirmations are rooted in Scripture and many are simply rephrased Bible passages. Here again, as you observe how I have done this for ninety days, you will be able to transform Bible verses into affirmations on your own. I cannot overemphasize the importance of these affirmations. I believe they are an extremely powerful component of this ninety-day program.

Practical Actions

God cares about every area of your life, not just the spiritual stuff like prayer. He cares about your total well-being: mental, emotional, relational, and practical. He's concerned about your home, your family, your career, and your finances. He cares about your physical well-being: what you eat and how you care for your body. The Bible is filled with advice for every area of our lives. *Becoming the Woman God Wants Me to Be* will address your total well-being in the following ways.

Implementing Learning

Each day I will give you some action to take to implement in a practical way what you're learning. This is your opportunity to apply the force of your will toward a positive end. It's not enough to think new thoughts or adopt a new belief system; you must take action. Each day we'll take a small step forward together.

Keeping a Personal Notebook

To follow the program as it is intended, you must begin on a Monday. To keep you busy until Monday rolls around, your first assignment is obtaining your Personal Notebook. Other than this book and your Bible, the most important component of this program is your Personal Notebook. It will become your brains and your base of operations. Rather than jotting things on slips of paper or relying on your memory, you'll discover how much more effective you can be when you let your notebook do the remembering for you. The only way the Personal Notebook will work for you is if you make a firm commitment to carry it with you everywhere you go for the next ninety days.

You'll have specific assignments concerning your notebook, so you'll need to purchase the "ingredients" right away. In addition to this personal organizer, which you can buy at an office supply store, you'll find photocopy-ready forms at the back of this book. All of the forms are also available for download-and-print at www.donnapartow.com/forms.

A Jumpstart

As you experience this 90-Day Jumpstart, it's important to remember that it's intended to give you a jumpstart—a fresh start—in a wide variety of areas. It's not intended to be a comprehensive overhaul of any one area. For example, if your home is a mess, you'll get a jumpstart toward transforming it into your dream house. But we're not redecorating it together. If your finances are in disarray, you'll start to get a handle on things and discover some powerful tools that can set you up for life financially. But you'll still have more work to do on day 91. And, of course, that's the whole idea. I want to whet your appetite by giving you a taste of living the Proverbs 31 life so you'll want to continue the always unfolding process of becoming the woman God wants you to be.

I want you to know that I'm excited for you and I'm praying that God will transform your life from the inside out. So let's get jumpstarted!

What You'll Need

What You'll Need to Get Started

Before beginning your 90-Day Jumpstart, you will need to visit an office supply store or personal organization specialty shop. Franklin Covey has stand-alone stores around the country. For the location nearest you, visit www.franklincovey.com. Your Personal Notebook is at the heart of the 90-Day Jumpstart. To begin, you will need

- ☐ a daily planner/organizer designed to hold 5.5" x 8.5" paper (I purchased a combination binder/purse from an office supply store that works extremely well for my needs. If you cannot afford a professional organizer, purchase a three-ring binder.)
- ☐ 5.5" x 8.5" filler paper
- ☐ monthly calendar
- ☐ five blank tab dividers
- ☐ pocket pages (some with and others without zippers)
- ☐ single-hole punch or a hole-punch specifically designed for use with your planner

To begin, insert the monthly calendar and the pocket pages in the front of the binder. Then put in the five tab dividers along with some filler paper after each tab. You will assemble the rest of your Personal Notebook as we progress along this 90-Day Jumpstart together. Get in the habit of carrying it with you *everywhere you go.*

WEEK ONE
FAITH FOUNDATIONS

Place Your Full Confidence in God

Scripture to Memorize

A wife of noble character who can find?
    She is worth far more than rubies.
Her husband has full confidence in her
    and lacks nothing of value.

Proverbs 31:10–11

Passage to Read

"For your Maker is your husband—
    the LORD Almighty is his name—
the Holy One of Israel is your Redeemer;
    he is called the God of all the earth.
The LORD will call you back
    as if you were a wife deserted and distressed in spirit—
a wife who married young,
    only to be rejected," says your God.

Isaiah 54:5–6

Guided Prayer

Dear heavenly Husband, how I thank you for choosing me to be your bride! I don't pretend to understand all that this means, but I do know your Word says it's true. You are my Husband. You are the one who loves, protects, and provides—even if you do it through my earthly husband. I acknowledge that you are the one behind every good thing in my life. It's awesome to know that you are almighty. You have all might, all power in your hands. Therefore no situation in my life and no challenge I'll encounter during these next ninety days will be more than you can handle. Thank you for being a redeemer, the one who can take something worthless and transform it into something valuable. I invite you to redeem every area of my life that has potential for greater value.

Thank you for calling me back to a closer walk with you. At times I have felt deserted, distressed, and abandoned, sometimes by people in my life and sometimes—I want to be honest enough to admit—I've even felt like you have deserted me. Thank you for promising to never leave me or forsake me. The truth is, whenever there's been a distance between us, I'm the one who has walked away from you. I long to draw near to you once more; draw me close to you through the pages of this book. Thank you for calling me back once again. Amen.

Personal

We place the highest value on the scarcest commodities. M&M's are made from cheap ingredients and available for easy grabbing on your way out the door at any convenience store. But you won't find diamonds within reach on aisle nine. No, high-quality diamonds are locked away behind the counter, and only serious buyers get to take a closer look.

Today, more than ever before, a woman of noble character is hard to find. To be noble means to be dignified and gracious. In the Amplified Bible, the word for *noble* is rendered "capable, intelligent, and virtuous." A woman like that is not easy to come by anymore.

God wants us to stand out as women who know we have something valuable to offer the world. We are capable, intelligent, and virtuous women who inspire full confidence in those who rely on us most, whether our husband, children, employer, or co-worker. The people around us can have full confidence in us because we have full confidence in God and we live accordingly.

You can have full confidence in God no matter what season of life you're in right now. Maybe you're a mother at home with small children. Or an empty nester. You may be single . . . or single again. I don't know what situation you're in, but I do know who is in the midst of that situation with you: a loving God who cares so much for you that he paid the ultimate price so you and he never have to spend even one day apart. He laid down his life to ensure that someday you'll be the honored guest at the ultimate wedding in heaven, when Jesus celebrates the church as his eternal bride (see Revelation 21). In today's Passage to Read, God declares himself our Husband. Since we'll be studying in depth the Proverbs 31 woman—the wife of noble character—the passage in Isaiah is an ideal place to start.

You may or may not have an earthly husband, but you do have a heavenly Husband. Married or single, God wants you to be *his* wife of noble character. So this study of Proverbs 31 is relevant to all of us. I want to encourage you to listen for his encouragement along your journey, whether or not you receive any positive feedback from anyone else. You may live with a critical husband or be in an otherwise difficult marriage or family relationship. Remember, you are on the road to becoming the woman *God* wants you to be. Ideally, everyone shares the same goals for you as God does. Hopefully, everyone you know wants you to be the very best you can be, but that's not necessarily the case. Some of you live with people who seem determined to discourage you or people who want to drag you down. Don't focus on human feedback. Focus on your relationship with your heavenly Husband and live to please him.

As God transforms your life, you'll become an ever more beautiful bride and a woman whose noble character eventually brings her praise from the most important people in her life, whether that's your husband, children, extended family, or circle of friends. It may not happen overnight, but I believe someday our children (whether physical or spiritual) will stand up and acknowledge what God has done in and through our lives (see Prov. 31:28). Meanwhile, enjoy the inner satisfaction that comes from becoming the woman God wants you to be.

To begin our journey together, I want you to complete a simple but important exercise: writing your Personal Vision Statement.[1]

1. List two of your unique personal qualities (e.g., creativity, enthusiasm).

2. List one or two ways you enjoy expressing those qualities when interacting with others (e.g., through supporting, inspiring).

3. Assume the world is perfect. Then describe it as you see it—what are people doing, how are they interacting, what does it feel like (e.g., everyone is freely expressing his or her talents in harmonious and loving ways)?

4. Combine your three answers above into a single statement (e.g., "My personal vision statement is to use my creativity and enthusiasm to support and inspire others to freely express their talents in a harmonious and loving way.").

It's really pretty simple. Here's what I wrote:

1. Energetic, powerful
2. Challenging, motivating
3. Everyone is actively serving God by serving others, thereby making the world a better place.

Therefore:

4. My Personal Vision Statement is to use my energetic, powerful communication skills to challenge and motivate Christians to go into all the world, impacting lives and making the world a better place.

There you have your first assignment and your first step toward becoming the woman God wants you to be.

Affirmation: I place my full confidence in God. He has a good purpose for my life.

Practical

Now it's your turn. Become the woman *you* want to be—start with a clear Personal Vision Statement.

1. Two unique personal qualities:

_____

_____

2. How you enjoy expressing these qualities:

_____

_____

3. What people are doing in the ideal world:

_____

_____

4. Combine into one sentence:

_____

_____

Notebook: Assemble your notebook as described on page 19, if you haven't done so already. Write your Personal Vision Statement on the first page of your notebook.

Day 2

Commit Yourself to Time Alone with God

Scripture to Memorize

A wife of noble character who can find?
She is worth far more than rubies.
Her husband has full confidence in her
and lacks nothing of value.

Proverbs 31:10–11

Passage to Read

Very early in the morning, while it was still dark, Jesus got up, left the house and went off to a solitary place, where he prayed. Simon and his companions went to look for him, and when they found him, they exclaimed: "Everyone is looking for you!"

Jesus replied, "Let us go somewhere else—to the nearby villages—so I can preach there also. That is why I have come." So he traveled throughout Galilee, preaching in their synagogues and driving out demons.

Mark 1:35–39

Guided Prayer

Dear Jesus, thank you for coming to earth to show me how to live. I marvel that even though you are the divine Son of God, you still took time to pray to your Father in heaven. Just like me, you had people demanding your time and attention. I chuckle as I can almost hear Simon exclaiming, "Everyone is looking for you!" Sometimes I feel like the whole world wants a piece of me, too. I delude myself into thinking I'm too busy or that I can skip time with the Father and still stay on track. Forgive me, Lord! I notice too, Jesus, how you refocused on your life mission and set your agenda for the day after your time alone. I invite you, Holy Spirit, as my counselor, to show me a solitary place where I can get my priorities straight. I will consider this place and time your official invitation to call me there, morning by morning. Amen.

Personal

The Proverbs 31 woman got up while it was still dark, just as Jesus did. The Bible tells us Jesus left the house to find a solitary place to pray and thus meet with the Father. That may or may not be a realistic option for you on a daily basis. In either case, I encourage you to create a Prayer Oasis. Find an area in your house that you can transform into a beautiful place to meet with God each day. It may be a closet or a corner of a room. (Don't laugh. I used a closet-turned-prayer room for *years*—and it wasn't a walk-in closet, either!) Even if you have only three beautiful decorative items (painting, vase, etc.), put them in a corner with your Bible, Personal Notebook, and pen.

Prayer is an important enough priority that I eliminated our formal dining room (I gave away the furniture!) and transformed it into our family prayer chapel. I outfitted it with a comfortable couch, two rocking chairs, Bibles, prayer and devotional books, small tables with plants, a tabletop fountain, and mementos from various mission trips we've taken. The walls are covered with sacred items: Scripture plaques, crosses, and inspirational artwork.

Henri Nouwen said, "Discipline is the human effort to create the space in which God can be generous and give us what we need."[2] By setting up a specific place to pray, you are creating space in your life for God to bless you. Create the space and make the time to meet with God.

The reason the Proverbs 31 woman's husband could have full confidence in her is because she had full confidence in God. Confidence in a relationship comes from investing time in that relationship. If we want to have something valuable to offer the world, we must first have something of value to offer. It must be more than material things. True, we can rush out the door first thing in the morning in pursuit of stuff to buy and give to our loved ones, but the things of this world are fleeting and have no lasting value. Instead, let's invest our time seeking heavenly treasures, like spiritual insight, knowledge of Scripture, the power to demonstrate the fruit of the Spirit, and the ability to carry the presence of God with us wherever we go.

Any determined, hardworking woman can bring home the bacon and fry it up in a pan. That's no great accomplishment. A woman who is so wise she has figured out how to get the bacon to *come to her* and has trained her children to be servant-hearted enough to *do the frying*—now that's a valuable woman! That's a woman who will inspire confidence in her husband and everyone else who meets her.

If you want to be an inspiration to everyone you meet, meet with God first. If this were an important business meeting, you would make the time and instruct your staff to set up the best conference room in the building and have everything ready in advance. Well, you have important business to do with God, so set up the conference room and have everything ready.

Bruce Wilkinson, author of *The Prayer of Jabez*, observed: "I have yet to find a respected spiritual leader throughout history who had devotions at night."[3] Although I enjoy reading a devotional or Christian book at night, I concur with Wilkinson's observation about the importance of morning time alone with God. Every book and biography I've ever read by spiritual leaders, past and present, and every person ever used mightily of God indicated that meeting with God was their first order of business. Morning devotions set the agenda *and the tone* for the day.

Before you meet with your family, before you face the world, before you do anything else, meet with God. Give him the first half hour or so of your day. This step alone will transform your life. Just think how different your life will be ninety days from now if you take time, every day, to meet with God first! I promise it will be dramatic.

Affirmation: I commit myself to time alone with God.

Practical

Create a specific place for time alone with God, a place where you do nothing else but spend time with him. Equip it with all the tools you need for Bible study, prayer, and meditation. Place your Bible, this book, your Personal Notebook, pens, index cards, tissues, lip balm, and Post-it notes in a small basket. Make it the most inviting place in your entire home and you will be drawn to it like an oasis in the desert.

Establish a lifetime habit of TAG (Time Alone with God). Give God the first thirty minutes (or more) of every day.

Note where you'll meet with God: _____

What time? _____

Write out your commitment to TAG, then sign and date below:

Dear Lord, I hereby commit myself to giving you the first _____ minutes of my day for the next ninety days. I believe you are a rewarder of those who diligently seek you, so I have set my heart on seeking you first. I believe, by faith, that one of the rewards you will give me is supernatural wisdom and the ability to conduct the affairs of my day with greater efficiency so that my TAG will in no way diminish my effectiveness but will in fact increase it. I sign this on _____ (date).

With love,

_____ (your name)

Noteook: Label the first tab divider in your notebook TAG. (We'll be adding more labels and contents to the notebook in the days to come.)

Day 3

Meditate on God's Word

Scripture to Memorize

A wife of noble character who can find?
She is worth far more than rubies.
Her husband has full confidence in her
and lacks nothing of value.

Proverbs 31:10–11

Passage to Read

How can a young [woman] keep [her] way pure?
  By living according to your word.
I seek you with all my heart;
  do not let me stray from your commands.
I have hidden your word in my heart
  that I might not sin against you. . . .
I meditate on your precepts
  and consider your ways.
I delight in your decrees;
  I will not neglect your word.

Psalm 119:9–11, 15–16

Guided Prayer

Dear Lord, it's not easy to keep my way pure in the midst of an increasingly corrupt world. Sexual innuendo is everywhere. Standards of modesty become more and more lax, and I'm hard-pressed to find clothing that honors you and protects the purity of the men around me. The only answer is living according to the principles set forth in your Word, not the standards of this world. Today I'm seeking you with all my heart. Holy Spirit, empower me to walk in obedience, not straying from your commands. Help me as I hide the Word in my heart, so I won't stumble into sin. Train me to do as Jesus did: use the Word of God as a weapon against temptation. Teach me the art of meditation. There's so much mumbo jumbo and distortion in the world, it can be intimidating. But you are my Teacher, so teach me your way of meditation. Right now, I renew my commitment: I will not neglect your Word but will take delight in it. Amen.

Personal

If we are serious about our goal of becoming a capable, dignified, virtuous woman of noble character, we will have to do more than casually read the Bible. We have to meditate on it so it seeps deep down into the fiber of our being. If we want to be women who can stand firm in the face of Satan's onslaught of temptations, then we need the Word of God on our lips. The Bible says, "Out of the overflow of the heart the mouth speaks" (Matt. 12:34). That's why we meditate on the Word and store it in our heart, so that it can flow from our mouth when we need it.

When Satan tempted Jesus in the wilderness (Matt. 4:1–11), Jesus responded with confidence. He *knew* exactly what God's Word said and he used it as a weapon. We need to learn to do the same. When Satan says something to you, you need to open your mouth and say to the devil: "You've got it wrong! *This* is what the Bible says!" Don't be duped like Eve, who fell for Satan's oldest line: "Did God really say . . . ?" (Gen. 3:1). Remember, Satan is the father of lies. The only way to cut through his lies is with the truth. Jesus said, "You shall know the truth, and the truth will set you free" (John 8:32). Memorizing Scripture also helps keep our thoughts pure. When we fill our mind with Scripture, there's less room for all the other junk we usually have hanging around up there.

Unfortunately, New Age gurus and Eastern mystics have given meditation a bad name. When we think of meditation, we think of chanting "ummmmm" with our legs crossed, trying to drive away bad karma. Christian meditation almost sounds like an oxymoron, doesn't it? Nevertheless, meditation is an important tool for our transformation. We need to take back meditation! It was God's idea and his gift to us as his children.

This 90-Day Jumpstart incorporates Scripture memorization as a tool for meditation. Let me encourage you to go beyond rote memorization to genuine meditation. Take time to think about what you are memorizing, to pray over the words even as you say them over and over again in your head. Ask the Holy Spirit to teach you the meaning and application of each word, and let his instruction begin to transform who you are and how you live.

Over the course of the next three months, you will memorize the entire passage of Scripture describing the Proverbs 31 woman. We'll take it one bite-sized portion at a time. I find it particularly helpful to write, write, and rewrite a passage I'm trying to memorize. Go ahead and use any white space available on these pages to rewrite your verse each day or just use scratch paper. Then, every Sunday afternoon you will face your weekly challenge: to fill in the blanks in the cumulative memory Scripture. Each week, the challenge will become harder and harder as we build to the finale. Stay with it. What an amazing accomplishment it will be to commit this vital passage of Scripture to memory! But more than an accomplishment, it will be an awesome opportunity for spiritual growth and will provide material on which you can meditate for years to come.

Affirmation: I meditate on God's Word day and night.

Practical

Cut out the Scripture memory verse cards at the back of this book, place them in one of the binder pockets in the front of your Personal Notebook, and begin carrying these cards around with you wherever you go. Spend an extra fifteen to thirty minutes writing out the verses on index cards and/or Post-it notes. Place these around the house, in your car, anywhere you might have a few extra minutes to review your Scripture memory verses.

Notebook: Create a page labeled SCRIPTURE MEMORY and put it in the TAG section of your notebook. Whenever you encounter a verse you would like to memorize, write it out here for future reference, memorization, and meditation. Add additional SCRIPTURE MEMORY pages as needed.

Day 4

Be a Woman Worthy of Confidence

Scripture to Memorize

A wife of noble character who can find?
    She is worth far more than rubies.
Her husband has full confidence in her
    and lacks nothing of value.

Proverbs 31:10–11

Passage to Read

A wife of noble character who can find?
    She is worth far more than rubies.

Her husband has full confidence in her
and lacks nothing of value.
She brings him good, not harm,
all the days of her life.

Proverbs 31:10–12

Guided Prayer

Dear heavenly Husband, my deepest desire is to become a wife of noble character for you. I know the real test of my character is who I am when no one is watching but you. It's not what I do to impress others or please myself that counts. What matters are those choices I make simply because I want to honor you. I want you to be able to have full confidence in me. I want you to be able to call on me and count on me to do the right thing. Although I'll never attain perfection this side of heaven, I don't want to use this as an excuse for sloppy living. Instead, I want to be a valuable asset to your cause on the earth. I want to bring you good, not harm, all the days of my life. Thank you for loving me. Empower me to live a life of grateful service in response. Amen.

Personal

The Proverbs 31 woman's husband had full confidence in her because she brought him good and not harm all the days of her life. Can your husband or employer or friends have full confidence in you? Do you bring them good, not harm?

As we have already seen, God is our spiritual husband. Are you the kind of woman that God can have full confidence in? Have you ever thought about the idea of bringing God good and not harm?

First, how might we bring him harm? The most obvious way to harm a husband, earthly or heavenly, is driving him to jealousy by pursuing other exclusive relationships. The very first commandment reveals how important this issue is to God. Throughout the Old Testament, God's anger burned against Israel for their adulteries—meaning they pursued other relationships and priorities more than him. Jesus reiterated this when he said, "Seek first his kingdom and his righteousness" (Matt. 6:33). God wants to be first, and when we get our priorities mixed up—when we give him second, third, or tenth place in our heart and on our schedule—we bring him harm.

By contrast, we bring God good by living in such a way that he can have full confidence in us. One of the best messages I ever heard was titled "Can God Trust You?" A good wife is one who does the right thing even when her husband isn't watching, who remains faithful and diligent no matter the circumstances. She is trustworthy.

Can God have full confidence in you? Do you do the right thing even when no human is watching? In private are you the same woman you proclaim to be in public? The Bible assures us that what is done in secret will eventually be shouted from the rooftops (Luke 12:2–3). Don't tell yourself, *This little pet sin of mine isn't doing anyone any harm.* Be trustworthy in secret things so God can have full confidence that you will bring him good, not harm, all the days of your life.

Honestly examine your life. Is there anything you are doing, or failing to do, in your private life that you excuse because it is "secret"? Imagine that your little pet sin became public. Would it harm your reputation, your family, employer, or church? If so, you are already harming God in the eyes of the "great cloud of witnesses" (Heb. 12:1) and have the potential to do far greater harm in the future. Resolve, with God's help, to deal decisively with potentially harmful practices in your life.

When dealing with difficult areas, it helps to have at least one person, an accountability partner, with whom we can be completely open about our struggles, someone who will love us enough to tell us when we are heading in the wrong direction. Be sure you have such a person available to you. If necessary, reach out for help from your local church or support group.

Now is the time, while you are on the journey to becoming the woman God wants you to be, to deal decisively with anything that might hold you back from that goal. Be determined that nothing will prevent you from becoming someone worthy of confidence.

Affirmation: I bring God good, not harm, all the days of my life.

Practical

Identify areas in your life that might hold you back from becoming the woman God is calling you to be. Know your weaknesses, be honest about them, and determine to deal decisively with them. Find an accountability partner and/or support group to help you.

Notebook: In the TAG section of your Personal Notebook, label a blank piece of paper POWER TOOLS. Here you can list Scripture verses, practical tips, and resources to strengthen yourself in weak areas. Also note the name of one person you can call on for help in each area of weakness.

Day 5

Choose to Focus on the Positive

Scripture to Memorize

> A wife of noble character who can find?
> She is worth far more than rubies.
> Her husband has full confidence in her
> and lacks nothing of value.

Proverbs 31:10–11

Passage to Read

Rejoice in the Lord always. I will say it again: Rejoice! Let your gentleness be evident to all. The Lord is near. Do not be anxious about anything, but in everything, by prayer and petition, with thanksgiving, present your requests to God. And the peace of God, which transcends all understanding, will guard your hearts and your minds in Christ Jesus.

Finally, brothers, whatever is true, whatever is noble, whatever is right, whatever is pure, whatever is lovely, whatever is admirable—if anything is excellent or praiseworthy—think about such things. Whatever you have learned or received or heard from me, or seen in me—put it into practice. And the God of peace will be with you.

Philippians 4:4–9

Guided Prayer

Dear Lord, I rejoice in you! Let the joy and rest I find in knowing you be manifested in my life as a gentle and quiet spirit. Thank you for being near. Today I choose, by faith, not to be anxious about anything. Instead, I'm presenting it all to you and trusting you to work all things together for my good. Thank you, Lord. You've been so good to me.

Holy Spirit, teach me how to recognize and remain in the peace of God, even when my circumstances are anything but peaceful. I know that peace guards my heart, my mind, and my health, too. Forgive me for those times when I get so focused on everything that's wrong with my life. That gets me nowhere. Instead, I'm fixing my thoughts on what is *right* in my life: everything that's true, noble, pure, lovely, admirable, excellent, and praiseworthy. Since that sums up Jesus perfectly, all I really have to do is fix my eyes on you. Thanks for making it so simple, Lord. Amen.

Personal

The Proverbs 31 woman was noble and dignified. But there is nothing noble or dignified about a complaining woman. Capable women don't complain. They take action to change the situation or have enough faith to accept the things they cannot change. The best gift you can give yourself and those around you is an optimistic, can-do attitude. Our physical health and emotional well-being are directly tied to our mental state. Scientific research, including a study done at the University of Maryland, has proven this beyond a doubt: joy and laughter are healers. Negativity—and the stress it creates—is a destroyer.[4] Of course, the Bible said it first: "A joyful heart is good medicine but a crushed spirit dries up the bones" (Prov. 17:22 ESV).

One of the most comprehensive studies ever conducted on aging well was the Harvard study. They concluded that people in late midlife with an optimistic viewpoint were 50 percent more likely to live another thirty years than those with a negative outlook.[5]

Lately, I have been spending time with my husband's 104-year-old great-grandfather, Mike "The Chief" Nasco. He still lives independently, drives, works from home several hours a day, and even does his own grocery shopping. In short, he's more active than many people half his age. As of this writing, he was on his way to spend a month at an RV resort to enjoy socializing and boccie ball.[6] Recently he hosted a yard sale with his son. I kid you not! Here's what he had to say about the role of attitude:

> I have always chosen to look at the world—and everyone in it—from an optimistic viewpoint. I find that, when I believe the best in people, it brings the best out of them. Recently I began to second-guess my convictions. All we hear on the news is bad news about the world gone wrong. I began to wonder if there was goodness left in people. So one morning I decided to conduct an experiment. I would greet fifty total strangers and see how they responded. I walked to the nearby bus stop, took a seat, and began greeting passersby. I'm happy to report that forty-nine out of fifty people cheerfully greeted me in return.

People treat us the way we treat them. There is good in everyone if we choose to see it. By believing the best, we bring out the best. The same is true for circumstances that, after all, are largely influenced by people. There is good in every circumstance, even if that good is merely the opportunity to become a more patient, more compassionate, or wiser person. Look for the lesson; look for the positive. Seek and you will surely find.

Of course, if you look for the negative, you can always find that as well. But why would you want to? To me, it's a simple choice. You can choose to see the glass as half empty and be mad or half full and be glad. You can look at all that's right with the world and the people in it and be happy. Or you can look at all that's wrong with everyone and everything and be miserable.

Not only will such a perspective bring you down, rob you of peace, steal your joy, ruin your health, and possibly erase years from your life; it will make the people around you unhappy as well. In fact it will bring others down, rob their peace, steal their joy, and—if they have to live with you—cheat them out of a long, happy, healthy life. So, if you aren't willing to choose optimism for yourself, choose it out of concern for those around you. They'll thank you for it!

A huge step in the journey to becoming the women God wants us to be—capable, dignified, virtuous women—is learning to discipline our minds to focus on what's *right* rather than what's *wrong*. During this 90-Day Jumpstart, I want you to turn your attention to the positive by reprogramming your mind with the truth of God's Word.

"Be transformed by the renewing of your mind" (Rom. 12:1). The mind is a primary battlefield and will either help or hinder our goal of becoming the women God wants us to be. By renewing your mind with positive, personal statements of God's truth, your thoughts become your ally rather than your enemy. That's the reason the daily Affirmation is such a vital part of this program. Keep in mind, however, that it won't be enough simply to read the Affirmation. Frankly, that will do you very little good. You will need to recite the Affirmations aloud, over and over and over, until they begin to transform you from the inside out. As you fill your mind with the truth about who God is and all the good things he has done in the past and desires to do in the future, the negative will eventually get washed away.

As you think new thoughts, your attitude will begin to change. Gradually, with a new attitude, the words you speak and the way you respond will change. Your behavior—the actions you take—will change. Then something wonderful will begin to happen. You'll notice that people respond to you differently. Your circumstances begin to change. It becomes a positive cycle of blessing. Soon you and everyone around you will believe you *are capable* of handling anything that comes your way—with dignity and without complaint. And it all begins with your daily Affirmation.

Affirmation: I choose to focus on the positive, especially the truth of God's Word; therefore my life is filled with positive outcomes.

Practical

Begin reciting your Affirmations daily. Each morning, you can rewrite the day's Affirmation on a Post-it note or index card and carry it with you everywhere you go.

Notebook: Write the daily Affirmations on a sheet of paper labeled AFFIRMATIONS in the TAG section of your Personal Notebook and begin noting any that are especially meaningful to you. You can also write your own affirmations. The friend who introduced me to the power of reciting affirmations devotes an hour a day to this spiritual discipline and credits it with completely transforming her life. Turn to your AFFIRMATIONS page anytime you have a few spare minutes to redeem the time by renewing your mind.

Day 6

Weekly Checkup

Cumulative Scripture Review

> A wife of noble character who can find?
> She is worth far more than rubies.
> Her husband has full confidence in her
> and lacks nothing of value.

Proverbs 31:10–11

Turn verses 10–11 into a Scripture-based prayer:

_____

_____

_____

Practical

Saturday is your day to review and catch up on any unfinished items. Check to confirm that you have completed the following one-time tasks:

- ☐ I created and have begun using a Personal Notebook.
- ☐ I wrote a Personal Vision Statement and recorded it on the first page of my notebook.
- ☐ I created and have begun using a special prayer place.
- ☐ I committed to spend Time Alone with God (TAG).

- ☐ I added the following items to my Personal Notebook: TAG section divider, SCRIPTURE MEMORY page, POWER TOOLS page, and AFFIRMATIONS page.
- ☐ I've confronted areas of secret sin and am developing a battle plan to deal with them.
- ☐ I've found an accountability partner. I cut out the Scripture cards from the back of the book and have put them in the binder pocket.

Check to confirm you are routinely incorporating the following positive changes into your daily routine:

- ☐ I'm using my Personal Notebook.
- ☐ I'm regularly reviewing my Personal Vision Statement.
- ☐ I'm spending time in my prayer place, enjoying TAG.
- ☐ I'm dealing proactively with my secret sins.
- ☐ I'm completing this study every day, practicing the memory verse, and reciting Affirmations daily.

Day 7

Weekly Reflection

Sunday is a great day to devote extra time meditating on the entire Proverbs 31 passage, memorizing your assigned verses, praying, and preparing your heart for the week ahead. Take one day out of every seven to rest and reflect. Do *not* catch up on assignments you did not complete, but *do* schedule them for the coming week.

Fill in the remainder of Proverbs 31:10–11 from memory:

A _____ ___ _____ _____ who can find?

    She is worth ____ _____ _____ _____ .

    Her husband ____ ____ _____ ___ ____

        and lacks _____ ___ _____ .

Weekly Evaluation

1. Am I listening for and hearing God's voice? What is he saying to me?

   _____

   _____

2. Am I increasingly manifesting the fruit of the Spirit: love, joy, peace, patience, kindness, goodness, faithfulness, gentleness, and self-control (Gal. 5:22–23)? What areas look encouraging? What needs prayer?

   _____

   _____

3. What did God teach me during my TAG?

   _____

   _____

4. Which priorities did I live by? Which goals did I pursue?

   _____

   _____

5. Which priorities or goals did I neglect?

   _____

   _____

6. What new thing did I learn—about life, God, my family, and the people around me?

   _____

   _____

7. What are my specific priorities/goals for the coming week?

_____

_____

Take out your notebook and schedule your priorities or goals for the coming week.

WEEK TWO
GODLY HABITS

Day 8

Become Consciously Selective

Scripture to Memorize

> She brings him good, not harm,
> all the days of her life.
> She selects wool and flax
> and works with eager hands.
>
> Proverbs 31:12–13

Passage to Read

> She brings him good, not harm,
> all the days of her life.
> She selects wool and flax
> and works with eager hands.
>
> Proverbs 31:12–13

Guided Prayer

Dear Lord, help me to become more selective! I want to be more selective about the music I listen to, the movies and television programs I watch, and the people I allow to influence my life. Holy Spirit, empower me to be more selective about where I invest my time, money, energy, and other resources. I want to work with eager hands—to be diligent and not self-indulgent. In particular, I recognize the need to be less self-indulgent of my taste buds and far more selective about the food I put in my mouth and on my table. Everything matters to you, and I want to please you in all things. Lord, you know sometimes I have trouble getting in gear in the mornings. I believe you'll give me extra energy as I'm faithful to awake a little earlier each day, just to spend time with you and to get myself and my family off to a good start. Help me to provide for the basic needs of my family and others who rely on me for guidance. Lord, give me supernatural selectivity. Amen.

Personal

The Proverbs 31 woman was selective—she *selected* the wool and flax that was good enough for her to invest her time working with. To be selective means to be discriminating, discerning, and choosy—to be careful about the choices you make. It's the opposite of the mindless living that characterizes so many of us today. The first MK (missionary kid) I ever met had been raised in the Amazon jungle. She said the first time she walked into an American grocery store (as a teenager), with instructions to pick up a box of cereal, she nearly had a nervous breakdown. Why? The selection was overwhelming. The cereal aisle alone contained more food than her entire village grocery. She was faced with so many choices, her head spun.

I've traveled to remote villages in Asia, Africa, and Latin America where people have very few options. There's only one place to draw water, only one market to purchase or barter for goods, only one food staple. Life is difficult yet simple. The more complex the society we live in, the more we need to exercise the art of selectivity. Whether we realize it or not, we're making selections every day. We choose which way we dress and present ourselves to the world. We select the music we listen to, the movies and programs we watch, what we read and believe. We choose how we spend our time and with whom we spend it. We select our friends and even our enemies (although sometimes they select us!).

Unlimited options and unending choices are both a blessing and, in some ways, a tremendous burden. To cope with the complexity, some people let others select for them. They go with the flow and unquestioningly follow the crowd. They take the path of least resistance. They listen to whatever music the radio station puts on the air, watch whatever programming the networks or cable channels choose, wear whatever is popular in the fashion magazines and at the mall.

If we're going to become the women God wants us to be, we're going to have to begin being consciously selective, which means we ask ourselves questions like: Is this the best use of my time, money, energy, and resources? Is this God's highest and best for me? Is it the healthiest thing for my spirit, soul, and body? Is this outfit glorifying to God? Is it modest or does it draw attention to my physical attributes? Do my daily choices reflect my true values or am I taking the path of least resistance simply to avoid the hard work of making conscious selections?

Being selective also applies to this 90-Day Jumpstart. No woman will be able to fully complete every project idea that is introduced here. Carefully consider which areas will be of most benefit to you and your family and focus your attention there.

Begin today to practice being consciously selective.

Affirmation: I am consciously selective about how I invest my time, money, and other resources.

Practical

Analyze each of the following areas, rating yourself on a scale of 1 to 10, with 1 meaning you take the path of least resistance (conforming to the world) and 10 meaning you are consciously selective in that area.

Reading material
Media exposure
Fashion sense
Financial priorities
Family time
Home life
Diet/food selection
Personal appearance
Time usage

What changes do you need to make?

Notebook: Label the fifth tab divider PROJECTS. (We will fill in the other tabs as we proceed.) Here you can list projects and worthwhile things to do with your time. Label one sheet SELECTIVITY. Divide it into three columns with the headings BOOKS TO READ, RECOMMENDED MOVIES, and POSITIVE PROJECTS. You can continually update these lists. As you progress through this Jumpstart, many great ideas will spring to mind that you won't be able to act on because you're too busy with each day's assignments. Write them down! In the future, when you have time available, you can *select* how you want to invest it.

Day 9

Stay Planted in the Word of God

Scripture to Memorize

> She brings him good, not harm,
>   all the days of her life.
> She selects wool and flax
>   and works with eager hands.
>
> Proverbs 31:12–13

Passage to Read

> Blessed is the man
>   who does not walk in the counsel of the wicked
> or stand in the way of sinners
>   or sit in the seat of mockers.
> But his delight is in the law of the LORD,
>   and on his law he meditates day and night.
> He is like a tree planted by streams of water,
>   which yields its fruit in season
> and whose leaf does not wither.
>   Whatever he does prospers.
>
> Psalm 1:1–3

Guided Prayer

Dear Lord, thank you for blessing me. I renew my commitment to you today not to walk with the wicked, stand with sinners, or sit with mockers. Holy Spirit, show me anyone or anything in my life that would lead me in the wrong direction. Help me to find my delight in the study of God's Word by granting me insight. Bring it to life for me as only you can. Teach me how to meditate on Scripture, revealing those passages you want me to focus on. I'm so glad I have you as my personal Bible tutor. Thank you for promising that as I stay planted in the Word, I will be like a tree that yields its fruit in season. I want to be fruitful and to prosper in whatever I do. Now I know the secret: meditating on God's Word. All that I have to do is remain in it. Help me, Lord! Amen.

Personal

The Proverbs 31 woman brings good, not harm, to those who love her—including her heavenly Father and her earthly family. That doesn't happen by accident. This week's memory verse tells us she works with eager hands. If we are to become capable, dignified, and virtuous women, it will take a lot of hard work over the course of many years. And it will mean persevering even when we don't see instant results.

I live in an area of Arizona filled with citrus trees. Last year we didn't get a single lemon from our lemon tree. When everyone else in the neighborhood had trees in full bloom, we didn't have even one flower on any of our three trees (orange, grapefruit, and lemon). Needless to say, I was very unhappy. Frustrated and indignant, too! *Everyone* else in the neighborhood had trees in bloom. How unfair! How bizarre! Then I discovered that my husband had turned off the watering system to do some yard work six months earlier and had forgotten to turn it back on. Mystery solved.

So often, we're tempted to look at the blooms or fruit on someone else's "tree" and feel frustrated or indignant. Why are they prospering when we're not? Is it a mystery? Sometimes, yes. However, for the most part, the world makes sense. It's governed by basic laws like cause and effect, sowing and reaping, and so on. Of course, there are exceptions, disasters, and mysteries. But exceptions are exceptions, disasters are rare, and most of life is not that mysterious. Typically, we reap what we have sown. Things happen for a reason.

God's Word says that a person who meditates on Scripture—who remains faithful and sinks deep roots into the living water—that person will prosper *in season*. However, *in season* may not mean next week. That's the problem for most of us. We want instant results. But the picture God gives isn't instant. A tree begins as a seed planted in the ground. It's watered and nurtured, day after day, without any visible results. That's when so many of us are tempted to give up. Years pass before it yields fruit and even then, only in season.

The person who will be blessed is the one who stays *planted*, who sinks her roots deep into the soil of God's Word. Let me urge you to become a more serious student of the Bible—to study, memorize, and meditate. As you do, God has promised something: you *will* yield fruit in season. Everything you do will ultimately prosper. The Proverbs 31 woman didn't become God's ideal woman overnight, and neither will we. But eventually she became the kind of woman everyone honored—a woman clothed with strength and dignity—and so will we.

Affirmation: I study God's Word so my life is fruitful; everything I do prospers.

Practical

Spend some extra time reading and studying God's Word today.

Notebook: Photocopy the BIBLE STUDY WORKSHEET from the back of this book or download and print it from www.donnapartow.com/BibleStudyWorksheet. Place seven copies in the TAG section of your Personal Notebook. You can begin using your TAG worksheets today or, if it is too overwhelming, keep them on hand for use after you've completed this study.

Day 10

Devote Yourself to Prayer

Scripture to Memorize

> She brings him good, not harm,
>   all the days of her life.
> She selects wool and flax
>   and works with eager hands.
>
> Proverbs 31:12–13

Passage to Read

And the prayer offered in faith will make the sick person well; the Lord will raise him up. If he has sinned, he will be forgiven. Therefore confess your sins to each other and pray for each other so that you may be healed. The prayer of a righteous man is powerful and effective.

Elijah was a man just like us. He prayed earnestly that it would not rain, and it did not rain on the land for three and a half years.

James 5:15–17

Guided Prayer

Dear Lord, I confess this morning that my prayers are not always offered in faith. They are too often offered as a last resort, clouded by doubt and unbelief. I've become so conditioned to the mindset of this world that my first response to sickness (or any other difficulty) is a man-made solution.

Thank you for promising to hear our prayers and raise up those who are sick. This morning I bring before your holy presence all who battle various sickness and disease. Send your healing in our day, just as you did when Jesus and the first disciples walked the earth.

I confess my sins so that nothing will hinder my prayers today. Forgive me, Lord, especially for my tendency to _____. Holy Spirit, show me someone I can trust to confess my sins to so that I might be healed, someone who can hold me accountable and challenge me to become more than I am.

Thank you for the blessed assurance that the prayer of a righteous person is powerful and effective. I stand on the righteousness of Christ. It is through his sacrifice that I have the right to ask and believe that I will receive answers when I pray. What a blessing that we have Elijah as an example! It's so tempting to think, *He was a super-prophet! No wonder his prayers were powerful and effective, but I'm no Elijah!* You've made it a point in your Word to remind us that Elijah was just like us.

If prayers are powerful enough to heal the sick and control the rain, there's nothing prayer cannot accomplish. Holy Spirit, cleanse me of all unrighteousness so that, with Christ's righteousness on me, I can pray with great power and effectiveness. Amen.

Personal

The Proverbs 31 woman worked with eager hands, but I believe she also understood that some work can only be accomplished on our knees. It's been aptly said, "When we work, we work. But when we pray, God works." A discerning woman knows when to cease from human labors and fold her eager hands in prayer.

The great revival preacher Leonard Ravenhill accurately proclaimed: "No Christian is greater than his prayer life." We often hear teaching on the importance of tithing our money. Let me suggest that you seriously consider tithing your time in prayer. You can do the quick math: that's about two and a half hours per day. Before you toss this book across the room, stop and think for a minute. How many hours a day do you breathe? When praying becomes as natural as breathing, you'll soon discover you can pray without ceasing.

Prayer is not just something we do. Prayer is a mindset, an attitude, an atmosphere we create. As we learn to cultivate the presence of God, walking moment by moment with a conscious awareness that we have a friend who sticks closer than a brother, a counselor who is always near, a teacher who is always speaking, then every waking hour becomes a prayer.

Paul admonished us: "Devote yourselves to prayer, being watchful and thankful" (Col. 4:2). It begins with what saints in former times called the morning watch. We begin our day watching for God, asking him what his priorities for the day are. Then we continue watching, with an attitude of gratitude, for the opportunities he has prepared in advance for us. Watch and pray throughout the day and you'll find you have plenty to be thankful for.

Be especially alert to what I call God-prompted prayer—those prayer requests that obviously come directly from God's heart to ours. Think about promptings that come in the middle of the night or out of nowhere. Think about promptings to pray for things we weren't even thinking about. *Those* are the prayers that often get the most dramatic and immediate results. But we will miss them if we are not watching.

Recently my friend Carla shared an experience she had with prompted prayer. Her daughter had broken her arm and was returning to the doctor for a one-week follow-up visit. God prompted Carla to pray that the arm would be completely healed and the cast removed that very day, even though the emergency room doctor had projected many weeks of recovery. Her adolescent son, who is struggling with his faith, was sitting in the backseat of the car as Carla prayed aloud over her daughter before entering the doctor's office.

"That's so ridiculous, Mom," he said contemptuously. "You know that's not going to happen."

Carla continued praying, "Lord, I ask you to do this to show my son just how real and powerful you are."

After X-rays to determine how well the bone was setting, a doctor (not the one they had seen at the emergency room) came in and began cutting off the cast, asking casually how many weeks it had been in place. When her daughter replied, "Six days," the doctor said there must be some mistake. But he reexamined both sets of X-rays and declared it a miracle! Her arm was perfectly sound. To prove it, she even did a handstand!

The purpose of prayer is to bring *heaven's power to bear on earth's circumstances*. We can literally invite heaven to invade earth, declaring to God the Father: "Your kingdom come, your will be done on earth as it is in heaven." Then prayer becomes the bridge that links heaven and earth. But we must listen to those promptings.

Two weeks ago, I emailed a woman I hadn't seen in nearly a decade, telling her the Lord had laid it strongly on my heart that her mother needed prayer for her health. The woman did not acknowledge my email, but I just found out this morning that her mother had a heart attack yesterday. Would more focused prayer have averted the heart attack? Only God knows for sure.

As you spend time in prayer, each morning and throughout the day, take time to *listen*. If you have your notebook handy, write down what you sense *God* is saying and focus your prayer effort accordingly. Too many of us have a one-sided approach to prayer. Our total focus is on what *we* want to say to God. Let your prayers become a two-way conversation and see what a difference it makes. Prayer can be the ultimate adventure. Or it can be nothing more than a glorified gripe session. The second approach will do you no earthly good; the first will bring down the power of God. Which do you prefer?

Ask the Holy Spirit to teach you how to be prayerful, watchful, and thankful. You'll be amazed what a difference it makes in your life—and what a difference you begin to make in the lives of others. God will use a woman of prayer to bring about much good in the world all the days of her life.

Affirmation: I devote myself to prayer, being watchful and thankful.

Practical

Begin today with an attitude of prayer and watchfulness. Then carry that with you throughout the day: being prayerful, watchful, and thankful.

Notebook: Create a PRAYER page in the TAG section of your Personal Notebook. Note prayer requests that people share with you. More important, note those things God lays on your heart.

Day 11

Sleep in Peace

Scripture to Memorize

> She brings him good, not harm,
>   all the days of her life.
> She selects wool and flax
>   and works with eager hands.

> Proverbs 31:12–13

Passage to Read

> To the LORD I cry aloud,
>   and he answers me from his holy hill. *Selah*
> I lie down and sleep;
>   I wake again, because the LORD sustains me.
> I will not fear the tens of thousands
>   drawn up against me on every side.

> Psalm 3:4–6

Guided Prayer

Dear Lord, I cry to you and I believe you will answer me. Forgive me for all the times I've cried to everyone else instead of you. Forgive me for expecting answers from mere mortals when you alone have the wisdom and power I need.

Thank you for the healing gift of restful sleep. As I trust in you, my sleep will be sweet. Holy Spirit, I invite you to take charge of my sleep patterns. Teach me how to unwind so I can maximize my sleep, and guide me to the correct number of hours for sleep. I may not be getting enough or perhaps I'm indulging in too much sleep. You created me, so you know how much I need. Please reveal that to me.

Lord, I release all fear, knowing you are the God of the universe and you will work all things together for my good, for I love you and have been called according to your purpose. This knowledge alone frees me to release my anxiety and to sleep in peace. I give it all to you because I trust you. Thank you for being so trustworthy. Amen.

Personal

The Proverbs 31 woman worked with eager hands, not exhausted ones. Although the passage tells us she did indeed burn the midnight oil when the occasion demanded it, her ability to consistently perform at a high level would have required the right amount of sound sleep. Tomorrow we're going to talk about the importance of waking up and jumpstarting your day. But before we do, we have to look at one of the major reasons people *don't* get a great start each day. They don't sleep well at night.

Insomnia is now an epidemic in America. Too many of us lie awake half the night, wracked with anxiety. If you think that doesn't take a toll on your physical, emotional, and spiritual health, think again. Sleep deprivation is a critical factor in weakening our immune system and making us vulnerable to a broad range of ailments. Researchers indicate that people need seven to eight hours of restful sleep each night. For the record, research also proves that "catching up" on missed sleep doesn't work.

The psalmist declared: "I will lie down and sleep in peace, for you alone, O LORD, make me dwell in safety" (Ps. 4:8). Notice the phrase "I *will.*" It's a decision. You don't have to remain a victim of insomnia. There are several practical things you can do to prevent anxiety from robbing you of needed sleep.

Modify your eating habits. Ideally, you should eliminate caffeine altogether. Of course Americans consume four hundred million cups of coffee *per day*, so I'm probably wasting my breath. Besides, I enjoy the occasional cup of Starbucks myself. But a cup is a far cry from *a pot*, which is what many people are now drinking. At the very least, stop consuming caffeine by noon. You should minimize your sugar intake and eliminate all sweets and refined carbohydrates after dinner. If you must have a treat, have it at lunch rather than dinner.

Create the right environment. The ideal sleep atmosphere is dark, quiet, and cool. Several hours before bed, turn down the lights in your house to signal that sleep time is approaching. It's better not to exercise at night, particularly within two hours of bedtime. Your mattress should be supportive and less than ten years old. For maximum health and comfort, be sure to wash your linens weekly. Use your bedroom for sleep only; do not pay the bills or operate a home business from a desk next to your bed. Having those distractions so close to your pillow will surely interrupt your sleep.

Establish a nighttime routine. Find a way to unwind. Take a bath, read to your children, read a devotional, review your Scripture verses, drink a cup of hot lemon water, or do something else relaxing. The important thing is *routine*. Do the same thing every night. Always end your routine by getting into bed at the exact same time. The routine cues your mind and body that sleep time is coming. Make sure your nighttime routine *excludes* television. Watching television in bed is one of the leading predictors of insomnia. If you have a TV in your bedroom, remove it immediately.

Keep your Personal Notebook by your bed. One reason we toss and turn is because the minute our head hits the pillow, we start thinking of a million things that need to be done or issues that are bothering us. When this happens, reach for your notebook, jot down your concerns, and forget about them. You'll be amazed how quickly you fall asleep and how much more peaceful that sleep is when you empty your mind of your concerns and put them into your Personal Notebook.

Engage in positive conversation. Many couples make the mistake of complaining about the day or disputing about the bills after the children are in bed at night. Big mistake on every level. You and your husband can and should pray together about your concerns, turning your anxieties into prayer requests. But don't have a gripe session right before sleeping and then wonder why (1) your love life is in a rut and (2) you don't sleep well.

You can dramatically improve the quality of your sleep by improving your diet, establishing a nightly routine, turning your concerns into prayers, and choosing to think and talk about what's right in the world rather than what's wrong. I promise you'll see improvement in your spiritual, mental, emotional, and physical health. As a result, you'll make better decisions and be able to work with eager hands throughout the day.

Affirmation: I lie down and sleep in peace.

Practical

Write out a proposed bedtime ritual along with some thoughts on how following this routine will improve your life. Now, go to bed on time, today and every day!

Commit to a specific bedtime: _____.

Notebook: Label the second tab divider PERSONAL in your Personal Notebook. Create a page entitled EVENING ROUTINE. Rewrite your proposed bedtime ritual, including a specific bedtime. You'll refine this in the days to come.

Day 12

Be Diligent

Scripture to Memorize

> She brings him good, not harm,
> all the days of her life.
> She selects wool and flax
> and works with eager hands.
>
> Proverbs 31:12–13

Passage to Read

> Go to the ant, you sluggard;
> consider its ways and be wise!
> It has no commander,
> no overseer or ruler,
> yet it stores its provisions in summer
> and gathers its food at harvest.
> How long will you lie there, you sluggard?
> When will you get up from your sleep?
> A little sleep, a little slumber,
> a little folding of the hands to rest—

and poverty will come on you like a bandit
and scarcity like an armed man.

Proverbs 6:6–11

Guided Prayer

Dear Lord, thank you for the example of the ant. I want to consider its ways and become wise. I marvel at how self-motivated the ant is. It doesn't need the promise of a paycheck or the corner office to keep busy. It doesn't need a calendar to recognize the times and seasons. It's driven by an internal sense of mission and controlled by an internal clock. Lord, that's what I desire.

I confess that in the past I've found it difficult to stay on task unless I had someone hovering over me or some other external motivator. I've struggled to find self-motivation born of self-control. Yet I know self-control is part of the fruit of the Holy Spirit. Teach me how to nurture that fruit.

Lord, I also confess that sometimes I sleep more than my body requires. I sleep for emotional reasons—to escape my responsibilities or to indulge my yearning for comfort. Other times, I don't sleep enough as I frantically try to do it all and be it all. Holy Spirit, I invite you to bring your wisdom and conviction to bear on my sleep habits. I want to be well balanced, even in the area of sleep, because I know my adversary, the devil, prowls around like a roaring lion looking for someone to devour . . . or someone to lull to sleep. Lord, be my alarm clock. Wake me morning by morning, inviting me to spend the day with you. Amen.

Personal

I did it. I went out and watched an anthill last night just to get fresh inspiration. Ants work relentlessly! I'm not sure I'd recommend we start lugging around food that weighs twice as much as we do (although I've seen people do it at buffets), but the Bible does say, in the Passage to Read, that we can learn a lesson from the ant.

You don't have to run yourself ragged to please God, but he does call us to hard work and diligence. Like the Proverbs 31 woman, we should work with eager, not reluctant, hands. Even if you have a job outside the home, with a boss hovering over you to keep you motivated, you are your own boss when it comes to running your household. (Well, you may have a husband who's in charge!) The message of the ant is particularly relevant for those of you who, like me, spend most of your time at home. The easiest thing in the world is to become lackadaisical; the hardest is to stay focused and on task. I don't have all the answers to self-motivation, but I do have one secret weapon that helps: put the laws of physics to work for you.

Newton's first law of motion states that a body at rest tends to stay at rest, while a body in motion tends to stay in motion. Get the law of inertia working for you, rather than against you, by getting in gear early. I'm not a morning person, but I've figured out (the hard way) that the direction I set in the morning is where the day heads.

Snooze, snooze, you lose. I'm sure the snooze button was inspired by the devil. It's *his* secret weapon against Christians. The devil is never too busy to rock the cradle of a sleeping saint. If he can get you to snooze away the thirty minutes you would have, could have, and should have spent with God, the devil has the upper hand against you for the rest of the day. Think about it.

Commit to a specific wake-up time, which should ideally be at least thirty minutes before the rest of your family awakens. Don't lie there dreading the day. Don't keep hitting the snooze button. Don't tell yourself "in a few minutes." Get up and get going. The first words out of your mouth should be, "This is the day that the Lord has made. I *will* rejoice and be glad in it." Jump up out of bed and announce, "Look out, world, here I come!" In fact I want to live my life in such a way that when my feet hit the floor in the morning, the devil yells, "Oh, no, she's up!" Your morning sets the tone for the entire day, so make sure it's a positive note.

My father worked as a truck driver for almost thirty years and never once set an alarm clock. Instead, each night before he went to bed, he asked God to wake him up on time. He said God never failed him. So go ahead and set your alarm clock but try an experiment. Ask God to awaken you when you've had enough sleep. You may find, as I have recently, that he wakes you up just before the alarm rings. It's so wonderful to awake naturally rather than being jarred into consciousness by a blaring noise.

God may even show you that you need less sleep than you think you do. As we age, our bodies need less sleep. I am not advocating sleep deprivation. But I am advocating wisdom—listening to God and listening to your body. If you awaken an hour earlier than normal and find that you are dragging through the day, lesson learned. But if you feel fine—or maybe even better—you've added an hour to your day and vitality to your hours. Oversleeping is just as bad for you as inadequate sleep.

God promises that if we ask him for wisdom, he will answer without finding fault. Ask him to show you the right amount of sleep for you. When you've had your sleep, get up and get going so you can work with eager hands to bring good, not harm, to those you love.

Affirmation: I am diligent like the ant. I consider its ways and grow wise.

Practical

Set your alarm for seven hours (eight hours if you are under thirty-five) from your appointed bedtime. When the alarm goes off (or if you awaken having had a reasonable amount of sleep), get up and get going. Try this for a week. Then adjust fifteen minutes upward or downward, depending on your energy level, until you determine the ideal number of sleep hours for you.

Make it an adventure to see how many mornings you can awake *before* your alarm goes off. God will do this for you. Let God prove himself faithful to awaken you morning by morning. Set your alarm as a backup, but don't rely on it. When you awake, don't lie there waiting for the alarm to ring. Get up and get going. When it rings, go turn it off and praise God for the jumpstart you've had on the day. Reflect on all the tranquility you've experienced and how much less stress you and your family will experience.

Notebook: Add a MORNING ROUTINE page to the PERSONAL section of your notebook. Create a routine that puts the law of inertia to work for you.

Day 13

Weekly Checkup

Cumulative Scripture Review

> A wife of noble character who can find?
> She is worth far more than rubies.
> Her husband has full confidence in her
> and lacks nothing of value.
> She brings him good, not harm,
> all the days of her life.
> She selects wool and flax
> and works with eager hands.
>
> Proverbs 31:10–13

Turn verses 12–13 into a Scripture-based prayer:

_____

_____

_____

Practical

Saturday is your day to review and catch up on any unfinished items. Check to confirm that you have completed the following one-time tasks:

- ☐ I created a PROJECTS section tab in my notebook.
- ☐ I began a list of positive books, movies, and projects (for future reference).
- ☐ I printed out several copies of the BIBLE STUDY WORKSHEET and inserted them into my Personal Notebook.
- ☐ I started a PRAYER page in my notebook.
- ☐ I created a PERSONAL section tab in my notebook.
- ☐ I created an EVENING ROUTINE page in my notebook.
- ☐ I created a MORNING ROUTINE page in my notebook.

Check to confirm you are routinely incorporating the following positive changes into your daily routine:

☐ I'm using my Personal Notebook.

☐ I'm regularly reviewing my Personal Vision Statement.

☐ I'm spending time in my prayer place, enjoying TAG.

☐ I'm dealing proactively with my secret sins.

☐ I'm completing this study every day, practicing the memory verse, and reciting affirmations daily.

☐ I'm becoming consciously selective about how I dress and how I use my time and resources.

☐ I'm becoming a more serious student of the Bible.

☐ I'm practicing the presence of God, being watchful, thankful, and prayerful.

☐ I'm following my EVENING ROUTINE and going to bed on time.

☐ I'm inviting God to awaken me each morning, saying no to the snooze button, and following a MORNING ROUTINE.

Day 14

Weekly Reflection

Sunday is a great day to devote extra time meditating on the entire Proverbs 31 passage, memorizing your assigned verses, praying, and preparing your heart for the week ahead. Take one day out of every seven to rest and reflect. Do *not* catch up on assignments you did not complete, but *do* schedule them for the coming week.

Fill in the remainder of Proverbs 31:10–13 from memory:

A _____ ___ _____ _____ who can find?

She is worth ____ _____ _____ _____.

Her husband _____ ____ _____ ___ ____

and lacks _____ ___ _____.

She brings him _____, _____ _____,

    all the _____ ____ _____ _____.

She selects _____ _____ _____

    and works _____ _____ _____.

Weekly Evaluation

1. Am I listening for and hearing God's voice? What is he saying to me?

2. Am I increasingly manifesting the fruit of the Spirit: love, joy, peace, patience, kindness, goodness, faithfulness, gentleness, and self-control (Gal. 5:22–23)? What areas look encouraging? What needs prayer?

3. What did God teach me during my TAG?

4. Which priorities did I live by? Which goals did I pursue?

5. Which priorities or goals did I neglect?

6. What new thing did I learn—about life, God, my family, and the people around me?

_____

_____

7. What are my specific priorities/goals for the coming week?

_____

_____

Take out your notebook and schedule your priorities or goals for the coming week.

Week Three
Healthy Eating

Purge Your Pantry of Harm

Scripture to Memorize

> She is like the merchant ships,
>   bringing her food from afar.
> She gets up while it is still dark;
>   she provides food for her family
>   and portions for her servant girls.
>
> Proverbs 31:14–15

Passage to Read

> She is like the merchant ships,
>   bringing her food from afar.
> She gets up while it is still dark;
>   she provides food for her family
>   and portions for her servant girls.
>
> Proverbs 31:14–15

Guided Prayer

Dear heavenly Father, thank you for blessing us with the gift of food. Thanks for taste buds that can savor all the wonderful things you've created, and even for the gift of sight and smell that enhance the dining experience. Lord, I confess that sometimes I've allowed my senses to overrule common sense. I've served my family food that was convenient but wasn't really food at all. I want to become like the Proverbs 31 woman who brought her family food from afar. She was willing to go the extra mile to provide the very best for her family.

Holy Spirit, empower me to resist the ever-present temptation to feed my family convenience foods rather than real, healthy food. Give me wisdom to make necessary changes with grace and humor, so my family will be able to adjust and even share my enthusiasm for healthier living.

God, thank you for providing for us so abundantly that we have choices about which foods to eat. I pray, right now, for people around the world who don't have enough to eat and lack clean drinking water. Help me to be grateful without forgetting those in need and without becoming self-indulgent. Amen.

Personal

The Proverbs 31 woman went the extra mile to bring her family quality food, whether that meant spending the extra money for imported goods or getting up early to make sure everything was prepared properly. Even though she had household help, she was still in charge of providing the food. Her family may not have even been aware she was going to so much extra trouble, but she knew and God knew.

There are some things we do for our family just because we know it's the right thing to do. They may not appreciate it; they may even resent us for it. Sometimes they fight us tooth and nail, and the battle hardly seems worth waging. One of those right things is trying to ensure that our family eats a healthy diet. What a challenge that is in today's culture!

I made a hilarious mistake the other day while working on this manuscript. I typed, "She brings him food, not harm, all the days of her life." When I reread it, I laughed so hard I almost fell on the floor. Then I called my husband, and he thought it was a great idea to bring him *food, not harm*. He declared (joking, of course), "You've brought me enough harm. Can I have some food now?" Unfortunately, a lot of what we bring our families is harm, not food.

Today we're going to take a quantum leap forward toward our goal of bringing our family food—real food—and not harm. We're going to purge the pantry. It's not difficult. In fact, last month my eleven-year-old daughter did it and filled two trash bags while watching television. Use this three-step process:

1. If it's been sitting in there for more than a year and it's unlikely you'll use it in the next year, throw it out. I don't care if it has a shelf life of eternity. Throw it out.
2. Now check labels for expiration dates. If it's expired, throw it out, unless you have a compelling reason to keep it.
3. While checking labels, if it has a list of ingredients you can't pronounce, then it's not really food at all. It's a bundle of man-made chemicals with tremendous potential to bring harm to your family; it's not good. Throw it out. This is where you need to be battle-hardened, because your children may be very unhappy indeed when you throw out their favorite nonfood food. But your arms are strong for the task, so never fear.

After you've done these three things, if you still have time and energy, you can organize what remains. I would give you an elaborate organizational system, but it's beyond the scope of this book. This program is designed to jumpstart you in a broad range of areas. Now is not the time to get bogged down in minutia. We're dealing with the big picture. For now, do what can be done in the pantry *in one day*. Tomorrow we'll move on to another area. If you want to devote extra time to the pantry—or any other area—on Saturday, that's terrific. Saturday is your catch-up day.

One final suggestion: although I like warehouse stores for some items, I don't buy pantry items there. They tend to come in huge containers. Unless you are feeding six mouths or more, you're probably better off stocking your pantry with the reasonable-sized containers found at your local grocery store.

Affirmation: I bring my family food, not harm!

Practical

Purge your pantry using the three-step process.

Day 16

Resolve to Control Your Eating Habits

Scripture to Memorize

She is like the merchant ships,
bringing her food from afar.
She gets up while it is still dark;
she provides food for her family
and portions for her servant girls.

Proverbs 31:14–15

Passage to Read

But Daniel resolved not to defile himself with the royal food and wine, and he asked the chief official for permission not to defile himself this way. Now God had caused the official to show favor and sympathy to Daniel, but the official told Daniel, "I am afraid of my lord the king, who has assigned your food and drink. Why should he see you looking worse than the other young men your age? The king would then have my head because of you."

Daniel then said to the guard whom the chief official had appointed over Daniel, Hananiah, Mishael and Azariah, "Please test your servants for ten days: Give us nothing but vegetables to eat and water to drink. Then compare our appearance with that of the young men who eat the royal food, and treat your servants in accordance with what you see." So he agreed to this and tested them for ten days.

At the end of the ten days they looked healthier and better nourished than any of the young men who ate the royal food.

Daniel 1:11–15

Guided Prayer

Dear Lord, thank you for including the story of Daniel in the Bible. I know everything that's written was included for my encouragement and instruction. It's amazing to think that these four teenagers had the courage to take a stand against the culture, even though they were captives in a foreign land. They weren't willing to *go with the flow*, not even in the area of diet.

I must confess that my tendency is to be conformed to the pattern of this world when it comes to my eating habits. What an inspiration to read about believers who were willing to say God is God over every area of our lives, not just the so-called spiritual stuff!

What's really encouraging about this story is the outcome. When they chose food *you provided* (vegetables and water) rather than food the world had prepared, they were blessed.

Holy Spirit, strengthen me to make better food choices. Help me escape autopilot mode and really begin to think before I eat. I resolve, beginning today, to put this to the test for the next ten days. I'm going to eat *your food* (specifically, vegetables and water). At the end of that time, let's see how I look and feel. I'm excited about this new adventure. But I'll need your help, Holy Spirit, to stand firm in this resolve. I know you'll help me. Amen.

Personal

The Proverbs 31 woman brought her food from afar. She was willing to go to extra trouble to ensure that she and her family ate right. Daniel is another example of someone who believed it was important to observe healthy eating habits, even when doing so involved a lot of extra effort. The Proverbs 31 woman didn't eat healthy because it was convenient; she was willing to do what was inconvenient. The same is true for Daniel. He put himself on the line and put his guardian to a great deal of inconvenience to eat healthily. If you hope to follow in their footsteps, don't expect eating healthily to be convenient for you. Eating healthily has always taken extra effort and it always will. But it's worth it.

You've probably heard the old joke about Daniel. It's said that the reason the lions couldn't eat him was because he was all backbone. Unfortunately many Christians today are all wishbone and no backbone. We need to be like Daniel. He took control of what he ate and, when the real test came, even the lions couldn't eat him up.

What's eating you? Maybe if you resolve to control what you eat, you would make some progress in the battle against what's eating you. If you're like most women, one item high on your list is your concern about weight gain. It seems almost everyone these days is battling at least an extra ten or fifteen pounds. If you're like me, it's a constant battle: up and down, up and down like a yo-yo. Sound familiar?

Daniel *resolved* to take charge of his eating habits. The word *resolve* is fascinating. It means:

1. to reduce to first principles
2. to remove obscurity by analysis
3. to fix in opinion or purpose
4. to determine in mind
5. (in Algebra) to bring all the known quantities to one side of the equation, and the unknown quantities to the other, in order to resolve an equation

The last definition is perhaps the most helpful. If you want to know what to eat and what *not* to eat, let resolve be your guide. Move all the known quantities to one side (if you *know* what it is, you can eat it). Move all the unknown quantities to the other side (if you can't even *pronounce* it and have no idea what it is, *don't* eat it). Pretty simple formula, isn't it? And I'll bet you sat in Algebra class saying, "When will I ever use this in the real world?"

You can read the rest of the story about Daniel and his three teenage friends for yourself. In a nutshell, it says they not only *looked better*, they were healthier physically. Can a change in diet have that dramatic of an impact? I believe the answer is yes. Don't take my word for it. Put it to the test yourself. For the next ten days, resolve to eat and drink only vegetables and water. At the end of ten days, see how much better you look and feel.[1]

Best of all, research indicates that children take their eating cues from the adults in their lives. You've heard it said, "You are what you eat." Well, your kids are what you eat, too. If you live on junk food, so will they. If you model healthy eating, there's a fighting chance they might just follow in your footsteps. Make the changes for your sake and your family's sake.

Affirmation: I resolve to exercise control over my eating habits.

Practical

Take the ten-day vegetable-and-water-resolve challenge and begin your new diet today.

Notebook: Mark your calendar for ten days of eating and drinking only vegetables and water. If the thought of living without protein horrifies you, add tofu, nuts, seeds, some peanut butter, or cheese to your celery sticks.[2]

Day 17

Limit Your Sugar Intake

Scripture to Memorize

She is like the merchant ships,
    bringing her food from afar.
She gets up while it is still dark;
    she provides food for her family
    and portions for her servant girls.

Proverbs 31:14–15

Passage to Read

When you sit to dine with a ruler,
    note well what is before you,
and put a knife to your throat
    if you are given to gluttony.
Do not crave his delicacies,
    for that food is deceptive.

Proverbs 23:1–3

Guided Prayer

Dear Lord, I'm so blessed to share all my meals with the King of kings. Thank you for all the good things you provide, including my daily bread. I acknowledge that it's often a challenge to eat wisely when I dine out at restaurants with family and friends or when I go to special events. I don't want to hurt anyone's feelings by making an issue about food, but at the same time, I want to exercise wisdom.

I'm amazed how strongly worded this proverb is—that I'd be better to put a knife to my throat than give in to gluttony. Help me to view gluttony as the serious sin that it is and to take my eating habits as seriously as you do. I confess that sometimes I *do* crave the delicacies that are put right in front of me and don't often enough exercise proper self-control. Instead, I allow myself to be deceived by food that looks good, even though it isn't good. Holy Spirit, empower me to escape any bondage in my life in the area of food, so that I can glorify God at all times, in every area of my life. Amen.

Personal

The Proverbs 31 woman provided food for her family and portions for her servant girls. Since everyone rose up and called her blessed, I believe it's safe to assume she fed them the right food in the right portions. Have you ever noticed that overweight parents often have overweight children? It's not genetics. It's eating habits! Today we'll discuss the type of food we choose for our families and ourselves; tomorrow we'll explore the issue of portion control.

I think it's interesting that the very first recorded sin involved a woman being tempted by food that looked too good to pass up. I don't know about you, but I am certainly in no position to judge Eve! I *love* food that looks good to eat, like donuts, cookies, and cakes. I'm always tempted to indulge my taste buds even though I know these foods will lead me into sin. How? They alter my blood sugar and make me irritable within thirty minutes. Then I get depressed because my clothes don't fit. I find it fascinating that Adam and Eve both needed new outfits after demonstrating their inability to resist food temptations. Wow! Things haven't changed that much after all these centuries, have they?

For now, let's look at "delicacies," specifically sugar. Now, I love sugary treats as much as anyone. I've definitely been known to eat my share of Oreos, especially when someone hurts my feelings. But just because we do it, doesn't mean it's wise. Proverbs 25:28 says, "Like a city whose walls are broken down is a man who lacks self-control." Imagine in ancient times, two neighboring cities constantly at war with one another. Their first line of defense against enemy attack was the city walls. That's the reason it was so important that they be strong and fortified, and they had to be guarded at all times with watchmen up on the towers. Now imagine how foolish it would be if one city decided to tear down its *own* walls, literally making itself defenseless against the enemy. How stupid is that?

Did you know that sugar literally breaks down your immune system? If you don't exercise self-control in your consumption of sweets, your body is just like an unprotected city. The walls of your defense system are broken down, opening the way for colds and flu, not to mention hypoglycemia, diabetes, and weight gain, which leads to a host of illnesses, including heart disease. Once again, we see that every word in the Bible was written for our benefit, not to spoil our fun. Even the statements in the Bible that appear metaphorical turn out to be literally true.

Consider this:

- Six teaspoons of sugar in one sitting will decrease your immune function by 25 percent.
- Twelve teaspoons of sugar will decrease your immune function by 60 percent.
- Twenty-four teaspoons of sugar will decrease your immune function by 92 percent.[3]

You're probably thinking, *Good thing I don't consume that much sugar.* You're probably wrong. The average American adult consumes thirty-two teaspoons of sugar per day. That's 120 pounds of sugar per year. One can of Coke contains more than eight teaspoons of sugar. Remember, twenty-four teaspoons was enough to just about shut down your entire immune system. And we wonder why we feel sick and tired.

You have an enemy. In fact you have three of them: the world, the flesh, and the devil. The entire world system is your enemy. When you refuse to exercise self-control, you leave yourself wide open to destruction. Self-control is your personal city wall. It's your first line of defense. Don't be like a city with broken-down walls. Protect your immune system by limiting your sugar intake. And don't forget to protect your family's immune systems by providing them with the right kind of food, too.

Affirmation: I limit my sugar intake, lest I become like a city whose walls are broken down.

Practical

Pray right now, asking the Holy Spirit if you've been guilty of the sin of gluttony. Begin to limit your intake of sugar.

Remember: Today is day two of vegetables and water.

Day 18

Eat Reasonable Portions

Scripture to Memorize

> She is like the merchant ships,
>   bringing her food from afar.
> She gets up while it is still dark;
>   she provides food for her family
>   and portions for her servant girls.
>
> Proverbs 31:14–15

Passage to Read

> My [daughter], pay attention to what I say;
>   listen closely to my words.
> Do not let them out of your sight,

keep them within your heart;
for they are life to those who find them
and health to a man's whole body.

Proverbs 4:20–22

Guided Prayer

Dear heavenly Father, I come before you as your daughter today. I'm choosing to pay close attention to your words and have committed myself to keep your Word before me through regular reading. Holy Spirit, strengthen me with wisdom and diligence as I study and store the Word in my heart.

Thank you for the promise that your Word will bring life and health to my whole body. I believe that I can experience wholeness in spirit, soul, and body. As I keep my mind at peace, meditating on the Word, I'll be enabling my body to do what you created it to do: heal and restore itself. Thank you for the power of your Word. Not only does it renew my mind, strengthen my will, and soothe my haywire emotions, it even brings health to my body. You are such a wise and loving God! Thank you. Amen.

Personal

The Proverbs 31 woman provides both food and *portions* for those under her care. Not only is it important for us to provide those we love with the right quality of food, we also need to exercise control over the portions we serve. Americans are suffering from a severe case of *portion distortion.* We no longer have a realistic sense of what a reasonable portion of food even looks like.

A study at Rutgers University:

compared what people currently perceive to be a typical portion size to what was perceived as appropriate two decades ago. More than 175 young adults were invited to select typical portions of 8 meal items for breakfast or 6 for lunch and dinner. Their selections were compared with a similar study conducted 20 years previously. The foods with the greatest difference in portion size between the two studies were those served and consumed from a cup or bowl. Servings of orange juice, cornflakes, and milk increased by 40, 20, and 30 percent, respectively.[4]

To get an idea of what a reasonable portion of food looks like, draw an imaginary line through the middle of your plate. One-half of your plate should be filled with vegetables and fruits. Divide the other half into two equal parts: one section for protein and the other for whole grains.

America has become a nation of inadvertent gluttons, thanks to the supersizing that abounds in restaurants and homes. Once upon a time, gluttony was considered one of the most serious sins a Christian could commit. It was included on the list of the seven deadly sins. The church took overeating seriously because they knew it had far-reaching ramifications. At its core, gluttony proves we value the flesh more than the spirit. That's a very destructive mindset. But have you ever heard a sermon preached against overeating?

What we eat, and how much we eat, has a profound impact on our body, soul, and spirit. God's ideal woman, as portrayed in Proverbs 31, doesn't just live for the moment. She lives with an eye on the future. She proactively plans to age well. According to the Harvard Study described in *Aging Well* by George Vaillant, being overweight is one of the top six hindrances to aging well.[5] Literally, it's right up there with smoking and alcohol abuse.

Conversely, one of the leading predictors of longevity is moderate eating and a healthy body weight. Almost every known centenarian had a lifelong habit of low caloric intake. I had a dear friend who lived to be 103. Whenever I visited him, he would serve tea and cookies, Fig Newtons to be precise. He gave each guest one or two. Not half a bag—one or two.

Smaller portions are the key. If you must have M&M'S, eat a handful, not an entire king-size bag. If you are dying for a cookie, eat one. Don't bake and eat an entire batch. One of my best friends has a small square of Hershey's dark chocolate every day. That's her chocolate fix. She knows it's there for her, so she doesn't act like a parched woman in the desert when she's faced with the temptation to gorge herself on chocolate.

Moderation. It's anti-American. That probably explains why—despite our vast resources and advanced health care system—we are among the unhealthiest people on the planet. The United States recently ranked forty-second in longevity among nations of the world, *behind* Guam and Jordan.

Digestion is one of the most taxing jobs our body must undertake. When we force our body to devote too much time and energy to digestion, it becomes a drain on the entire system. Overeating is truly one of the most destructive things you can do to your own body, right behind living a stressful (translate that: refusing to trust God) lifestyle.

Here's a simple strategy you can begin to implement immediately: never clean your plate. That's right. I'm suggesting you do the *opposite* of what your mother taught you. Always make it a point to leave a little of each food item on the plate, with the exception of raw or steamed vegetables. You're protesting: "Oh, but that's wasteful!" Would you rather be wasteful or have a full waist? When confronted with the choice, ask yourself this question direct from Scripture: "Is not life more important than food?" (Matt. 6:25). Which is more important: a few scraps of wasted food or killing yourself by overeating? If you really feel that strongly about not wasting food, you can gather up the fragments that remain and eat them at your next meal. But remember to leave something on the plate at *that* meal, too.

And while you're at it, begin to watch the portions you serve to others. The Proverbs 31 woman gave *portions* to her servant girls. She didn't hand over the whole bag of Fritos and turn them loose. She exercised wisdom.

Psalm 103:5 says that God "satisfies your desires with good things." Learn to satisfy your hunger with good things: time with God or good friends, fresh air, long walks. When you're feeling blue, feed on the Word of God instead of downing a gallon of ice cream. Don't live to eat; eat to live. One of the most practical ways to transition from living to eat to eating to live is by reducing your portion sizes. That's precisely your assignment, beginning today.

Affirmation: I eat reasonable portions.

Practical

Begin using an eight- or nine-inch plate, rather than the typical eleven- or twelve-inch dinner plate. Don't take seconds of anything but vegetables. Consciously reduce your portion sizes and never, ever clean your plate! One helpful tool is The Portion Plate, available at www.theportionplate. com, a nine-inch plate with visual aids to remind you, at every meal, exactly what a reasonable portion looks like. They have two plates, one for adults and one for children.

Remember: Today is day three of vegetables and water.

Day 19

Plan Ahead for Healthier Eating

Scripture to Memorize

> She is like the merchant ships,
>   bringing her food from afar.
> She gets up while it is still dark;
>   she provides food for her family
>   and portions for her servant girls.
>
> Proverbs 31:14–15

Passage to Read

This day I call heaven and earth as witnesses against you that I have set before you life and death, blessings and curses. Now choose life, so that you and your children may live and that you may love the LORD your God, listen to his voice, and hold fast to him.

Deuteronomy 30:19–20

Guided Prayer

Dear Lord, thank you for the gift of choice, even though it sometimes feels like a burden. It seems life would be better if everyone just automatically did the right thing all the time. But you created us in your image, granting us the power to choose which path to follow. I'm so thankful that you've given us your Word and in it you've set before us life and death, blessings and curses. All of heaven and earth bear witness that you've made clear to humanity what the consequences of obedience and disobedience look like.

Today I choose life, not just for my own sake but for the sake of my children and all who will come after me. Holy Spirit, lead me in right pathways and empower me to choose wisely. I love you, Lord. I'm listening for your voice and holding fast to you. Speak to me and hold me, too. Amen.

Personal

We began this week by purging our homes of all the nonfood food hiding in our pantries. Today we talk about America's favorite source of harmful not food: fast-food restaurants. The Bible tells us that the virtuous woman is like the merchant ships, bringing her food from afar. We all know the grocery store is always farther than the nearest fast-food restaurant. And the grocery store with healthy food is always even farther! But even if it means we have to get up while it is still dark to provide food, real food, for our family, that's what we need to do.

Fast-foodaholism is rampant. If you have any doubt about that, drive down most any street in America—or pretty much anywhere else in the world these days—and the number of fast-food places testifies to our obsession. More often than not, we pull into a fast-food place because we're hungry, we're in a hurry, and it is *not* "from afar"—it's right in front of us. Because we didn't take time to plan or prepare ahead, our waistlines (and cholesterol levels) will pay the price.

You realize, of course, that the reason it's called fast food is because it's better to fast than to eat the food? In recent years, many of these restaurants have begun offering healthy alternatives. Still, even though we choose the healthier options, the food is much more expensive than eating at home.

The way to save money and calories is by eating the old-fashioned way: home cooking. Your Personal Notebook can help. Once a week, take time to plan your meals using the combination MENU PLANNER/GROCERY LIST that you will add to your notebook today. If you notice something running low during the week, note it on the grocery list in your notebook, rather than on the refrigerator door. After all, you won't be taking the refrigerator door to the grocery store, but hopefully, you've disciplined yourself to carry your Personal Notebook with you at all times. By planning ahead and shopping accordingly, you avoid the late-afternoon panic: *What's for dinner?* and the even more exasperating, *If only I had* _____, *I could fix* _____.

Be sure to have on hand plenty of fresh fruits, vegetables, seeds, nuts, and whole grains. Then, before you run out the door, you can grab some *healthy* snacks to take with you. A little preparation goes a long way, especially when you have to go *afar* to pick up your kids at soccer practice on the way to the orthodontist.

Let me introduce two secret weapons that may help. First, the Crock-Pot. If you don't have one and haven't discovered the joy of Crock-Pot cooking, you are really missing out. What I love is that everyone can have dinner at a different time without too much disruption. I can spoon out a bowl for Tara at 4:00 p.m. and sit and chat with her while she enjoys dinner; then when my husband comes in at 8:00 p.m., I can serve him a bowl that's just as delicious and nutritious without making another mess in the kitchen. You can throw the ingredients in the Crock-Pot the night before or early in the day and just let it simmer.

For those evenings when you know everyone can sit down at the same time (miracle of miracles), the easy answer is the meal-assembly kitchens that have popped up in shopping centers all over the nation. The one a block from my home is called My Girlfriend's Kitchen and their motto is "The best idea since the invention of the wife." They take care of all the grocery shopping, recipe planning, chopping, slicing, dicing, and cleanup. You can schedule an appointment to go in and assemble twelve "ready to cook" entrées to store in your fridge or freezer. The session takes about two hours but will feed your family for two weeks. Each entrée comes in a disposable aluminum pan, so there's no cleanup either during or after the meal. That alone is worth the price of admission in my book. The advantage of planning and cooking ahead should be obvious.

You don't have to assemble twelve meals, although you get a discount. You can go in and assemble just one dinner, if you are so inclined. Also they offer the option of ordering a meal to be assembled on your behalf, which you can then simply pick up or have delivered to your home—for an additional fee. Find out if there is a location near you by visiting www .mygirlfriendskitchen.com or check your newspaper for local alternatives. My best friend in Ohio uses Entrée Vous (www.entreevous.com), which actually sounds even more affordable. The cost is comparable to a delivered pizza, so it's a great deal.

If the price of delivered pizza is outside your budget (and let's be honest, for many families today, it certainly is), let me suggest the book *Once-a-Month Cooking* by Mary-Beth Lagerborg and Mimi Wilson. You can also check out www.frugalmom.net or simply google the phrase "once a month cooking" for recent additions. Don't forget to involve your kids in the cooking process too. It's good for them and good for you, too.

With a little advanced planning, you and your family can eat healthier, and probably you won't have to go that far to make it happen.

Affirmation: I plan ahead for healthier eating.

Practical

Investigate meal-assembly kitchens in your area.

Notebook: Label the third tab divider HOUSEHOLD. Photocopy from the back of the book or download and print the MENU PLANNER/GROCERY LIST worksheet (www.donnapartow.com/grocerylist). Insert several copies. Print a few extras and store in one of the pockets.

Remember: Today is day four of vegetables and water.

Day 20

Weekly Checkup

Cumulative Scripture Review

A wife of noble character who can find?
    She is worth far more than rubies.
Her husband has full confidence in her
    and lacks nothing of value.
She brings him good, not harm,
    all the days of her life.
She selects wool and flax

and works with eager hands.
    She is like the merchant ships,
        bringing her food from afar.
    She gets up while it is still dark;
        she provides food for her family
        and portions for her servant girls.

Proverbs 31:10–15

Turn verses 14–15 into a Scripture-based prayer:

_____

_____

_____

Practical

Saturday is your day to review and catch up on any unfinished items. Check to confirm that you have completed the following one-time tasks:

- ☐ I purged my pantry of nonfood foods.
- ☐ I resolved to follow Daniel's example by eating vegetables and water for ten days.
- ☐ I switched to smaller plates to help control food portions.
- ☐ I added a HOUSEHOLD section tab to my notebook.
- ☐ I added MENU PLANNER/GROCERY LIST worksheets to my notebook.
- ☐ I have found a meal-assembly kitchen near my home.

Check to confirm you are routinely incorporating the following positive changes into your daily routine:

- ☐ I'm using my Personal Notebook.
- ☐ I'm regularly reviewing my Personal Vision Statement.
- ☐ I'm spending time in my prayer place, enjoying TAG.
- ☐ I'm dealing proactively with my secret sins.
- ☐ I'm completing this study every day, practicing the memory verse, and reciting affirmations daily.

☐ I'm becoming consciously selective about how I dress and how I use my time and resources.

☐ I'm becoming a more serious student of the Bible.

☐ I'm practicing the presence of God, being watchful, thankful, and prayerful.

☐ I'm following my EVENING ROUTINE and going to bed on time.

☐ I'm inviting God to awaken me each morning, saying no to the snooze button, and following a MORNING ROUTINE.

☐ I'm exercising control over my eating habits and limiting sugar intake.

☐ I'm using smaller plates and controlling food portions.

☐ I'm planning ahead for healthier eating.

Remember: Today is day five of vegetables and water.

Day 21

Weekly Reflection

Sunday is a great day to devote extra time meditating on the entire Proverbs 31 passage, memorizing your assigned verses, praying, and preparing your heart for the week ahead. Take one day out of every seven to rest and reflect. Do *not* catch up on assignments you did not complete, but *do* schedule them for the coming week.

Fill in the remainder of Proverbs 31:10–15 from memory:

A _____ ___ _____ _____ who can find?

    She is worth ____ _____ _____ _____.

Her husband ____ ____ _____ __ ___

    and lacks _____ __ _____.

She brings him _____, ____ ____,

    all the _____ __ ___ ____.

She selects _____ _____ _____

    and works _____ _____ _____ .

She is like _____ _____ _____ ,

    bringing her _____ _____ _____ .

She gets up _____ ___ ___ _____ _____ ;

    she provides _____ ____ ____ _____

    and portions _____ ____ _____ _____ .

Weekly Evaluation

1. Am I listening for and hearing God's voice? What is he saying to me?

   _____

   _____

2. Am I increasingly manifesting the fruit of the Spirit: love, joy, peace, patience, kindness, goodness, faithfulness, gentleness, and self-control (Gal. 5:22–23)? What areas look encouraging? What needs prayer?

   _____

   _____

3. What did God teach me during my TAG?

   _____

   _____

4. Which priorities did I live by? Which goals did I pursue?

   _____

   _____

5. Which priorities or goals did I neglect?

_____

_____

6. What new thing did I learn—about life, God, my family, and the people around me?

_____

_____

7. What are my specific priorities/goals for the coming week?

_____

_____

Take out your notebook and schedule your priorities or goals for the coming week.

Remember: Today is day six of vegetables and water.

Week Four
STRENGTHENING YOUR BODY

Day 22

Walk to Boost Energy

Scripture to Memorize

She considers a field and buys it;
> out of her earnings she plants a vineyard.
She sets about her work vigorously;
> her arms are strong for her tasks.

Proverbs 31:16–17

Passage to Read

Do you not know that in a race all the runners run, but only one gets the prize? Run in such a way as to get the prize. Everyone who competes in the games goes into strict training. They do it to get a crown that will not last; but we do it to get a crown that will last forever. Therefore I do not run like a man running aimlessly; I do not fight like a man beating the air. No, I beat my body and make it my slave so that after I have preached to others, I myself will not be disqualified for the prize.

1 Corinthians 9:24–27

Guided Prayer

Dear Lord, thank you for calling me to run the race of life with you. Forgive me for the times when I've sat idly on the sidelines or failed to put forth my best effort. Too often I've done the bare minimum and wondered why there was no joy in the journey. I want to run in such a way as to get the prize, and that means going into strict training. Holy Spirit, I need you to be my personal trainer. I don't want to run like a man running aimlessly or fight like a man beating the air. I want to run like a woman who knows there's a crown in store. Thank you for promising me a crown that will last forever.

Everything around me beckons me to seek comfort and convenience. So few people are running. So many are taking the path of least resistance. That's not what you have in mind for me. It's not what I want either. Empower me to beat my body and make it my slave. Teach me the secret of self-control so that after I've preached to others, I myself will not be disqualified for the prize.

Lord, I want to run a race that honors you. I need your help to run with perseverance the race marked out for me. Thank you for promising to get me across that finish line. I'm fixing my eyes on you. Amen.

Personal

The Proverbs 31 woman set about her work vigorously, and her arms were strong for her tasks. To be vigorous means energetic and full of life; it's the opposite of sluggishly dragging yourself through the day, downing cups of coffee to keep yourself moving. Instead of relying on caffeine to get you going in the morning, why not rely on a morning walk instead? It's the fastest, safest, and easiest way to stay vigorous and strong.

Walking burns about the same number of calories per mile as running but is easier on the joints and has a much lower risk of injury. Studies have shown that brisk walking is associated with substantial declines in the incidence of coronary problems in women,[1] can reduce or eliminate high blood pressure,[2] strengthens bones,[3] and increases levels of HDL (good cholesterol), reducing the risk of coronary artery disease. A Harvard study found that women who take a brisk walk each day can cut their risk of developing type 2 diabetes *in half*. According to the Centers for Disease Control and Prevention, regular physical exercise performed most days of the week will reduce your risk of dying prematurely, reduce high blood pressure, and reduce your risk of developing colon cancer.

But perhaps the greatest benefits of walking are not physical but spiritual and emotional. Walking is a great time for praying and meditating on Scripture. It even boosts endorphins, the neurotransmitters that elevate your mood and overall sense of well-being.

Make the commitment to walk at least three mornings per week, and soon you'll discover that you really are able to set about your work more vigorously. And if you swing your arms in the air as you walk, you'll find that they will be strengthened for your tasks. As an extra bonus, you'll save lots of time getting dressed in the morning, because all your clothes will fit and look great.

You can walk alone, of course, but there are some definite advantages to having a walking partner. And it shouldn't be hard to find one, because almost every woman wants to:

- improve her overall vitality and energy level
- lose a few pounds
- spend quality time with a friend
- have a prayer partner

Walking with a partner will accomplish all these goals and more. Although I try to pursue an active lifestyle, I find it much easier to stay committed when I have a walking partner. Knowing that someone is counting on you is the best motivation to get up and go. Otherwise it's just too tempting to make up excuses. Believe me, I know. The Bible says no temptation has seized us except what is common to woman. And God is faithful. Whenever we are tempted he will provide a way of escape (see 1 Cor. 10:13). A walking partner is the way of escaping the temptation to hit that snooze button and indulge in extra time under the blankets.

By the way, it's important to resist the urge to gossip or complain while you walk. Your walking partner can also be your prayer partner. Each morning, you can quickly exchange an update on what's new, then pray for the remainder of your walk.

Pick up the phone today and offer someone the exciting opportunity to partner with you. Both of you will be glad you did. If you absolutely, positively can't find a partner, ask the Holy Spirit to stand in the gap with you until you find someone. Either way, get out there prayer walking. You'll be amazed how much more energy you have, enabling you to set about your work vigorously and keeping your arms strong for your tasks.

Affirmation: I walk because I'm in strict training.

Practical

Find a walking partner.

Buy good quality shoes designed specifically for walking. *Do not buy a cheap pair.* You *must have good quality walking shoes*, especially if you are over age thirty-five. Otherwise, you can do more harm than good by wearing shoes that do not provide enough support, which can lead to injuries.

If you are out of shape, begin walking just fifteen minutes a day. Ultimately your goal should be sixty minutes a day. It may take you a month or a year to build up to that level. Just go at your own pace and listen to your body.

Notebook: Add PRAYER WALK to your MORNING ROUTINE page in the PERSONAL section of your notebook.

Remember: Today is day seven of vegetables and water.

Day 23

Purify Your Body with Enhanced Water

Scripture to Memorize

> She considers a field and buys it;
>   out of her earnings she plants a vineyard.
> She sets about her work vigorously;
>   her arms are strong for her tasks.
>
> Proverbs 31:16–17

Passage to Read

Since we have these promises, dear friends, let us purify ourselves from everything that contaminates body and spirit, perfecting holiness out of reverence for God.

2 Corinthians 7:1

93

Guided Prayer

Dear Lord, thank you for giving me your book filled with wonderful promises. I know you have great plans for my life. Plans to give me a hope and a future, plans to prosper and not to harm me. I confess that I've wanted all of your promises to be unconditional. But I know that, although your love for me is absolutely unconditional, you've chosen to reserve your promises for those who choose to walk in obedience. Father, I want to be one of your obedient children who enjoys the fullness of all you've promised.

Holy Spirit, guide and empower me as I seek to purify myself from everything that contaminates body and spirit. You know my enemies: the world, the flesh, and the devil. It seems that everything around me conspires to defile me. Purity is a rare commodity these days. But I know, with your grace enabling, I can pursue purity in every area of my life: spirit, soul, and body. Although I'll never reach perfection this side of heaven, my heart is chasing after holiness out of reverence for you. Lord, I know you are with me everywhere I go. I don't want to expose you to *anything* that would grieve you or break your heart. I choose the path of purity out of respect for you. You're worth it! Amen.

Personal

One thing we can be certain of, when we read about the strength and vigor of the Proverbs 31 woman, is that she didn't drink soda all day. I never buy soda when I grocery shop. Nevertheless, my kids have managed to acquire a taste for it and their friends guzzle it by the gallon. The other day my teenager walked in the house with a giant fast-food cup of soda. I asked her why on earth she went for the super size. It turns out she didn't; it was a *medium* soda (more portion distortion).

If I were to give you just one directive that had the power to make a significant difference in how you look and feel, it would be drink *more water*. This is true, if for no other reason than the more water you drink, the less soda, iced tea, and coffee you're likely to drink. But water does more than prevent you from doing harm to yourself. Water cleanses your internal system, promotes weight loss, clears skin, fights fatigue, gives energy, increases metabolism, prevents dehydration (and the dizziness and brain fog that go with it), helps reduce your total caloric intake by promoting a feeling of fullness, and even *carries fat out of the body.*

How about developing a new habit? Before putting anything in your mouth, ask yourself: will this purify or contaminate my body?

Water is a purifier. And if you add a little extra to it, it can even decontaminate. One of the easiest things you can do to decontaminate your body is starting each day with a cleansing drink.

First thing each morning, heat eight ounces of water and add *fresh-squeezed* lemon juice. Start with one-eighth of a lemon. If your stomach handles it okay, increase to one-quarter and finally to one-half a lemon. Be forewarned. If your system is contaminated with toxins, this will upset your stomach and may even give you a headache. That's a *good sign*. It means the lemon is doing its work.

Lemon is a natural antiseptic, which cleanses bacteria, impurities, and even decomposed tissue from your lymphatic system. It aids the digestion process, speeds waste elimination, and promotes healthier bowels. Lemon also stimulates the liver's detoxification processes, which makes every cell in your body healthier.[4]

Now I realize that hot lemon water will not appease your sweet tooth. I can't tell you how many women have asked me, "Can I add an artificial sweetener to it?" That defeats the purpose. Your taste buds, if they are anything like those of the average American, are entirely too accustomed to sweets. And they are demanding, too, aren't they? You try to sneak in something that's *not* sugary and your mouth pitches a fit. Don't give in.

Even if your stomach joins the protest, stand strong. And believe me, if your system is clogged, it will protest. But work through it. Lemon water is wonderful for you. If you have a cup of warm lemon water first thing in the morning and another before you go to bed, I promise you'll gradually feel better. As a bonus, people will begin commenting on your improved complexion.

The second way to increase water's effectiveness is by adding *a very small amount of unsweetened* cranberry juice. Buy at least two thirty-two-ounce bottles of *unsweetened* cranberry juice. Pour three-quarters of the first bottle into another container. Now fill the bottle that contains one-quarter cranberry juice with water. Drink it by noon. Refill one-quarter of the bottle with unsweetened cranberry juice and three-quarters with water. Finish this bottle before you go to bed. Repeat this process every day for a month. Warning: if you do not have healthy eating habits, this may make you feel sick. Again, that's a good sign. It means your body is detoxifying itself from chemicals, excess sugar, caffeine, and other harmful substances.

Because variety is not only the spice of life but also good for your body, you shouldn't drink cranberry water every day for the rest of your life. Mix it up a bit. Some days you can fill your two thirty-two-ounce containers with just plain water. Or you can squeeze in fresh lemon, lime, grapefruit, or orange juice. The important thing is to finish both bottles before you go to bed.

Obviously you can pour some of your water into smaller containers and drink it on the go. Purchase a Nalgene[5] bottle for this purpose. Do *not* refill ordinary plastic water bottles, which are not made to be reused and may retain harmful bacteria. As crazy as this may sound, *first, fill your two thirty-two-ounce bottles with water* and then pour it into the smaller bottle, so that, when you have emptied the large containers, you know for sure you have fulfilled your daily quota.

Drinking enhanced water is one of the simplest ways to increase your body's ability to work vigorously throughout the day.

Affirmation: I purify myself from everything that contaminates body and spirit.

Practical

Buy lemons and begin each day with warm lemon water.

Buy two thirty-two-ounce bottles of unsweetened cranberry juice.

Notebook: Turn to your EVENING ROUTINE page and add, "Be sure to finish water for the day." Expand your MORNING ROUTINE page and add, "Fill two thirty-two-ounce water bottles" and "Consume cleansing drink."

Remember: Today is day eight of vegetables and water.

Day 24

Give Your Body Time to Digest

Scripture to Memorize

She considers a field and buys it;
    out of her earnings she plants a vineyard.
She sets about her work vigorously;
    her arms are strong for her tasks.

Proverbs 31:16–17

Passage to Read

Let the morning bring me word of your unfailing love,
    for I have put my trust in you.
Show me the way I should go,
    for to you I lift up my soul.

Psalm 143:8

Guided Prayer

Dear Lord, thank you for mornings. I'm so grateful for the constant reminder that each day is another chance to start fresh. Each day is brand-new with no mistakes in it. Thank you for reminding us in your Word that your compassions are new every morning. You never run out of grace, mercy, or forgiveness. Your love never fails. I confess my tendency to put my trust in all the wrong places. "Some trust in chariots and some in horses" (Ps. 20:7)—sometimes I trust in my employer, my education, my accomplishments, my possessions. You alone are trustworthy. Today I choose to put my trust entirely in you.

Holy Spirit, show me the way I should go. Help me to make good decisions today and every day. To you, O Lord, I lift up my soul. I offer you my mind, my will, and my emotions. I submit every thought, action, and feeling to your lordship. You're in charge of my life. I belong to you. I trust you. Thank you for being so easy to trust. Amen.

Personal

The Proverbs 31 woman set about her work vigorously, and her arms were strong for her tasks. If we want to be equally vigorous and strong, it's important for us to sleep soundly and maintain a healthy weight. One way to promote both of these goals is this: stop eating at least three hours before you go to bed. For optimum performance, our digestive system requires approximately twelve hours of rest. When we give our body what it needs to do its job, it returns the favor by providing us with energy to carry out the tasks of the day. When we eat late at night, especially if we have a heavy, carbohydrate-intense or sugar-laden meal, we wake up with a food hangover. That's because we don't sleep as well when our body is digesting; nor does our body digest as well when we're not moving.

Most people don't recognize the symptoms of a food hangover. They assume: *That's just how I feel in the morning* or *I'm not a morning person.* Try giving your body a full twelve hours to focus on digestion, with a three- to four-hour head start before you lie down, and you will marvel at how much better you feel. If you really want to help the process, take a leisurely walk after dinner. Notice how much better you feel the next day.

In the future, anytime you violate this principle (and inevitably you will), you will immediately notice the difference. And you'll declare: "Donna was right. I *have* been suffering from food hangovers!"

Eating at night also stimulates insulin production, which in turn stimulates fat storage. You don't have to be a scientist to know right away: that *can't* be good.

Eat a healthy dinner at least three to four hours before bedtime. Then, if you *feel* hungry later in the evening, remind yourself: *This isn't real. I just ate __ hours ago. I can't possibly be hungry.* What you *think* is hunger is either thirst (so drink some water) or a craving (so just say no—if it helps, promise yourself you can eat whatever it is you are craving *tomorrow morning*).

The next morning you should flush out what's been digested overnight by drinking your lemon water first thing. You'll be well on your way to a great day of vigorous work.

Affirmation: I give my body time to digest.

Practical

Stop eating at least three hours before going to bed. Consider taking a leisurely stroll after dinner.

Notebook: Turn to your ever-expanding EVENING ROUTINE page in your notebook. Subtract three hours from your bedtime and note: "No eating after _____ p.m." (So if you are committed to being in bed by 10 p.m., no eating after 7 p.m.) You can also add EVENING WALK if you are so inclined.

Remember: Today is day nine of vegetables and water.

Day 25

Grow Strong by Defying Gravity

Scripture to Memorize

> She considers a field and buys it;
> out of her earnings she plants a vineyard.
> She sets about her work vigorously;
> her arms are strong for her tasks.
>
> Proverbs 31:16–17

Passage to Read

Therefore, I urge you, brothers, in view of God's mercy, to offer your bodies as living sacrifices, holy and pleasing to God—this is your spiritual act of worship. Do not conform any longer to the pattern of this world, but be transformed by the renewing of your mind. Then you will be able to test and approve what God's will is—his good, pleasing and perfect will.

Romans 12:1–2

Guided Prayer

Dear Lord, thank you for your mercy. Jesus, I stand amazed that you would endure the cross, scorning its shame, just to open the gates of heaven to me. You offered the ultimate sacrifice. No sacrifice I might make in return could even compare, yet I choose to offer my body as a living sacrifice, holy and pleasing to you. It's my way of worshiping you. I confess my natural tendency is to conform to the pattern of this world. It's a constant temptation to go with the flow and follow the crowd down the path to self-destruction.

Holy Spirit, transform me as I renew my mind with the Word of God. I hear you challenging me to put your Word to the test, to discover for myself how much better life can be when I live it your way. I want to experience not just your good and pleasing will—but your *perfect* will for my life. This can happen only when I offer my body as a living sacrifice. Here I am, Lord. Take me. I'm yours. Amen.

Personal

The Proverbs 31 woman was probably able to remain vigorous and strong simply by going about the daily tasks of life. However, in today's modern world filled with conveniences like cars, escalators, washing machines, dishwashers, and the like, we don't automatically have enough exercise. We need a strategy to stay fit.

If you are a gym rat or an aerobics nut or if you already have some other fitness routine that works for you, today is your day off. Go volunteer at a soup kitchen or something! For the rest of us mere mortals, I've discovered the fastest, simplest way to get a total body workout: rebounding.

Rebounding is a fancy word for jumping lightly on a mini-trampoline. It's quick, powerful, efficient, and effective. According to Albert Carter, founder of the American Institute of Reboundology, rebounding "is like doing push-ups with every cell in the body all at once. All other strength exercises are designed to strengthen only the muscles and generally only one group at a time. While strengthening muscles is necessary, it is also important to have strong bones, connective tissue and strong vital organs. Rebounding strengthens the whole body, cell by cell."[6]

For me, as a middle-aged woman, the greatest benefit is that rebounding reduces cellulite, something no amount of walking will accomplish. The up-and-down motion of rebounding stimulates the lymphatic system, promoting more efficient cell-cleansing processes. This explains why pockets of cellulite (notice the word *cell*) begin to dissipate, even though they've remained impervious to other forms of exercise.

A healthy lymphatic system is absolutely essential. It's responsible for eliminating toxins, poisons, and metabolic waste products while destroying bacteria, viruses, germs, dead cells, and other unhealthy material that doesn't belong in your body. If your lymphatic system were to stop circulating for just twenty-four hours, you'd be dead. That's the reason a diagnosis of lymphoma or a report that cancer has spread to the lymph nodes is so dire. It means the very system designed to purify your body has itself been contaminated. It's like trying to mop the floor with a dirty mop, except your very life is at stake.

Research conducted by NASA, comparing running to rebounding, found rebounding is 68 percent more efficient in producing similar physiological results. According to NASA research, the straight up-and-down movement of the body while rebounding exposes the human body to g-force (pull of gravity). Each time you resist the pull of gravity (by jumping up) your entire body becomes stronger. This takes the concept of resistance exercise to a whole new level. Even if you're not an astronaut, you've probably noticed that gravity is doing weird things to your body. Fight gravity by defying gravity. Start jumping! If it's good enough to keep astronauts in condition, think what it can do for the rest of us earthlings.[7]

You can place your rebounder in front of the television, thereby redeeming time that would otherwise have been spent on the couch. I like to multitask by bouncing when I'm on the phone.

Your children will love it, too. A depressing number of children are currently overweight. Rebounding provides your children with an efficient total body workout, and they will have no idea they are getting their exercise. They think they're having fun.

I do need to offer two words of warning:

1. *Bounce lightly.* Do *not* leap in the air. In fact, in the beginning your feet should remain in contact with the rebounder at all times. Gradually you can begin to lift your feet off the rebounder in more of a jumping motion. Begin with just two to three minutes per day and build up to fifteen to twenty minutes for best results. Visit www. donnapartow.com/Rebounder for more details.
2. *Do not buy a cheap rebounder.* There are at least two different brands that I recommend on my website, or you can do your own research. But please do *not* buy a cheap mini-trampoline. You will hurt yourself. The difference is in the impact. Each time your feet hit the ground during any exercise, your entire body is impacted or "jarred." That's why jogging and high-impact aerobics have such a high rate of injury. Shins and ankles give out long before the lungs and heart do. Jog in place and feel for yourself how your entire body reacts when your feet hit the floor. If you're really brave, jump up in the air and land on both feet. Does the word *ouch* spring to mind? A cheap rebounder is little better than jumping on concrete. Choose a rebounder with a cushioned landing.
3. Check with your doctor. Do not rebound if you are or may become pregnant.

One of the best ways to stay vigorous and build strength is by defying gravity. Give it a try!

Affirmation: I grow strong by defying gravity.

Practical

Consider the purchase of a rebounder.
Remember: Today is the last day of your vegetable and water fast.

Day 26

Purify Body and Soul

Scripture to Memorize

She considers a field and buys it;
    out of her earnings she plants a vineyard.
She sets about her work vigorously;
    her arms are strong for her tasks.

Proverbs 31:16–17

Passage to Read

Have mercy on me, O God,
    according to your unfailing love;
according to your great compassion
    blot out my transgressions.
Wash away all my iniquity
    and cleanse me from my sin.
For I know my transgressions,
    and my sin is always before me.
Against you, you only, have I sinned
    and done what is evil in your sight,
so that you are proved right when you speak
    and justified when you judge. . . .
Cleanse me with hyssop, and I will be clean;
    wash me, and I will be whiter than snow.

Psalm 51:1–4, 7

Guided Prayer

Have mercy on me, O God, according to your unfailing love; according to your great compassion blot out my transgressions. Wash away all my iniquity and cleanse me from my sin. For I know my transgressions, and my sin is always before me. Against you, you only, have I sinned and done what is evil in your sight, so that you are proved right when you speak and justified when you judge. Cleanse me with hyssop, and I will be clean; wash me, and I will be whiter than snow. Amen.

Personal

If we want to remain vigorous and energized, it's important to take time to care for our bodies. One of the best ways to do that is to be sure to eat cleansing foods. Here's an example of the healthy cleansing diet set forth in my previous book, *Becoming the Woman I Want To Be*:[8]

- ☐ On arising, drink a cup of cranwater (one-quarter unsweetened cranberry juice and three-quarters water) with 1 tablespoon of freshly ground flaxseed (use a coffee grinder).
- ☐ Drink a cup of hot lemon water (one-quarter to one-half fresh squeezed lemon).
- ☐ Breakfast: two eggs scrambled with vegetables (for example, broccoli, onion, garlic, peppers) *or* a protein shake made with one cup cranwater, one cup frozen blueberries, one-quarter cup frozen cranberries, one tablespoon flax oil, and one scoop of protein powder.[9]
- ☐ Midmorning: one serving of fruit or vegetable.
- ☐ Lunch: salad with one palm-sized serving of protein.
- ☐ Midday: one serving of fruit or vegetable.
- ☐ Dinner: one palm-sized serving of protein, along with steamed or stir-fried vegetables and a whole grain.
- ☐ Before bed: one cup of cranwater with one tablespoon ground flaxseed.

In addition to eating right, one of the kindest things you can do for yourself, body and soul, is taking time to bathe. Did you know that bathing is important for your physical well-being? A shower may be convenient, but it doesn't accomplish the same degree of cleansing as a bath can. A cleansing bath can purify your body from the toxins that have built up in your body. This is especially important when you start to exercise and eat foods that promote detoxification. Ironically, you can actually begin to feel *sicker* as your body is trying to make itself healthier. That's because your body is throwing off toxins. It's like stirring up a hornet's nest. And the more toxic your system, the sicker you'll feel.

Furthermore, if toxins are not rapidly eliminated from the body, they can become reassimilated.

For your bath, pour two cups of Epsom salts, two cups of baking soda, and a few drops of lavender or arnica oil into a hot bath. Soak until the water turns cold but not longer than thirty minutes. Be aware that you may feel dizzy when you emerge. That means the bath did its job. This process draws out the toxins and enables your body's digestive system to function more efficiently.

Incorporate a cleansing bath into your EVENING ROUTINE at least once or twice a week. It's a simple, pleasant way to care for your body, God's temple. Light an aromatic candle, put on some relaxing praise music, and it will simultaneously do wonders for your soul and spirit. Another thing you might do is meditate on Psalm 51 as you soak, asking God to cleanse your spirit even as you cleanse your body.

Affirmation: I purify body and soul.

Practical

Eat a cleansing diet.

Obtain ingredients for your cleansing bath and incorporate it into your weekly or daily schedule.

Notebook: If desired, add CLEANSING BATH to your EVENING ROUTINE page.

Day 27

Weekly Checkup

Cumulative Scripture Review

> A wife of noble character who can find?
>   She is worth far more than rubies.
> Her husband has full confidence in her
>   and lacks nothing of value.
> She brings him good, not harm,
>   all the days of her life.
> She selects wool and flax
>   and works with eager hands.
> She is like the merchant ships,
>   bringing her food from afar.
> She gets up while it is still dark;
>   she provides food for her family
>   and portions for her servant girls.
> She considers a field and buys it;
>   out of her earnings she plants a vineyard.
> She sets about her work vigorously;
>   her arms are strong for her tasks.

Proverbs 31:10–17

Turn verses 16–17 into a Scripture-based prayer:

_____

_____

_____

Practical

Saturday is your day to review and catch up on any unfinished items. Check to confirm that you have completed the following one-time tasks:

- ☐ I have suitable shoes for walking without injury.
- ☐ I began walking three to five days per week.[10]
- ☐ I found a walking partner.
- ☐ I purchased lemons and unsweetened cranberry juice and began consuming detoxifying drinks.
- ☐ I added "fill water bottles" and "consume cleansing drink" to my MORNING ROUTINE.
- ☐ I established a new routine to allow my body sufficient time to digest.
- ☐ I evaluated the purchase of a rebounder.
- ☐ I purchased the ingredients for the cleansing bath and took my first one.
- ☐ I added CLEANSING BATH to my EVENING ROUTINE.

Check to confirm you are routinely incorporating the following positive changes into your daily routine:

- ☐ I'm using my Personal Notebook.
- ☐ I'm regularly reviewing my Personal Vision Statement.
- ☐ I'm spending time in my prayer place, enjoying TAG.
- ☐ I'm dealing proactively with my secret sins.
- ☐ I'm completing this study every day, practicing the memory verse, and reciting affirmations daily.
- ☐ I'm becoming consciously selective about how I dress and how I use my time and resources.
- ☐ I'm becoming a more serious student of the Bible.
- ☐ I'm practicing the presence of God, being watchful, thankful, and prayerful.
- ☐ I'm following my EVENING ROUTINE and going to bed on time.
- ☐ I'm inviting God to awaken me each morning, saying no to the snooze button, and following a MORNING ROUTINE.
- ☐ I'm exercising control over my eating habits and limiting sugar intake.
- ☐ I'm using smaller plates and controlling food portions.
- ☐ I'm planning ahead for healthier eating.
- ☐ I'm prayer walking three to five days per week.
- ☐ I begin each day with a cleansing drink and consume sixty-four ounces of water every day.
- ☐ I stop eating several hours before bed.
- ☐ I'm using a rebounder to fight gravity and cellulite (optional).
- ☐ I routinely take cleansing baths.

Day 28

Weekly Reflection

Sunday is a great day to devote extra time meditating on the entire Proverbs 31 passage, memorizing your assigned verses, praying, and preparing your heart for the week ahead. Take one day out of every seven to rest and reflect. Do *not* catch up on assignments you did not complete, but *do* schedule them for the coming week.

Fill in the remainder of Proverbs 31:10–17 from memory:

A _____ __ _____ _____ who can find?

She is worth _____ _____ _____ _____.

Her husband _____ ____ _____ ___ ____

and lacks _____ __ _____.

She brings him _____, ____ _____,

all the _____ __ ____ _____.

She selects _____ ___ _____

and works _____ _____ _____.

She is like _____ _____ _____,

bringing her _____ _____ _____.

She gets up _____ ___ __ _____ _____;

she provides _____ ____ ____ _____

and portions ____ ____ _____ _____.

She considers _ _____ ____ ____ ___;

out of her earnings ____ _____ __ _____.

She sets about ____ ___ _____;

her arms ____ _____ _____ _____.

Weekly Evaluation

1. Am I listening for and hearing God's voice? What is he saying to me?

_____

_____

2. Am I increasingly manifesting the fruit of the Spirit: love, joy, peace, patience, kindness, goodness, faithfulness, gentleness, and self-control (Gal. 5:22–23)? What areas look encouraging? What needs prayer?

_____

_____

3. What did God teach me during my TAG?

_____

_____

4. Which priorities did I live by? Which goals did I pursue?

_____

_____

5. Which priorities or goals did I neglect?

_____

_____

6. What new thing did I learn—about life, God, my family, and the people around me?

_____

_____

7. What are my specific priorities/goals for the coming week?

_____

_____

Take out your notebook and schedule your priorities or goals for the coming week.

WEEK FIVE
MANAGEMENT TOOLS

Day 29

Maximize Each Day

Scripture to Memorize

She sees that her trading is profitable,
  and her lamp does not go out at night.
In her hand she holds the distaff
  and grasps the spindles with her fingers.

Proverbs 31:18–19

Passage to Read

Now listen, you who say, "Today or tomorrow we will go to this or that city, spend a year there, carry on business and make money." Why, you do not even know what will happen tomorrow. What is your life? You are a mist that appears for a little while and then vanishes.

James 4:13–14

Guided Prayer

Dear Lord, thank you for today. It's all I have. Help me to make the most of it. I confess that, in the past, I've been quick to make great boasts and predictions about all the great things I was going to do *tomorrow.* Sometimes I can be the Queen of Great Intentions. But great intentions for tomorrow mean nothing. What counts is my obedience today. Holy Spirit, help me to find balance between planning for the future (which is important) and giving place to grand illusions (which is foolishness). You know the dreams and desires of my heart. You've said in your Word that you will *give me the desires of my heart.* I rest in that. My time here on earth is so short—a mist that vanishes. Enable me to make the most of each moment by focusing on things that truly matter for eternity. Amen.

Personal

The Proverbs 31 woman saw to it that her trading was profitable. She made sure she had a good return for her investment of time and money. Her strategy is outlined in our two verses for this week. First, she worked long hours. Second, she had the right tools to succeed. We will discuss the concept of generating income from home in Week 8. But for this week, our focus is on the work *all* women do from home, namely, managing ourselves, our family, and our household effectively.

Since none of us has a guarantee about tomorrow or next year, all we can do is make the most of each day. To see to it that your days are profitable, your Personal Notebook will serve as your distaff and spindle. So take it out and grasp it in your fingers. Turn to the PERSONAL section and write EVERY DAY on the top of a blank sheet of paper. Now divide the paper into six sections labeled:

SPIRITUAL

PHYSICAL

RELATIONAL

PERSONAL

MINISTRY

FINANCIAL

Reread your Personal Vision Statement, then ask: *What would I need to do* every day *in each category to fulfill my vision statement?* For example, if I'm going to "use my energetic, powerful communication skills to challenge and motivate Christians to go into all the world, impacting lives and making the world a better place," then every day I need to do the following:

SPIRITUAL—spend at least an hour cultivating spiritual disciplines.
PHYSICAL—eat right and exercise to preserve my energy.

113

RELATIONAL—balance the needs of my family with the needs of a hurting world (*include my family in my mission whenever possible*).

PERSONAL—continually develop my communication skills and stay informed about God's work in the world.

MINISTRY—say yes only to churches and organizations that are looking for a speaker who will challenge them (and not just entertain).

FINANCIAL—give generously and strategically to advance the kingdom around the world. Invest wisely so I'll have more to give and the resources needed to fulfill my mission.

Now we need to bring four items together: your Personal Vision Statement, your monthly calendar, your EVERY DAY list, and the DAILY PAGE. I *promise* this isn't complicated. I can't stand organizational overkill.

As part of your EVENING ROUTINE, plan for the next day by filling out a DAILY PAGE. As mentioned on Day 11, "Sleep in Peace," this exercise will go a long way toward creating a mental environment that's conducive to sleep. Transferring everything from your brain to your notebook is a powerful peace producer.

Review your Personal Vision Statement first. Remind yourself why on earth you're on the planet. Next, glance at the monthly calendar. If there's anything time specific, put it in the first section of your DAILY PAGE, noting details like who, what, when, where, and so on. Next, using your EVERY DAY list as a reference, write *one thing* you need to do in each category on the DAILY PAGE—not a dozen things, just one thing. You can always do *more*, but the *one thing* is your minimum requirement. Here's what my list might look like:

- [ ] SPIRITUAL: *TAG*
- [ ] PHYSICAL: *rebounder*
- [ ] RELATIONAL: *bike ride with Tara*
- [ ] PERSONAL: *register for conference*
- [ ] MINISTRY: *write 1 hour*
- [ ] FINANCIAL: *call Realtor*

Check off items as they are completed.

Next, make a list of ten additional things you need to do. Any items that remain unfinished at the end of the day should be transferred to the next day for completion. This is important. The very act of writing out your list of ten things will force you to focus. You may notice that there are one or two items that never get done. Eventually, you'll get so sick of writing them every day that you'll do them just to get them off your list! It's a great way to put an end to never-ending procrastination.

I believe gratitude blesses the heart of God, and he often rewards our grateful hearts by sending us even more blessings for which to be grateful. So each morning, make a list on the DAILY PAGE of five things you can be grateful for throughout the day. As you review the list of things that need to be done, review your gratitude list as well. It's a great way to keep your heart at rest.

Your DAILY PAGE also includes room to list two items to pray about. They might be specific to that date (someone having surgery, for example) or just whatever God lays on your heart.

Notice that this system doesn't try to predict exactly what time you'll do all these things. If you were a corporate executive, you would *need* that level of detail. Or if you were naturally detail oriented, you would *want* it and you would already have a system in place. So my focus is on the ordinary woman like me who just wants to make the most of her day. I believe the DAILY PAGE is a powerful tool to help you watch over the affairs of your household and avoid eating the bread of idleness.

Affirmation: I maximize each day.

Practical

Begin using your DAILY PAGE to manage your life more effectively.

Notebook: You should already have a month-at-a-glance calendar in the front of your Personal Notebook. Record birthdays, events, appointments, and such on the calendar instead of on scraps of paper. If you have not already done so, take the time to do this now. The whole idea of your Personal Notebook is to minimize the paper blizzard and help you keep your head on straight.

Photocopy from the back of the book or download and print thirty copies of the DAILY PAGE at www.donnapartow.com/dailypage. Insert ten in the front of your notebook, then place the remainder in the binder pocket or a file folder where you keep extra forms. Using the above guidelines, make your plans for tomorrow.

Turn to the EVENING ROUTINE page and add "Complete daily page" to the list of things you do before going to bed each night.

Day 30

Apply the 80/20 Rule

Scripture to Memorize

She sees that her trading is profitable,
and her lamp does not go out at night.
In her hand she holds the distaff
and grasps the spindles with her fingers.

Proverbs 31:18–19

Passage to Read

A discerning man keeps wisdom in view,
but a fool's eyes wander to the ends of the earth.

Proverbs 17:24

Guided Prayer

Dear Lord, help me to become more discerning. I want to live each day with wisdom in view. But I confess that, more often than not, I take my eyes off the prize. I let my mind and heart wander. I get distracted by things that don't matter and lose sight of the things that do. Holy Spirit, empower me to fix my eyes on Jesus. Help me to stay on task and on target, today and every day. I'm counting on you, trusted Teacher, to constantly call me back to the path of wisdom. Amen.

Personal

The Proverbs 31 woman saw to it that her time and money went into the most profitable enterprises. Today we're going to explore yet another modern-day version of the spindle and distaff: the 80/20 rule. The rule arises from the work of an Italian economist who observed that the world is governed by a nearly universal 80/20 rule, also known as the Pareto Principle. In practical application: 20 percent of salespeople produce 80 percent of the sales results; 20 percent of customers generate 80 percent of business income; 20 percent of any given congregation do 80 percent of the work in the church; you call 20 percent of your friends 80 percent of the time; you watch 20 percent of your television channels 80 percent of the time; you make 20 percent of the recipes in your collection 80 percent of the time (did your husband just shout amen or oh no?), the top 20 percent of the world's wealthies people control 80 percent (or more) of the world's wealth, and so on.

Put this rule to work for you. Focus on the 20 percent of activities that will yield the 80 percent return. Don't waste your time on the remaining 80 percent that will yield only an additional 20 percent return. In other words, don't be a perfectionist. It's not worth driving yourself to physical and emotional collapse to squeeze out an additional 20 percent return.

Review your DAILY PAGE every day and put an asterisk next to the two items on your TACKLE LIST that will yield the 80 percent return on your time investment. Do these two tasks first. Then, even if you don't accomplish any of the remaining items, you'll probably have achieved 80 percent effectiveness. *Do not allow yourself to work on anything other than the items with an asterisk until you have completed those two.*

Here are some other ways to apply the 80/20 rule:

Make a list of ten friends. Put a star next to the two most important ones and devote your attention to them. Be nice to everyone, of course, but focus your energies on the two you have identified.

Make a list of your ten favorite hobbies/free-time activities. Put a star next to the two you enjoy most. Invest in them.

If you are in business, make a list of your top ten customers and put a star next to the top two. Focus on them.

You spend 80 percent of your waking hours in 20 percent of your house (probably your kitchen and family room). Focus on making them fabulous and you'll be much happier at home.

Your children play with 20 percent of their toys 80 percent of the time. Give away or put away the rest.

Put the 80/20 rule to good use and let it simplify your life.

Affirmation: I use the 80/20 rule to help me simplify and prioritize my life.

Practical

Begin implementing the 80/20 rule by making the lists suggested above.

Notebook: Begin distinguishing between the 80 and the 20 on your DAILY PAGE. Put an asterisk next to the two most important items and *do not work on anything else* until those two are completed.

Day 31

Give Away Everything You Can

Scripture to Memorize

She sees that her trading is profitable,
and her lamp does not go out at night.
In her hand she holds the distaff
and grasps the spindles with her fingers.

Proverbs 31:18–19

Passage to Read

John [the Baptist] answered, "The man with two tunics should share with him who has none, and the one who has food should do the same. . . ."

[Jesus said,] "Give, and it will be given to you. A good measure, pressed down, shaken together and running over, will be poured into your lap. For with the measure you use, it will be measured to you."

Luke 3:11; 6:38

Guided Prayer

Dear Lord, thank you for filling your Book with such practical advice. I confess my tendency to pick and choose only those parts of the Bible that say what I want to hear. I love the parts that speak of blessing me, but I tend to skim over the parts that challenge me to be a blessing to others. Ironically, in seeking first to bless myself, I miss out on many of the greatest blessings.

Today's passage is a real challenge to me. You are clearly telling me that if I have more than I need of anything, I should give some away to someone who has a greater need. Although part of me believes I'll be happier if I cling to everything and keep it for myself, I will choose to believe, by faith, that you know what you're talking about and that this commandment is not designed to punish or rob me, but to bless me. I believe your Word is true: as I give, it will be given to me. I'll receive a good measure, pressed down, shaken together, and running over, poured out into my lap. I believe that with the measure I use, it will be measured to me. Holy Spirit, give me the courage to use a *huge* measuring cup in the coming days as I give to others. Amen.

Personal

If there's one thing that most intimidated me about writing a book based on the Proverbs 31 woman, it's this: I'm a lousy housekeeper. I'm one of those creative types who are just messy by nature, so it's always been a major challenge. So the bad news is: housekeeping isn't my forte. The good news is: I have a secret weapon in the war against messiness. I have the household management tool that makes the distaff and spindle even more obsolete than they already were! It's a weapon that's guaranteed to change your life! Are you ready? Here it is:

Give away everything you can.

The key to minimizing clutter and keeping an orderly home is a resolute commitment to give away everything you can. Give, give, give! Give until it hurts. And because it does hurt sometimes, you'll think twice about accumulating next time. Get your kids in on it; your husband, too.

Go through your house: room by room, cabinet by cabinet, closet by closet, drawer by drawer. If you can imagine life without it, give it away. Your life will be exponentially better with less clutter—less to clean, less to confuse. Less is absolutely, positively more. Do this exercise *quickly*. Don't overanalyze. Just do it.

Please do not think of this as merely de-cluttering your house, although it will certainly help with that. Think of it as ministry. Think of it as simple obedience to the command of Christ. Focus on the joy of *giving* and view this exercise as a ministry opportunity. In fact, if you are doing this study with a group, you may want to organize a massive giveaway party at your church. We did this at my church in Tempe, Arizona, and people were astonished when they walked into the auditorium filled with *free stuff*. We simply said, "Take what you need as a gift from your loving heavenly Father." I saw single moms in tears.

Go through your clothes, books, CDs, toys, kitchen gadgets—you name it. If you have two when one will do, obey the biblical directive to give one away. If you can even conceive of your life without it, give it away. If you can imagine anyone at all who needs it more than you, give it away.

You don't have to label four boxes (every book I've ever read on household management emphasizes the infamous four labeled boxes, dragged from room to room). Forget about all that. It's too complicated. You need only *one box* at a time. When it's full, fill another one. And another one. And another one.

The last time our family did this, we filled the back of our pickup truck and took everything to a group of families hit by an apartment fire. It was pure *joy*. It really is better to give than to receive. Be like the Proverbs 31 woman who opened her hands to the poor and extended her hands to the needy (v. 20). Isn't it interesting that the *very next verse* points out that, even as she has open hands to *give*, her family still has everything they need: "When it snows, she has no fear for her household; for all of them are clothed in scarlet" (v. 21). Never hesitate to be generous with what you have, trusting God to provide everything you need.

I do want to add a disclaimer here. If you are deeply in debt or otherwise in a financial bind, rather than giving away everything you can, you might consider selling everything you can. You can organize a yard sale or read Day 54 for ideas on selling your unneeded stuff on the Internet.

However, you don't have to host a yard sale to have profitable trading. Give to the Lord and see what he gives you in trade!

Affirmation: I give away everything I can.

Practical

Go through your house: every room, closet, cabinet, and drawer. Don't ask, *How long has it been since I used this?* Ask, *Can I possibly live without it? Do I have two when one will do? Does someone else need it more? Would someone else get greater use out of it?* Your mission is *not* to justify keeping it. Your mission is to give away as much as you possibly can. Obviously, if you come across stuff that neither you nor any other human being wants, *throw it out.*

If you want to take a tax deduction, you can donate to the Salvation Army or some other charity that accepts used items. Make a list of big-ticket items and a general description of smaller items (kitchen gadgets, clothing, and such) and ask the manager to sign and date it for you. But don't get bogged down over the tax deduction. It's not about that! Set a goal to fill at least five boxes. You'll be amazed how easy it is to do.

Tip: Before the purge, call your local Wal-Mart store manager and ask what time they replenish inventory (and have empty boxes). Ask if you can stop by to pick up ten. Usually they are happy to accommodate you. While you're there, purchase ten plastic storage containers. You'll also need a thick black felt marker.

Day 32

Stow Away as Much as You Can

Scripture to Memorize

She sees that her trading is profitable,
   and her lamp does not go out at night.
In her hand she holds the distaff
   and grasps the spindles with her fingers.

Proverbs 31:18–19

Passage to Read

Better a dry crust with peace and quiet
   than a house full of feasting, with strife.

Proverbs 17:1

Guided Prayer

Dear Lord, I know that you have called me to peace. I long to create a peaceful home that's a refuge in the midst of life's storms, a place where we live by your priorities rather than being driven by the media frenzy. Forgive me for buying into the cultural lies that say the only way to be happy is to accumulate and do more, more, more. The truth is less, less, less is almost always better. Thank you for reminding me today that a dry crust with peace and quiet is better than a house full of feasting with strife. That is the complete *opposite* message from the one that bombards me daily.

Holy Spirit, empower me to live differently. Teach me how to pursue peace rather than stuff. Train my heart to choose quiet rather than endless activity.

Prince of Peace, make your home with me. Amen.

Personal

Now that you've given away and thrown away as much as you can, it's time to stow away as much as you can. If you don't use an item every month, put it in an out-of-the-way place, such as the garage or attic. (We store Christmas and Thanksgiving bins in the attic; everything else is in the garage.)

This is obviously much more than a one-day job. Your objective today is to jumpstart the project and work on it, a little at a time, over the coming weeks. For example, you might place a bin in each of your children's rooms and instruct them to put away all off-season clothing. Ask your husband to do the same. (You'll be tackling your own closet later on, so don't start there.) You might also stow holiday dishes to open up more space in the kitchen, as well as tax records and children's school documents to de-clutter paperwork.

Before stowing anything, search your heart again. Is there any possible way you can live without it? Is there anyone else who needs it more? It's not too late to give it away. Just start another giveaway box. The more you give away, the less you'll have to stow away. Nevertheless, there are certainly some things you'll want to keep. Some of my bins include:

birthday celebration items

Easter/spring decorations

fall/Thanksgiving decorations

Christmas decorations (Don't tackle your Christmas stuff now! Come back to that chore when you've finished this study. Again, think jumpstart!)

off-season clothes (at least one box for every member of the family)

children's school memorabilia (You might want a separate bin for each child. This makes it easier—no sorting later!)

tax documents (keep five years)

arts and crafts supplies

dream-size clothes (more on this later)

miscellaneous holiday decorations (Valentine's Day, St. Patrick's Day, etc.)

123

Your bins will be different from mine. For example, I have a bin filled with jungle gear because I've taken three mission trips into the jungle and hope to be invited again. I certainly don't need my Indiana Jones–wannabe outfits taking up valuable closet space, so they're in a bin. You get the idea.

Affirmation: I store up treasures in heaven.

Practical

Buy ten plastic storage containers. Use a thick black felt pen to number them. Stow away any items you do not use every month.

Notebook: Create a page in the HOUSEHOLD section entitled BINS and write the numbers from 1 to 10 down the left-hand side, leaving several lines between numbers. Make a brief notation *in pencil* of what is contained in each bin. If you write in pencil, you can change contents if you need to without crossing out or re-creating the list.

Day 33

Transfer Problems to a Tackle List

Scripture to Memorize

She sees that her trading is profitable,
    and her lamp does not go out at night.
In her hand she holds the distaff
    and grasps the spindles with her fingers.

Proverbs 31:18–19

Passage to Read

The LORD is my shepherd, I shall not be in want.
    He makes me lie down in green pastures,
he leads me beside quiet waters,
    he restores my soul.

He guides me in paths of righteousness
for his name's sake.

Psalm 23:1–3

Guided Prayer

Dear Lord, thank you for being my shepherd. Because I have you to lead and guide me, I shall not be in want. I confess that sometimes I act like a needy person. But the reality is, when I rest in you, I must acknowledge you've supplied my every need. I acknowledge, too, that sometimes I need you to *make me lie down*! I'm like an overtired child, fussing, fretting, and making a spectacle. Thanks for loving me enough to *make me lie down*, for leading me beside quiet waters. Holy Spirit, restore my soul. Restore my mind, will, and emotions. Help me to think differently, to make better decisions, and to tame these wild emotions. Please guide me in right pathways, not just for my own sake but for the sake of your reputation. Lord, I desire to be a positive reflection on your name. I want people to look at my life and know I am well cared for because I have a good shepherd. Thanks for leading me this far. Amen.

Personal

We may look at the Proverbs 31 woman and all she accomplished and think, *Wasn't she completely exhausted?* Actually I get the sense of a woman who is energized—a woman who has discovered that the more you get done, the more energy is generated to tackle the next thing that must be done. The truth is, often the most exhausting thing of all is not what we've done, but what we've left undone. It's those unfinished tasks that haunt our quiet moments and drain the life from our soul—those unwritten letters, unspoken words, that unfinished baby blanket. The twenty pounds we need to lose or the disaster in the garage that we plan to organize some day, these are the things that drain the life from our soul, silently accusing us, reminding us of our own inadequacy and robbing us of much-needed energy.

The Proverbs 31 woman may have worked late at night, but she didn't lie awake at night wracked with anxiety. She achieved that ideal balance of a soul at rest and a body in motion. Too many of us live the opposite way. Our body is resting—sitting on the couch watching TV or surfing the Internet—but our soul is in absolute turmoil. Or we lie in bed for eight hours but we don't really sleep because we haven't learned to cast our cares on God.

The psalmist declared, "He restores my soul." Your soul includes your mind, will, and emotions. It encompasses the thoughts you think, the decisions you make, and the way you feel. (Often your feelings flow from the thoughts you think, and the consequences you reap from the decisions you make.)

Today we're going to do a simple exercise that has the power to help restore your soul. We're going to create a TACKLE LIST. You'll go from room to room and make note of everything that's unfinished, anything that bothers you, or things that need to be changed in some way. When you're done walking from room to room, sit down and search your mind. Anything else up there—phone calls to make, letters to write, classes to take, weight to lose? If it's bothering you, write it down. Get it out of your head and onto a piece of paper. When you record the item, estimate the amount of time it might take to resolve the problem. Sometimes we put something off for ten years that will take about ten minutes to complete. Meanwhile, we've been robbed of peace and drained of life because this "unfinished business" hangs over us.

Start your list and add to it whenever something else comes to mind. Then, when you have an extra ten, twenty, thirty, or sixty minutes, turn to your TACKLE LIST. Look for an item you've estimated will require the amount of time you have available and tackle it. You should also review your TACKLE LIST each night as you complete your DAILY PAGE to see if you can tackle at least one item per day.

Stop procrastinating, relying on the excuse that you are waiting for the "perfect time," which of course never arrives. It's amazing how much you can get accomplished in five or ten minutes. What's even more amazing is how much you can get done in a day when you make the most of those unscheduled moments, whenever they become available.

What unfinished tasks are haunting you right now? Resolve to roll up your sleeves and get to work. A task begun is half done. And I bet you'll feel energized by the momentum—so much so that you'll move on to the next task. And the next. And the next. Don't let your lamp go out tonight until you've finished one item on your TACKLE LIST!

Affirmation: He restores my soul.

Practical

With your notebook in hand, go from room to room. Note any items that need to be tackled, along with estimates of how long it will take to complete. This is an ongoing list. When you have free time, tackle an item on your TACKLE LIST. Also, be sure to review your TACKLE LIST each night as you prepare your DAILY PAGE for the next day. When you have a large number of crossed-out items, rewrite your TACKLE LIST.

Notebook: Create a page entitled TACKLE LIST in the HOUSEHOLD section of your Personal Notebook.

Day 34

Weekly Checkup

Cumulative Scripture Review

A wife of noble character who can find?
    She is worth far more than rubies.
Her husband has full confidence in her
    and lacks nothing of value.
She brings him good, not harm,
    all the days of her life.
She selects wool and flax
    and works with eager hands.
She is like the merchant ships,
    bringing her food from afar.
She gets up while it is still dark;
    she provides food for her family
    and portions for her servant girls.

She considers a field and buys it;
　　out of her earnings she plants a vineyard.
She sets about her work vigorously;
　　her arms are strong for her tasks.
She sees that her trading is profitable,
　　and her lamp does not go out at night.
In her hand she holds the distaff
　　and grasps the spindles with her fingers.

Proverbs 31:10–19

Turn verses 18–19 into a Scripture-based prayer:

_____

_____

_____

Practical

Saturday is your day to review and catch up on any unfinished items. Check to confirm that you have completed the following one-time tasks:

- ☐ I gained a basic understanding of the self-management system.
- ☐ I set my EVERY DAY goals.
- ☐ I printed out and began using the DAILY PAGE.
- ☐ I added "Complete DAILY PAGE" to my EVENING ROUTINE.
- ☐ I gained a basic understanding of the 80/20 rule and created the suggested lists (to simplify my life).
- ☐ I gathered up and gave away everything I could.
- ☐ I purchased bins and began stowing away as much as I could.
- ☐ I created a BINS list in my notebook to track what is stowed in each bin.
- ☐ I involved my family in the process of giving away or stowing as much as we could.
- ☐ I created a TACKLE LIST of unfinished business.

Check to confirm you are routinely incorporating the following positive changes into your daily routine:

- ☐ I'm using my Personal Notebook.
- ☐ I'm regularly reviewing my Personal Vision Statement.
- ☐ I'm spending time in my prayer place, enjoying TAG.
- ☐ I'm dealing proactively with my secret sins.
- ☐ I'm completing this study every day, practicing the memory verse, and reciting affirmations daily.
- ☐ I'm becoming consciously selective about how I dress and how I use my time and resources.
- ☐ I'm becoming a more serious student of the Bible.
- ☐ I'm practicing the presence of God, being watchful, thankful, and prayerful.
- ☐ I'm following my EVENING ROUTINE and going to bed on time.
- ☐ I'm inviting God to awaken me each morning, saying no to the snooze button, and following a MORNING ROUTINE.
- ☐ I'm exercising control over my eating habits and limiting sugar intake.
- ☐ I'm using smaller plates and controlling food portions.
- ☐ I'm planning ahead for healthier eating.
- ☐ I'm prayer walking three to five days per week.
- ☐ I begin each day with a cleansing drink and consume sixty-four ounces of water every day.
- ☐ I stop eating several hours before bed.
- ☐ I'm using a rebounder to fight gravity and cellulite.
- ☐ I routinely take cleansing baths.
- ☐ I'm using my DAILY PAGE and applying the 80/20 rule.
- ☐ I routinely give away everything I can.
- ☐ I'm tackling items on my TACKLE LIST.

Day 35

Weekly Reflection

Sunday is a great day to devote extra time meditating on the entire Proverbs 31 passage, memorizing your assigned verses, praying, and preparing your heart for the week ahead. Take one day out of every seven to rest and reflect. Do *not* catch up on assignments you did not complete, but *do* schedule them for the coming week.

Fill in the remainder of Proverbs 31:10–19 from memory:

A _____ ___ _____ _____ who can find?

   She is worth ____ _____ _____ _____.

Her husband ____ ___ _____ ___ ___

   and lacks _____ ___ _____.

She brings him _____, ____ _____,

   all the _____ ___ ____ _____.

She selects _____ ____ _____

   and works _____ _____ _____.

She is like _____ _____ _____,

   bringing her _____ _____ _____.

She gets up _____ ___ ___ _____ _____;

   she provides _____ ____ ____ _____

   and portions ____ ____ _____ _____.

She considers _ _____ ____ _____ ___;

   out of her earnings ____ _____ __ _____.

She sets about ____ _____ _____;

   her arms ____ _____ ____ ____ _____.

She sees that ____ _____ ___ _____,

   and her _____ _____ ____ ___ ____ ___ _____.

In her hand ____ _____ ____ _____

and grasps ____ _____ _____ ____ _____.

Weekly Evaluation

1. Am I listening for and hearing God's voice? What is he saying to me?

   _____

   _____

2. Am I increasingly manifesting the fruit of the Spirit: love, joy, peace, patience, kindness, goodness, faithfulness, gentleness, and self-control (Gal. 5:22–23)? What areas look encouraging? What needs prayer?

   _____

   _____

3. What did God teach me during my TAG?

   _____

   _____

4. Which priorities did I live by? Which goals did I pursue?

   _____

   _____

5. Which priorities or goals did I neglect?

   _____

   _____

6. What new thing did I learn—about life, God, my family, and the people around me?

_____

_____

7. What are my specific priorities/goals for the coming week?

_____

_____

Take out your notebook and schedule your priorities or goals for the coming week.

WEEK SIX
FINANCIAL PLANNING

Tithe

Scripture to Memorize

> She opens her arms to the poor
> and extends her hands to the needy.
> When it snows, she has no fear for her household;
> for all of them are clothed in scarlet.
>
> Proverbs 31:20–21

Passage to Read

"Will a man rob God? Yet you rob me.

"But you ask, 'How do we rob you?'

"In tithes and offerings. You are under a curse—the whole nation of you—because you are robbing me. Bring the whole tithe into the storehouse, that there may be food in my house. Test me in this", says the LORD Almighty, "and see if I will not throw open the floodgates of heaven and pour out so much blessing that you will not have room enough for it."

> Malachi 3:8–10

Guided Prayer

Dear Lord, I confess that I have robbed you in the past. There have been times when I've failed to bring my whole tithe into the storehouse. Forgive me, Lord. I want to honor you, but sometimes I allow my mind to be conformed to the beliefs and attitudes of this world. I fool myself into thinking the way to make sure I have food for my family, the way to insure our financial security, is to *keep* every penny for myself. That may be the world's truth, but it's not your truth. Your truth is that, as I give to you, you will provide for me.

I stand amazed at your offer to put you to the test in this. I'm going to take you up on that offer, beginning today. I'm committing myself to bring the whole tithe into your storehouse and I'm watching in expectation. Holy Spirit, I invite you to remind me of this commitment every time money comes my way. I believe you will be true to your promise. You will throw open the floodgates of heaven and pour out so much blessing that I will not have room enough to contain it all. Thank you, God, for your awesome provision. Amen.

Personal

The Proverbs 31 woman opened her hands to the poor and needy. She was able to do so because she had something in her hands to give. She had no fear for her household, because they were all well dressed and, it's safe to assume, well cared for. I won't go so far as to say that charity begins at home, but I will say charity begins with sound financial planning. That's the reason, this week, we're going to turn our attention to finances.

Probably the first thing I should say is, "Create a budget." But the fact is, either you have the personality type that does well with budgets or you don't. If you are a budget-keeping person, you already have one. You don't need my advice, especially considering that I've never stuck to a budget for more than a month in my entire life. If you are not a budget-keeping person, the best I can do is make you feel guilty. So let's not waste time creating a budget. Instead, let's get a handle on what matters most concerning your finances.

John Wesley had the right idea when he advised: "Earn all you can; save all you can; give all you can." Christians shouldn't be financially broke. We should be financially wise.

You really need to know and do only four things:

1. Tithe 10 percent.
2. Save/invest 10 percent.
3. Escape/avoid bad debt.
4. Spend less than you earn.

To effectively do any of these things, you don't need to keep track of every dime you spend. You just need to be smart. There's a better way and you're about to discover it. Today we begin with the tithe.

First, a math problem to solve. Which is greater: 90 percent plus God or 100 percent minus God?

If you answered 90 percent plus God, you are a winner. Actually that should be the easiest mathematical problem in the world to answer correctly, unless you honestly believe that 100 percent *without God's blessing* will somehow yield more financial return than 90 percent *with God's blessing*. Think about the absurdity of that for a minute! Are you telling me the God who created the entire universe doesn't hold the upper hand in that simple equation? This is a no-brainer.

Here's how to make it easy. Calculate 10 percent of your income (some say gross; some say net; it's between you and God). Determine where you are going to donate this money. Typically, it should go to your local church, but if the Lord directs you to support other Christian organizations, I think that's fine. Local pastors and deacon boards throughout the nation will pitch a fit over this advice, but that's okay. They'll like this next part. Determine exactly how much you are committed to donating to each organization. Contact them to see if arrangements can be made to *automatically deduct* the funds from your checking account each month. I've been giving automatically, every month, to a broad range of Christian ministries for *years*. I don't even have to think about it. Many churches are making this option available now.

The Bible says the Israelites gave God a tithe of their firstfruits. They had no guarantee that the second fruit was coming. When we give God our firstfruits—from our heart and for the right reasons—he makes sure we reap a harvest beyond our imagination. Wherever you decide to give, give with joy and because you *want* to, not because you have to or hope to get something in return. "Remember this: Whoever sows sparingly will also reap sparingly, and whoever sows generously will also reap generously. Each man should give what he has decided in his heart to give, not reluctantly or under compulsion, for God loves a cheerful giver" (2 Cor. 9:6–7).

The first step toward providing for your family and for those in need is giving to God first.

Affirmation: I tithe because I know that 90 percent plus God equals more than 100 percent without him.

Practical

Calculate 10 percent of your earnings. Determine where you want to give. See if you can make arrangements to have your donation automatically deducted. If not, be sure to tithe your income as it comes in.

Notebook: Label the fourth tab divider FINANCES. Label a page TITHE. Calculate (or estimate) your monthly income. List any organizations you are committed to giving to monthly, along with any you may want to make a one-time or occasional donation to in the future.

Day 37

Calculate Your Assets and Liabilities

Scripture to Memorize

She opens her arms to the poor
and extends her hands to the needy.
When it snows, she has no fear for her household;
for all of them are clothed in scarlet.

Proverbs 31:20–21

Passage to Read

No one can serve two masters. Either he will hate the one and love the other, or he will be devoted to the one and despise the other. You cannot serve both God and Money.

Matthew 6:24

Guided Prayer

Dear Lord, thank you for speaking the truth concerning money. I'm glad your Word is practical and shows me how to live my daily life. I confess that I've tried serving two masters and it didn't work very well. I became frustrated, exhausted, and irritable. It's so easy to get caught up in the rat race of earning money (or nagging my husband to earn more!). It's so easy to become a slave to money or a slave to my job. It's easy but it brings only discontentment. I don't want to live that way anymore. God, I believe you can give me the wisdom it takes to be set free from serving money. Instead, I want to discover how to make money work for me. I know I can't serve both God and money. From this day forward, I choose to serve you, Lord. Amen.

Personal

The Proverbs 31 woman had no fear for her household. If only that were true of more of us today. Many people are afraid of what would happen if the primary breadwinner in the family lost his or her job. And it is frightening, considering that the average out-of-work person will take up to twenty months to find a new job. The fact is that only 20 percent of American families have enough savings to survive for two months.[1] So how many would be able to survive for twenty months? Not many. That's the reason financial experts recommend you have an emergency savings account with enough money to cover three months of living expenses. If you are just beginning to get a handle on your finances, this should be your highest priority. Open a money market account (MMA) with check-writing privileges but then resist the temptation to write checks against it, except in the case of a true emergency. At the time of this writing, it's possible to earn 5.5 percent interest on an MMA. You can visit www. bankrate.com to hunt for the best current rates.

Dave Ramsey, author of *The Total Money Makeover*, recommends you begin by putting one thousand dollars in your emergency fund.[2] Then focus your energy on paying down your credit card debt. Once you are out of debt, build up your three-month savings reserve. In other words, it doesn't make much sense to put all your money in a 5 percent MMA while you are paying 17 percent interest on credit cards.

But you have to be *serious* about your goal of getting completely out of debt within a fixed amount of time and getting that reserve in place. Otherwise, you are just fooling yourself and that three-month reserve will never materialize. Ramsey suggests getting a second job, if that's what it takes. You might also consider starting a home enterprise and devoting all you earn from it to paying down your debt (see Week 8).

The underlying problem is that most of us are still living paycheck to paycheck. We're still working for money and the minute that paycheck stops, we are in a whole heap of trouble. Robert Kiyosaki, author of *Rich Dad, Poor Dad*, has rightly observed: "The poor and middle class work for money. The rich have money work for them."[3]

The rich have the right idea. Does that sound unspiritual? Let me ask you this: which is more spiritual—working for money or putting money to work for you?

I would suggest that a person who has money working on her behalf has much greater freedom to pursue the kingdom of God than someone who has to devote all day, every day working for money. Such a person is certainly in a much better position to extend her hand to the poor and needy and is surely better able to have no fear for her household. The Bible reminds us, "No one can serve two masters." The less time I spend serving my money, the better.

Why is it that some Christians think it's spiritual to take time to keep track of every penny they *spend* but unspiritual to take time and energy to generate additional income? Given the choice between *earning more* and *obsessively monitoring and controlling what I've already got*, I'd much rather focus on earning more. (Of course, our primary focus should always be the kingdom of God, not money, whether we have a little or a lot. Don't let building your asset column distract you from the more important pursuit: pursuing God.) Yes, I monitor my balance sheet each month, but it's not my focus. My focus is on building my asset column. Not only is generating income a lot more fun, it sets me on the path to financial freedom rather than continual slavery. That's why I love the writings of two modern financial gurus: Robert Kiyosaki (*Rich Dad*) and David Bach, creator of the Automatic Millionaire concept.

The simplest way to understand your money is in terms of assets and liabilities. Anything that brings you money is an asset. Anything that costs you money is a liability. The primary difference between the rich and the rest of us is that the rich acquire assets while the rest of us blow our money on liabilities.[4] Again, "an asset is something that puts money in my pocket. A liability is something that takes money out of my pocket."[5]

Assets include stocks, bonds, notes, real estate, intellectual property.

Liabilities include mortgage, loans, credit card debt, taxes, insurance, household bills, Disneyland.

Unfortunately, what most people do when they get more money is spend more money. They blow it on liabilities: big screen TVs, new cars, boats, furniture, and so on. Rich people invest that money in assets *and use the earnings generated by the assets* to buy liabilities like big screen TVs and new cars. In other words, all you need to do is *add one step between income and spending.* Put the income into an income-generating asset, *then you can spend, not once, but as long as the asset keeps generating income.*

Let me give you an example. Let's say Joan inherits fifty thousand dollars from her great-aunt. She goes out and buys a new car. The minute she drives the car off the lot, it depreciates 25 percent and, every day, it's worth less and less until, finally, she trades it in for another car. That fifty thousand dollars didn't go too far, did it? What if, instead, Joan took that fifty thousand dollars and put a hefty down payment on a small starter home that she rented out for the next thirty years. All of a sudden, that fifty thousand dollars generates monthly cash flow in the form of rent, year after year after year. Meanwhile, her renters are paying the mortgage while Joan's property appreciates. In thirty years Joan can sell the place and buy a fleet of new cars. That's the difference between buying assets versus liabilities. Assets put money in your pocket, month after month, year after year. Buy assets and use the income the assets generate to buy liabilities.

If you have not already organized your finances using a personal finance software program such as Quicken or Microsoft Money, that's an important step to take. Both are affordable and easy to use. You can purchase them in downloadable format direct from the Internet at www.quicken.com or www.microsoft.com. It took me a weekend of effort to set up all my savings, checking, and investment accounts online so that, once a week, they automatically download all transactions directly into Quicken. Once your accounts are set up online and linked into your financial software, you can get an overview of your assets and liabilities with the click of a button. You can always see, at a glance, exactly where most of your money is going and where you need to cut back. These programs even generate full-color pie charts so, if you can't read numbers, you can at least get the picture. And yes, both have a budget feature if you want to create one.

If your finances are in disarray, this will be a multiday assignment, but at least you can make a beginning. Your real mission, and what I want to jumpstart you toward, is building your asset column and shrinking your liability column. For the remainder of this week, we'll look primarily at ways to reduce your liabilities. In Week 8, we'll discover some exciting opportunities to create more assets.

Affirmation: I don't work for money; money works for me.

Practical

Create an overview of your current assets and liabilities.

Notebook: Place your completed Assets and Liabilities Worksheet (found on page 337) in the financial section of your Personal Notebook.

Day 38

Reduce Your Debt

Scripture to Memorize

> She opens her arms to the poor
> and extends her hands to the needy.
> When it snows, she has no fear for her household;
> for all of them are clothed in scarlet.

Proverbs 31:20–21

Passage to Read

When Sanballat heard that we were rebuilding the wall, he became angry and was greatly incensed. He ridiculed the Jews, and in the presence of his associates and the army of Samaria, he said, "What are those feeble Jews doing? Will they restore their wall? Will they offer sacrifices? Will they finish in a day? Can they bring the stones back to life from those heaps of rubble—burned as they are?"

Nehemiah 4:1–2

Guided Prayer

Dear Lord, thank you for the example of Nehemiah, who courageously worked to rebuild the walls around Jerusalem even as he was surrounded and threatened by enemies who wanted to distract or discourage him. As I begin dealing with the financial "rubble" in my life today, help me to not become discouraged. I know I won't be able to rebuild the wall, or even clear out the rubble, in a day. It took time to get me into my current financial situation and it will take time to get it straightened out. But Lord, I know you work miracles. You *can* bring stones back to life from heaps of rubble and you *can* enable me to get my finances in good order. Thank you, Holy Spirit, for all you're going to teach me about good money management. I'm doing my best to be a good student and a faithful wall builder. Help me today as I clear out the rubble. Amen.

Personal

The Proverbs 31 woman may have had the ideal assets and liabilities worksheet—no wonder she had no fear for her household and was able to help the poor and needy! But chances are, when you surveyed your own financial situation yesterday, you discovered two things:

1. You need more assets.
2. You have a mountain of liabilities.

If you are like most people, you are surrounded by "rubble" in the form of consumer debt. Today, if you're smart, you'll make a determined decision to do as the people did in Nehemiah's day: clear out the rubble. It won't be easy and you won't be able to do it overnight. But I want to give you a strategy to begin digging your way out. It's what Dave Ramsey, author of *The Total Money Makeover*, calls the Debt Snowball.[6] Here's how it works:

1. List your debts in order with the smallest payoff or balance first.
2. If you have two debts with similar payoffs, list the higher interest-rate debt first.
3. Pay off the smallest balance *first.* Anytime you get some extra money, put it toward paying off your debt rather than acquiring more stuff to clean, stow, and eventually give away. Meanwhile, be sure to make your monthly payments on all your debt.
4. Once you've paid off the first debt, apply the entire monthly payment that you used to pay toward the first debt toward the second debt on the list. (You will be paying out the same amount of money each month, but you will be paying down this debt twice as fast.)
5. When you've paid off the second item, apply the entire amount you were paying on debt number 1 and debt number 2 toward debt number 3.
6. Continue until you have paid off all consumer debt.

When your spiritual Enemy finds out you're determined to clear out the rubble of debt so you can rebuild your financial fortress, he will pitch a fit. Just like Sanballat mocked Nehemiah, the devil will ridicule you and tell you it's hopeless. Remember what he said: "Will they finish in a day?" Well, no, they didn't finish in a day, but they did finish in fifty-two days. And you won't get out of debt overnight, but you *will* get out of debt if you are determined to do so. Just as Nehemiah had to ignore the letter he received, inviting him to go to a meeting in the valley of Ono (read Nehemiah 6 for more details), you'll have to ignore all the invitations you receive to spend more or borrow more. When you get an offer in the mail, declare out loud: "I know what this is. It's an invitation to the valley of Ono—and oh no, I don't want to go there!" Don't listen to the voices of temptation that will try to drag you away to "the biggest sale of the year," "limited time only," "no money down," and "no payments for a year." That's the valley of Ono! In fact you can put a stop to these unwanted temptations and protect your identity by opting out of all those pre-approved credit card offers by visiting www.optoutprescreen.com or calling 1-888-5OptOut.

Stay focused on your task: clearing out the rubble. Once you do, you can rebuild the walls of your financial fortress and secure your family's future.

Like the Proverbs 31 woman, you will have no fear for your household and you'll be able to laugh at the days to come.

Affirmation: I clear out the rubble of debt.

Practical

Complete the Debt Reduction Strategy worksheet on page 338 and begin paying down your debt.

Notebook: Place your Debt Reduction Strategy worksheet in the finance section of your Personal Notebook.

Day 29

Pay Cash

Scripture to Memorize

She opens her arms to the poor
and extends her hands to the needy.
When it snows, she has no fear for her household;
for all of them are clothed in scarlet.

Proverbs 31:20–21

Passage to Read

Do not store up for yourselves treasures on earth where moth and rust destroy, and where thieves break in and steal. But store up for yourselves treasures in heaven, where moth and rust do not destroy and where thieves do not break in and steal. For where your heart is, there your treasure will be also.

Matthew 6:19–21

Guided Prayer

Dear Lord, forgive me for all the times I've stored up treasure here on earth, rather than storing up treasure in heaven. I admit that I've been foolish. This 90-Day Jumpstart has certainly shown me how much unnecessary *stuff* I've managed to accumulate. I can't help thinking how much kingdom work could have been accomplished with money I spent on things that have now been thrown away. Holy Spirit, help me to focus my attention on heavenly treasures. I don't want to store up for myself treasures on earth, where moth and rust destroy, and thieves break in and steal. I want to store up treasures in heaven. I know it's true: where my heart is, there my treasure will be also. May my heart seek after your kingdom and may all my most treasured investments be there, too. Amen.

Personal

As you are clearing out the rubble, trying to get out of debt, it's important that you *stay* out of debt. For centuries people have understood the pitfalls of debt and have worked and saved until they could buy with cash. It's a policy more of us should adopt. When people save up to buy a particular item, they have an opportunity to do something most of us have forgotten how to do: think it over. It's the opposite of impulse buying. You know, mindlessly throwing things into your shopping cart at the mall or on the Internet. If we had to save up and ponder our purchases, we wouldn't have closets filled with clothes we never wear and storage areas filled with junk we never use (but refuse to part with because we paid so much money for it).

Think back on all the stuff you have thrown away, given away, or stowed away, just since you've started this 90-Day Jumpstart. How many of those items were purchased with credit cards? How many items fall into the "I never would have bought it if I had had to save up to get it" category? Remember our good friend, the 80/20 rule? Why did you buy the 80 percent of clothes you never wear and toys your kids never use? No doubt it's because of your handy-dandy credit card and the impulse-buying mindset it creates.

The average American household has 8,400 dollars in credit card debt.[7] Even if they never put another dime on those credit card accounts, if all they do is pay the monthly minimum, it will take them forty-seven years to pay it back—and it will cost thirty-three thousand dollars.

Incidentally, you can cut your annual living expenses by 30 percent in less than one minute. Want to know how? Cut up your credit cards. Research indicates that consumers spend 30 percent more when purchasing with a credit card rather than cash.[8] Something about spending actual hard-earned dollar bills makes a person stop and think. Something about flashing a credit card makes a person half crazy.

The solution is this: become a cash person in a cashless society. From this day forward, either pay cash (that includes not only dollars but checks or a debit card that takes funds directly out of your checking account) or don't buy it. When you run out of money, stop spending. There's your budget right there! And isn't that easier than keeping track of every penny you spend? If you don't spend what you don't have, guess what? You'll quickly figure out the meaning of the word *budget* when you're eating macaroni and cheese out of a box every night for a week.

The only other option is disciplining yourself to pay off your entire credit card every month. However, only 40 percent of people are self-disciplined enough to do so.[9] Be honest with yourself. Are you one of them or are you among the 60 percent who will just heap up more rubble?

Another option is setting up your accounts on the Internet and paying off your credit cards *weekly*. Almost all major credit cards now offer the option of managing your account online. Check it out.

Stop and think before you buy. Ask yourself: is there any possible way I can live without this—at least until I can finish paying off all the stuff I've already accumulated? Does this fall into the 80 percent category of things I'll almost never use? If the answer is yes, have enough wisdom and self-control to walk away. If you do, you'll no longer have to fear for your household's financial future. Instead, your family will be clothed in scarlet and you'll be able to extend your hands to the needy.

Affirmation: I am a wise steward of my money.

Practical

Make all necessary arrangements to lead a cash lifestyle. This includes cutting up your credit cards (except one for true emergencies), scheduling cash withdrawals, obtaining a debit card to replace your credit card, and carrying your checkbook and a picture ID. Pay cash whenever possible. When the cash is gone for the week, stop spending. If you still want to use credit cards, set up your accounts online so you can pay them off *weekly*. Make it a practice to stop and think before you buy.

Day 40
Begin Automatic Savings and Investment

Scripture to Memorize

> She opens her arms to the poor
> and extends her hands to the needy.
> When it snows, she has no fear for her household;
> for all of them are clothed in scarlet.
>
> Proverbs 31:20–21

Passage to Read

> Pride only breeds quarrels,
> but wisdom is found in those who take advice.
> Dishonest money dwindles away,
> but he who gathers money little by little makes it grow.
>
> Proverbs 13:10–11

Guided Prayer

Dear Lord, I know that pride is at the heart of every quarrel, including the fights in my household over money. I confess that I've ignored the counsel of wise money managers in the past. Now I'm ready to listen. I won't be like the foolish people in this world who think they can get ahead of the money game through gambling, the lottery, or get-rich-quick schemes. They never work. What works is wisdom. What works is gathering money little by little and letting it grow over time. Holy Spirit, I invite you to bring wise counselors into my life who can teach me how to manage my finances more effectively. I thank you in advance for the lessons I'm going to learn and for the strength to apply them. Amen.

Personal

The Proverbs 31 woman had no fear for her household. Few things are more frightening than the prospect of divorce. And one of the surest predictors of divorce is fiscal irresponsibility on the part of one or both partners. Fifty-seven percent of divorced couples in the United States cited financial problems as the primary reason for the demise of their marriage, according to a survey conducted by Citibank.[10]

Jesus talked more about money than about heaven and hell combined. There are 125 verses in the Bible addressing our pocketbook, and many of Jesus's parables concerned money management. The Bible reminds us, "A man's life does not consist in the abundance of his possessions" (Luke 12:15), but it also teaches us the importance of financial wisdom. Clearly, money matters.

One of the best ideas I've ever heard is David Bach's Automatic Millionaire approach. Rather than saving what's left over, Bach teaches people: pay yourself first. Financial expert Robert Allen agrees. "The secret to financial success is to spend what you have left over after saving, instead of saving what is left over after spending."[11] We all know there's never anything left over. As of January 2007, the American personal savings rate was minus 0.7 percent.[12] However, if you save the money before it ever reaches your checking account, you can trick yourself into acting more financially savvy than you really are! Thanks to technology, this is literally a no-brainer. All it takes is a few hours to set up an automatic savings and investment plan. Trust me: if I can do it, anyone can. And I did it. Once you've done this, you are on the road to financial freedom by doing exactly what the Bible suggests: "He who gathers money little by little makes it grow."

Experts agree you should save 10 percent of your income. If your employer offers a 401(k) plan, schedule an appointment with the person who handles it *tomorrow*. Your spouse should do the same. Make arrangements for your employer to deduct 10 percent of your income automatically from your paycheck and invest it in the 401(k). Because they take pre-tax dollars, you will hardly notice the difference in your paycheck. Yes, it might "bite" a little, but it's worth the sacrifice, especially if the company matches your investment. By paying *yourself* before paying taxes, you save a considerable amount of money. (Learn more in chapter 3 of *The Automatic Millionaire*.)[13]

If your employer doesn't offer a 401(k), or if you are self-employed, you can still easily set up automatic savings and investment accounts. The whole key is to *make it automatic*. Choose the companies you want to save or invest with, decide how much you want to save or invest monthly, then set up an account authorizing the investment fund to *automatically* transfer money from your checking account into the savings or investment account *every month*. Do what the Bible says: gather money little by little. The whole secret is putting it on autopilot. Don't kid yourself by thinking, *Oh, I don't have to make it automatic. I'll just save and invest whenever I can*. You won't. David Bach worked as a private financial consultant for years, and he says he can count on one hand the number of clients who kept that commitment. You won't. Make it automatic.

The sooner you start, the more your money will grow. Just as an example, if you save $100 per month at 6 percent interest, it will *cost you* $48,000, but at the end of forty years, it will *pay you* $200,145. If you bump those numbers up a bit, the results are remarkable, thanks to the power of compound interest. According to David Bach: "If at age twenty-five you started putting $250 a month (or $3,000 a year) into an IRA that earned an annual return of 10 percent, by the time you were sixty-five, you'd have a nest egg worth nearly $1.6 million. Even if you waited until you were forty to get started, you'd still wind up with a hefty sum—roughly $335,000."[14]

You can set up automatic savings accounts with a fixed percent return, but once you have your three-month reserve in place, you should set up automatic *investment* accounts. Again, you don't have to be a Wall Street genius to generate income in the stock market. In reality, few so-called geniuses outperform good old-fashioned dollar cost averaging. As Robert Allen puts it, "You can be a total idiot and still win. You just buy every month, month after month. You buy during good times. You buy during bad times. You don't care what the headlines are saying. You ignore the experts on TV."[15] Instead, you automatically invest a fixed sum of money every month. When stock prices are low, your dollar goes *further* and you acquire *more stocks*. Then when the price goes up, the stocks you bought in the down market yield an even greater return than stocks you buy when the market is riding high. So for the long-term investor, a down market is actually good news. Sounds crazy, but it's true.

Over the past fifty years, the stock market has averaged an 11 percent annual return. That's no guarantee for the future, but stocks have *never* lost money over any ten-year period—and that includes the decade of the Great Depression. Your best choice is an index fund. These are offered by all major investment firms and incorporate stocks representative of a broad range of industries, giving you a balanced portfolio. But don't just take my word for it. Warren Buffett, the world's most successful investor, says, "The best way to own common stocks is through an index fund."[16]

One thing to be alert to is the management and other miscellaneous fees charged by the fund. These can add up over time and eat into your profits. You can visit www.morningstar.com for a ranking of index funds along with information on the percentage they charge. You should never pay more than 0.5 percent, and some funds charge far less. Index funds mimic the performance of a particular index (the most common is the S&P 500). Because these investment managers are not picking stocks, but rather allocating each dollar invested to the specific stocks represented by the index, they typically charge very low fees. With an index fund, you are guaranteed to earn the market return. In other words, you will earn the same percentage increase or decrease as the market average.

You will certainly want to research investing in much greater detail than I am able to provide as part of your jumpstart. Keep in mind the importance of having a diversified portfolio of assets, the up-and-down cycles of which don't run in sync: stocks (both U.S. and foreign, as well as large company and small), bonds (of varying maturities), cash, real estate, and commodities.

Trust the Bible's advice and follow David Bach's instruction: save little by little so your money will grow—and make it automatic. If you do so, you'll have no fear for your household's future.

Affirmation: I invest wisely.

Practical

Set up your savings and investment plan on autopilot.

Day 41

Weekly Checkup

Cumulative Scripture Review

> A wife of noble character who can find?
>   She is worth far more than rubies.
> Her husband has full confidence in her
>   and lacks nothing of value.
> She brings him good, not harm,
>   all the days of her life.
> She selects wool and flax
>   and works with eager hands.
> She is like the merchant ships,
>   bringing her food from afar.
> She gets up while it is still dark;
>   she provides food for her family
>   and portions for her servant girls.
> She considers a field and buys it;
>   out of her earnings she plants a vineyard.
> She sets about her work vigorously;
>   her arms are strong for her tasks.
> She sees that her trading is profitable,
>   and her lamp does not go out at night.
> In her hand she holds the distaff
>   and grasps the spindles with her fingers.

She opens her arms to the poor
and extends her hands to the needy.
When it snows, she has no fear for her household;
for all of them are clothed in scarlet.

Proverbs 31:10–21

Turn verses 20–21 into a Scripture-based prayer:

_____

_____

_____

Practical

Saturday is your day to review and catch up on any unfinished items. Check to confirm that you have completed the following one-time tasks:

- ☐ I calculated my tithe and committed to giving it.
- ☐ I arranged to make my giving automatic.
- ☐ I completed (or at least began work on) my ASSETS AND LIABILI-TIES WORKSHEET.
- ☐ I created a debt-reduction strategy and committed myself to "clearing out the rubble" in an orderly fashion.
- ☐ I made arrangements to lead a cash lifestyle (scheduling cash withdrawals, obtaining a debit card, carrying a checkbook, etc.).
- ☐ I set up (or began setting up) an automatic savings and investment program.

Check to confirm you are routinely incorporating the following positive changes into your daily routine:

- ☐ I'm using my Personal Notebook.
- ☐ I'm regularly reviewing my Personal Vision Statement.
- ☐ I'm spending time in my prayer place, enjoying TAG.
- ☐ I'm dealing proactively with my secret sins.
- ☐ I'm completing this study every day, practicing the memory verse, and reciting affirmations daily.

- ☐ I'm becoming consciously selective about how I dress and how I use my time and resources.
- ☐ I'm becoming a more serious student of the Bible.
- ☐ I'm practicing the presence of God, being watchful, thankful, and prayerful.
- ☐ I'm following my EVENING ROUTINE and going to bed on time.
- ☐ I'm inviting God to awaken me each morning, saying no to the snooze button, and following a MORNING ROUTINE.
- ☐ I'm exercising control over my eating habits and limiting sugar intake.
- ☐ I'm using smaller plates and controlling food portions.
- ☐ I'm planning ahead for healthier eating.
- ☐ I'm prayer walking three to five days per week.
- ☐ I begin each day with a cleansing drink and consume sixty-four ounces of water every day.
- ☐ I stop eating several hours before bed.
- ☐ I'm using a rebounder to fight gravity and cellulite.
- ☐ I routinely take cleansing baths.
- ☐ I'm using my DAILY PAGE and applying the 80/20 rule.
- ☐ I routinely give away everything I can.
- ☐ I'm tackling items on my TACKLE LIST.
- ☐ I'm tithing.
- ☐ I'm clearing out the rubble of debt and paying with cash.
- ☐ I have my savings and investments on autopilot.

Day 42

Weekly Reflection

Sunday is a great day to devote extra time meditating on the entire Proverbs 31 passage, memorizing your assigned verses, praying, and preparing your heart for the week ahead. Take one day out of every seven to rest and reflect. Do *not* catch up on assignments you did not complete, but *do* schedule them for the coming week.

Fill in the remainder of Proverbs 31:10–21 from memory:

A _____ __ _____ _____ who can find?

    She is worth ___ ____ ____ _____.

Her husband ____ ____ _____ __ ___

    and lacks _____ __ _____.

She brings him _____, ___ _____,

    all the _____ __ ___ ____.

She selects _____ ___ _____

    and works _____ _____ _____.

She is like ____ _____ _____,

    bringing her _____ ____ ____.

She gets up _____ __ __ _____ ____;

    she provides _____ ___ ___ _____

    and portions ___ ___ _____ _____.

She considers _ _____ ___ ____ __;

    out of her earnings ___ _____ __ _____.

She sets about ___ ____ _____;

    her arms ___ _____ ___ ___ _____.

She sees that ____ _____ _____,

    and her ____ ____ ___ __ __ __ _____.

In her hand ___ _____ __ _____

    and grasps ___ _____ ____ ___ _____.

She opens ___ _____ __ ___ ____

    and extends ___ _____ ___ ___ ____.

When it _____, she ___ __ ____ ___ ___

    _____;

    for all __ ____ ___ _____ __ _____.

Weekly Evaluation

1. Am I listening for and hearing God's voice? What is he saying to me?

_____

_____

2. Am I increasingly manifesting the fruit of the Spirit: love, joy, peace, patience, kindness, goodness, faithfulness, gentleness, and self-control (Gal. 5:22–23)? What areas look encouraging? What needs prayer?

_____

_____

3. What did God teach me during my TAG?

_____

_____

4. Which priorities did I live by? Which goals did I pursue?

_____

_____

5. Which priorities or goals did I neglect?

_____

_____

6. What new thing did I learn—about life, God, my family, and the people around me?

_____

_____

7. What are my specific priorities/goals for the coming week?

_____

_____

Take out your notebook and schedule your priorities or goals for the coming week.

WEEK SEVEN
PERSONAL APPEARANCE

Day 43

Stick with Your Core Color

Scripture to Memorize

She makes coverings for her bed;
> she is clothed in fine linen and purple.
Her husband is respected at the city gate,
> where he takes his seat among the elders of the land.

Proverbs 31:22–23

Passage to Read

I clothed you with an embroidered dress and put leather sandals on you. I dressed you in fine linen and covered you with costly garments. I adorned you with jewelry: I put bracelets on your arms and a necklace around your neck, and I put a ring on your nose, earrings on your ears and a beautiful crown on your head. So you were adorned with gold and silver; your clothes were of fine linen and costly fabric and embroidered cloth.... And your fame spread among the nations on account of your beauty, because the splendor I had given you made your beauty perfect, declares the Sovereign LORD.

Ezekiel 16:10–14

Guided Prayer

Dear Lord, I stand amazed at the beauty you intend for your women! All I can say is: clothe me, Lord. To think that you want me to wear embroidered dresses, leather shoes, fine linen, gold jewelry (I'm not so sure about that nose ring), and a tiara on my head. Wow! You really are an awesome God. Lord, I want to be a beautiful woman, inside and out. Yes, on the outside, too. Thank you for understanding that I want to look and feel beautiful. Holy Spirit, make me so radiate the love of God and the joy of being loved by him that no one notices the wrinkles or other imperfections. Amen and amen!

Personal

Whoever came up with the theology that God wants women to be frumpy must not have read the Old Testament. In today's passage from Ezekiel, God describes the outfits he personally picked for the women of Israel. He clearly states right up front: "I clothed you." God's fashion sense included embroidered dresses, leather sandals, fine linen, expensive clothes, and gold jewelry (specifically bracelets, necklaces, *nose rings*, earrings, and a tiara). The Bible says the Israeli women were so beautiful and well-dressed, their fame spread around the world. The Proverbs 31 woman was clothed in fine linen and purple, the equivalent of modern designer chic.

Okay, so now that we've dispensed with the silliness about how spiritual it is to look ugly, let's get to work. Step 1: Select a core color. As always, I learned this lesson the hard way. I was speaking at a church in Pittsburgh more than a decade ago. It's still vivid because it was that traumatic. At the end of a long Saturday, I retired to my hotel room only to realize I had been wearing navy blue stockings with my black dress all day long and none of my dear sisters-in-Christ bothered to mention it. (I have since forgiven them, of course.) That was the end of me and navy blue. I decided right then and there to finally implement advice I had heard many times, the same advice I'm giving you. Pick a core color and stick with it (I'll explain how in a minute). I promise you this is true: I went home and gathered up everything navy blue (shoes, dresses, purses) and gave them all away immediately.

I know a woman who carries a different colored purse every day to coordinate with her multicolored wardrobe. If that makes her happy, so be it. But my battle cry is simplify! Almost all of my shoes are black for winter (with some white for summer), and my life is easier when I simply carry one purse per season.

When I survey my closet, or when I conduct a periodic purge of items rarely worn, I almost always regret the items I've bought that don't somehow coordinate with black. Because I'm mindful of correct color, it always amazes me how *few* North American women wear the correct core color and, conversely, what a dramatic difference it makes when I see a woman who has got it right.

If you want to go to a color consultant or buy a book on the subject, you can certainly do that right after you finish your 90-Day Jumpstart. For now, the following simplified guidelines are enough to get you started in finding your correct core color:

- Dark hair and eyes—black
- Dark hair and blue or hazel eyes—go by skin tone: if dark, go with black; if light, go with navy
- Blonde hair and blue or hazel eyes—navy
- Red hair—brown
- Sandy hair and brown eyes—camel

When I traveled to Bogotá, Colombia, I marveled how fabulous *most* of the women looked. Truly, I have never seen so many gorgeous women anywhere in the world. It took me only a few days to figure it out. The vast majority of the women had dark hair and dark eyes and *almost every one* wore bold, vibrant colors in combination with a black core color. It's interesting that the stores made it easy by filling the racks with black and bold-colored clothing.

America is a melting pot and so shopping is not that simple. That's the reason most American women almost always *wear the wrong color*. You can't just walk into a store and assume that everything on the rack is going to look great on you. It won't, although it helps to shop in the right season. If your core color is brown, shop during late fall. If your core color is navy, shop in the summer. Black, shop in winter. And camel, shop in spring or fall. Although fabric and texture may be an issue, you can always add layers or use heavier items as accent pieces.

Just when you thought I couldn't possibly make you give anything else away, guess what? It's time to extend your hands to the needy one more time! (Or make another trip to your local consignment shop, if you prefer.) Pillage your closet, getting rid of everything that doesn't coordinate with your core color. Once again, it doesn't matter how much you paid for it, where you wore it, how nostalgic it is, or even how well it fits. What matters is that it's the wrong color and few things make a woman look worse than the wrong color.

Sometimes hard-learned lessons are the only ones we truly learn. So, as you gather up all those wrong-colored clothes for yet another 90-Day Jumpstart giveaway, let the message sink in. Only buy clothing that coordinates with your core color. In the future, before buying anything, ask yourself, *Does this work with my core color?* If it doesn't, don't buy it. No matter how fashionable, no matter how cute, even if it's 90 percent off, don't buy it.

This will save you time and money in the future. It will actually stretch your wardrobe because everything will coordinate with everything else. It will streamline your shopping expeditions, make buying decisions easier, speed up your morning routine, simplify travel, and, in general, free your energy to focus on more important things.

Keep it simple. Stick to your core color.

Affirmation: I wear my core color to simplify my life.

Practical

Purge your closet of anything that doesn't coordinate with your core color. Give it all away to someone who needs it more than you do anyway. If you are completing this study as part of a group, I encourage you to do what I've done on several occasions. Namely, participate in a clothing exchange. Set a date for all the women to bring *their very best clothing.* Loosely organize it into color sections and then *swap.* This is lots of fun and will lessen the pain of purging your closet.

Day 44

Determine Your Ideal Weight

Scripture to Memorize

She makes coverings for her bed;
    she is clothed in fine linen and purple.
Her husband is respected at the city gate,
    where he takes his seat among the elders of the land.

Proverbs 31:22–23

Passage to Read

When the woman saw that the fruit of the tree was good for food and pleasing to the eye, and also desirable for gaining wisdom, she took some and ate it. She also gave some to her husband, who was with her, and he ate it. Then the eyes of both of them were opened, and they realized they were naked; so they sewed fig leaves together and made coverings for themselves.

Genesis 3:6–7

Guided Prayer

Dear Lord, I have to confess: I can't cast the first stone at Eve. Although you've filled this world with wonderful food like fruits, vegetables, nuts, seeds, and whole grains, I'm continually tempted to eat all the wrong things. When I see food that looks good, even though it's *not good*, I fall for the deception. Like Eve, I take and eat it. I've also been guilty of giving deceptive food to my husband and children. It looks so good! It tastes so good!

Holy Spirit, open my eyes to see the truth. Enlighten my mind to understand just how deceptive food can be and give me wisdom to understand my eating habits. I know there are spiritual and emotional issues involved. Eating is not just a physical thing.

I also need to confess that, because I've failed to exercise self-control in the area of food, I'm just like Adam and Eve: I need new outfits! Forgive me for all the money I've spent buying more and more clothes, filling my closet with different sizes, simply because I was unwilling to exercise self-control concerning food.

Sometimes, I just feel so powerless in the face of the unrelenting onslaught of food that looks good and tastes good, even though it isn't good for me. I need your help. Heal those places in my soul that drive me to reach for food, rather than you, for comfort. Forgive me and heal me. Amen.

Personal

The Proverbs 31 woman was clothed in fine linen and purple. She wore the most expensive clothing available at the time. One way to position yourself to be able to afford better quality clothing is to limit yourself to buying *one size only*. If you have to spend money purchasing multiple wardrobes in multiple sizes, your wardrobe dollar is stretched to the limit. One of the best-dressed women I know is in her sixties. She's had some quality outfits in her closet for decades because they are well made, so they last forever; but more important, she has been wearing the same size for decades. If her clothing starts to get tight, as it does from time to time, she knows it's time to eat less and exercise more. It's *not* time to go out and buy clothing a size bigger.

An absolute essential for making the most of your wardrobe is having a one-size wardrobe. But what size is the right size? That's an important question that every woman who cares about her personal appearance needs to answer. As a chronic yo-yo dieter, I've thought a lot about my ideal weight. You can consult the Body Mass Index (BMI) chart at the end of this section for general guidelines concerning what's healthy and what's not. As long as you're within the healthy range, I believe: *Your ideal weight is the healthiest weight you can maintain while leading a sustainable lifestyle.*

Reread that: *Your ideal weight is the healthiest weight you can maintain while leading a sustainable lifestyle.* For example, if I live on nothing but egg whites and lemon water, I can get down to 120 pounds and wear a size 6. But that is *not* a sustainable lifestyle. Therefore, even though I would love to weigh 120 pounds and look fabulous in a size 6 (like I did when I was in my twenties and during the tail end of my forty-day fast in 2005), 120 pounds really isn't the ideal weight for me.

163

Unfortunately, when I begin eating for emotional reasons (like I did after the death of my father in June 2006), I can zoom up to the low 150s. I have photographic proof that this is *not* my ideal weight either. Besides, I can only sustain it by living on coffee and junk food while watching television and feeling sorry for myself. What's the answer? Somewhere in the middle.

If I am reasonably smart about my eating and perform moderate exercise three to four times a week, I hover around the low 130s and wear a size 8. That's a lifestyle I *should* maintain, and therefore, even though it doesn't enable me to look like a supermodel, size 8 is my ideal dress size and the low 130s is my ideal weight. My wardrobe, then, should consist almost entirely of size 8 clothing. When those clothes become too tight, I shouldn't go out and buy the next size clothing. That's poor stewardship of my clothing budget, not to mention poor stewardship of my body.

Please be realistic, not idealistic, when trying to determine your ideal weight. Factor in your height, your frame, your body type, and so on. Is it really worth tormenting yourself over those last ten pounds? It's ironic that many women who *should* be concerned about losing weight, because they are dangerously out of shape, aren't willing to put forth the effort it takes to reach a healthy size. And women who really look pretty good (age and other factors considered) live in absolute torment because they don't look like the women on the cover of the magazines.

Not only was the Proverbs 31 woman clothed in fine linen and purple, she was clothed with strength and dignity. We don't have to be supermodel thin but we shouldn't be flabby and sloppy either. Our physical appearance should convey strength and dignity. Again, be well-balanced. The devil is always looking for someone to devour, and his target is the person who is out of balance. Discover and commit to a healthy weight for life; then you can build your very best one-size wardrobe and enjoy top-quality clothing for years to come.

Practical

Determine your ideal weight and develop a plan to get to it and stick to it. The average weight loss on the 90-Day Renewal (as set forth in *Becoming the Woman I Want to Be*) is twenty pounds. You might consider undertaking the 90-Day Renewal after you have finished this 90-Day Jumpstart. For now, *put away any clothes that don't fit.*

It's okay to dream of returning to your ideal size. Just don't distract yourself by keeping clothes in your closet that don't fit. Put them away for now. Note the date you stow this bin on the list in your Personal Notebook. If you are not back down to that size within one year, then you must give away, sell, or consign all those cherished items. Meanwhile, let the impending deadline serve as your incentive to get back to your ideal size.

This exercise alone should go a long way toward de-cluttering your closet *and* simplifying your life. There's no point standing in your closet staring at clothes you can't wear. It's an emotional drain.

Notebook: Note the bin number and date you stowed your dream clothes. If you are not back into the clothes one year from now, you must get rid of them no matter how much you love them or how much money you paid for them!

Body Mass Index[1]

To use the table, find the appropriate height in the left-hand column. Move across the row to the given weight. The number at the top of the column is the BMI for that height and weight.

BMI (kg/m2)	19	20	21	22	23	24	25	26	27	28	29	30	35	40
Height (in.)							Weight (lb.)							
58	91	96	100	105	110	115	119	124	129	134	138	143	167	191
59	94	99	104	109	114	119	124	128	133	138	143	148	173	198
60	97	102	107	112	118	123	128	133	138	143	148	153	179	204
61	100	106	111	116	122	127	132	137	143	148	153	158	185	211
62	104	109	115	120	126	131	136	142	147	153	158	164	191	218
63	107	113	118	124	130	135	141	146	152	158	163	169	197	225
64	110	116	122	128	134	140	145	151	157	163	169	174	204	232
65	114	120	126	132	138	144	150	156	162	168	174	180	210	240
66	118	124	130	136	142	148	155	161	167	173	179	186	216	247
67	121	127	134	140	146	153	159	166	172	178	185	191	223	255
68	125	131	138	144	151	158	164	171	177	184	190	197	230	262
69	128	135	142	149	155	162	169	176	182	189	196	203	236	270
70	132	139	146	153	160	167	174	181	188	195	202	207	243	278
71	136	143	150	157	165	172	179	186	193	200	208	215	250	286
72	140	147	154	162	169	177	184	191	199	206	213	221	258	294
73	144	151	159	166	174	182	189	197	204	212	219	227	265	302
74	148	155	163	171	179	186	194	202	210	218	225	233	272	311
75	152	160	168	176	184	192	200	208	216	224	232	240	279	319
76	156	164	172	180	189	197	205	213	221	230	238	246	287	328

BMI	
18.5 or less	underweight
18.5–24.9	normal
25.0–29.9	overweight
30.0–39.9	obese
40 or greater	extremely obese

Day 45

Purge Personal Items

Scripture to Memorize

She makes coverings for her bed;
   she is clothed in fine linen and purple.
Her husband is respected at the city gate,
   where he takes his seat among the elders of the land.

Proverbs 31:22–23

Passage to Read

Therefore, since we are surrounded by such a great cloud of witnesses, let us throw off everything that hinders and the sin that so easily entangles, and let us run with perseverance the race marked out for us. Let us fix our eyes on Jesus, the author and perfecter of our faith.

Hebrews 12:1–2

Guided Prayer

Dear Lord, thank you for the great cloud of witnesses, those saints who have gone before who cheer me on toward the finish line. Thank you for preserving their stories in your Word and in Christian biographies, so I can be encouraged and challenged by their examples. I want to throw off everything that hinders and the sin that so easily entangles so that I, too, can run with perseverance the race marked out for me. Today I fix my eyes on you, Jesus, the author and perfecter of my faith. Thank you for running your race so faithfully even though it meant death on the cross. Help me today, Holy Spirit, to take up my cross and follow after Jesus. Amen.

Personal

We need to throw off everything that hinders us from becoming the women God has called us to be. Therefore, the purge continues! Gather up every ounce of hair care products, skin care products, and makeup you own. If you bought it more than a year ago, throw it out. If it's 90 percent empty, throw it out. If you don't use it, throw it out. I've said it before and I'll say it again: price isn't a factor. Even if you bought it at the Estée Lauder counter, if you don't use it or it doesn't look sensational on you, throw it out. Speaking of Estée Lauder—and Clinique and every other makeup counter in the mall—rid yourself of all the "gift with purchase" items you've acquired but never use. I know how warm and fuzzy you felt when they handed you that free container with thirty shades of eye shadow, but since you don't wear any of them, throw it out. And by the way, how many makeup cases do you need? When I did my makeup-counter purge, I gave away five of them.

Next, accessories. We're talking purses, belts, hats, scarves, and so on. You know the drill by now. If you never wear it, give it away. Apply the 80/20 rule (if you haven't done so already) and get rid of the 80 percent you wear only 20 percent of the time.

Finally, jewelry. We're getting ruthless now. Even if your mom gave it to you, even if your five-year-old made it for you, even if you bought it on your honeymoon in Tahiti, if you don't wear it, it's got to go. Now, if you can't put it in the trash can, I completely understand. Create a storage bin labeled NOSTALGIA and put it in there. And, yes, I have one of those bins!

When you purchase jewelry in the future, remember that the Proverbs 31 woman wore *fine linen* and that God adorned the Israelites with the purest gold. You might consider spending more money on a few quality pieces of jewelry rather than filling a giant jewelry box with low-cost pieces. If you are serious about simplifying your life, give away the 80 percent of your jewelry you almost never wear. Definitely get rid of anything that goes with only one outfit. Surely you can find something else that also works with that outfit. It might not match quite as perfectly, but remember: perfection is often the enemy of peace. Less is more.

Affirmation: I am clothed in fine linen and purple.

Practical

Purge your accessories and personal care items. Once again, if you are part of a group, you can organize an accessory exchange night. I've done it, and not only is it lots of fun, it's much simpler than the clothing exchange.

Day 46

The Importance of Being Modest

Scripture to Memorize

> She makes coverings for her bed;
>   she is clothed in fine linen and purple.
> Her husband is respected at the city gate,
>   where he takes his seat among the elders of the land.
>
> Proverbs 31:22–23

Passage to Read

I urge, then, first of all, that requests, prayers, intercession and thanksgiving be made for everyone—for kings and all those in authority, that we may live peaceful and quiet lives in all godliness and holiness. This is good, and pleases God our Savior, who wants all men to be saved and to come to a knowledge of the truth. . . .

I also want women to dress modestly, with decency and propriety, not with braided hair or gold or pearls or expensive clothes, but with good deeds, appropriate for women who profess to worship God.

1 Timothy 2:1–4, 9–10

Guided Prayer

Dear heavenly Father, today I pray for my country. I thank you for our leaders and ask you to give them great wisdom as they lead. I pray that our laws would be righteous in your sight. Lord, I desire to live a peaceful, quiet life in all godliness and holiness. I know you want all people to be saved and to come to a knowledge of the truth. Help me to gain a greater understanding of my role in bringing the gospel to my culture. I want to play a vital part in your kingdom work right here where I live.

Holy Spirit, help me to discern when it's best to conform to the culture for the sake of the gospel and when it's necessary to go against the culture. I know for sure that I cannot conform to the world when it comes to standards of modesty. Prepare my heart as I reevaluate my wardrobe to see if there is anything offensive or anything that might be a stumbling block to the men around me. I want to dress in fine linen and purple but, more important, I want to be clothed with strength and dignity. Give me spiritual eyes to see anything in my closet that makes me appear morally weak or undignified. Then give me the courage to refashion my wardrobe in a way that honors you, no matter what it takes. Amen.

Personal

Both the Proverbs 31 woman and her husband were acknowledged at the city gates, which represented the seat of political, economic, and social leadership in their culture. It was a combination of Congress, Wall Street, and the society page all rolled into one. The Bible tells us, "Her husband is respected at the city gate" and then adds, "Let her works bring her praise at the city gate" (vv. 23, 31). So there is nothing wrong with a Christian achieving fame, acclaim, or influence in politics, business, or society.

Today's passage urges us to pray for those in authority and do everything we can to live peacefully within the context of our culture *with a view toward* bringing salvation to our countrymen. However, the Bible does not teach total cultural conformity. We should go along to get along, but only to a point. The line Paul draws in the sand is modesty. Today's passage was written to Timothy, who was pastoring a church in Ephesus, a sexually decadent city where hundreds, perhaps even thousands, of women worked as prostitutes at the massive Temple of Artemis, the multibreasted goddess of fertility. It's hard for us to imagine now, but attending "worship service" meant having sex with strangers and even participating in massive sexual festivals. These temple prostitutes were wealthy and well dressed, much like our Hollywood and music stars today, who earn millions for dressing and behaving seductively.

To show the relevance of Paul's message for us today, here's what I believe he is saying: women in the church should not look like the women on the cover of *Cosmopolitan*, *Maxim*, or almost any other magazine for that matter. That may be how women in the culture dress, but it's not appropriate for God's woman. My comments today may offend some readers, but I feel strongly that while God's women *should be dressed in fine linen and purple*, they should wear enough of that fine linen and purple to cover key body parts.

I am absolutely shocked by the way some Christian women dress, *even at church*. Not long ago I attended a Christian event where one of the female speakers arrived dressed in a low-cut skin-tight blouse which showcased her obvious breast implants. Midway through the worship service, she took off her jacket to jump up and down in front of the mixed male-and-female audience. When I turned to the man standing next to me, I realized he was staring directly at her breasts. Sisters, this is not right! For the record, I didn't blame him for looking; I blamed her for flaunting.

Throughout these pages, I have talked about how less is more. That's almost always true, but there is an important exception: fabric. When it comes to fabric, more is more. Especially if you are a woman over forty, you need to wear more fabric—more fabric to cover your upper arms, more fabric to cover your knees, and—please, ladies, please—more fabric to cover your cleavage. It's offensive enough to see young Christian women baring cleavage, but to see a mature Christian woman revealing wrinkled, brown-spotted cleavage? Lord, have mercy on us all.

Remember, ladies, for the kingdom's sake, for modesty's sake, and, well, for mercy's sake: more fabric! And you may even have to spend more on fabric because expensive, higher-quality fabric is flattering on almost all women, while cheap, flimsy fabric can look great only when worn by skinny young women. I suspect the Proverbs 31 woman was over forty, which explains why she wore only expensive clothing.

One last thing in the more-is-more department: more coverage on the bottom, too. Unless you are in stellar physical condition, you will probably look better in a skirt than in pants. Other than those rare moments in history when I'm at my fantasy weight and wearing a size 6, I almost never wear pants, because I am a forty-something pear-shaped woman, and very few women over forty look their very best in pants. Conversely, almost all women look attractive in a well-made, properly fitting skirt that hits below the knee.

If you are still determined to wear pants, make sure they are well made in a firm fabric and that they fit your body type. The worst fashion invention since leggings is clothing made from stretch fabric (sometimes marketed as "travel clothing"). These may feel comfortable, but they reveal every lump and bump on your body.

Some apple-shaped women do look better in pants provided they wear long tunic-style tops. If you are a woman who carries every drop of excess weight above the waist (I'm insanely jealous, by the way), you can wear pants to your heart's content. But only on one condition: cover the cleavage. Chances are you have plenty of it. Good for you and good for your husband, but the rest of us don't need to see it. I may be old-fashioned, but I cannot think of one good reason a godly woman would have low-cut blouses or short skirts in her closet.

Certainly, a woman over forty should never wear a skirt above the knee. If you are trying to entice your own husband, wear a negligee. If you are trying to entice other men, get down on your knees and repent. If it still hasn't occurred to you that men are aroused by low-cut blouses and short skirts, you are living in la-la land.

Of course, my fashion observations are written with an American woman in mind. Having traveled around the world, I do know there are cultural differences when it comes to modesty. What is considered seductive dress in Turkey or Egypt is very different from what is considered seductive in the Hawaiian Islands or a remote village in Papua New Guinea. I've been to all of those places so I "get it." My point is: women *know* what is considered seductive in their culture and many of them deliberately dress to entice. As Christian women, we need to be aware of what is considered seductive in our culture so we can *avoid* dressing enticingly.

Here's something to think about: Jesus said when a man lusts after a woman in his heart, he has already committed adultery with her. How many people does it take to commit adultery? The last time I counted, it took two. I sincerely believe that a woman who dresses seductively is every bit as guilty of mental adultery as the men she causes to lust after her. No, you can't be responsible for the thoughts of every man around you but you can be responsible to dress modestly.

The Proverbs 31 woman is clothed with *dignity*. Sisters, it's past time for the women of God to dress with dignity, setting the example for our depraved culture. So take one more look at your wardrobe: is there anything seductive remaining? If so, get rid of it or wear it only in your bedroom.

Once again, my purpose here is to jumpstart your wardrobe. If you want to go further, visit your bookstore or library and peruse the indispensable book *What Not to Wear* by Trinny Woodall and Susannah Constantine.[2] I found some commentary on their website offensive and disagree with their standards of modesty, but there is plenty of good information in there. It's especially helpful in understanding whether you have a pear or apple shape, and what the fashion implications of each shape are.

Now that you've off-loaded all the wrong colors and styles (and previously you removed everything that doesn't fit or that you rarely wear), you can stow away your off-season clothing. Be sure to note the bin number on your BIN list. You can have as many off-season bins as you like, as long as you fill them with fashionable yet modest correct-color clothing that actually fits and flatters you.

By now, your closet should be a lean, mean fashion machine. Enjoy the peace and confidence it brings! You are clothed in fine linen and purple!

Affirmation: I am clothed in fine linen and purple!

Practical

Rethink clothing items that may not be flattering or appropriate.

Day 47

Evaluate Your Countenance

Scripture to Memorize

She makes coverings for her bed;
  she is clothed in fine linen and purple.
Her husband is respected at the city gate,
  where he takes his seat among the elders of the land.

Proverbs 31:22–23

Passage to Read

Your beauty should not come from outward adornment, such as braided hair and the wearing of gold jewelry and fine clothes. Instead, it should be that of your inner self, the unfading beauty of a gentle and quiet spirit, which is of great worth in God's sight. For this is the way the holy women of the past who put their hope in God used to make themselves beautiful.

1 Peter 3:3–5

Guided Prayer

Dear Lord, I don't want my beauty to come from the outside. I don't want people to think I'm beautiful just because I have the latest hairstyle and a great, fully accessorized wardrobe. I know such beauty can last only to a certain age. I want my beauty to radiate from the inside out. I want people to look at me and think, *There's something about her!*

Holy Spirit, you alone can transform me from the inside out. Only your power at work within my spirit, soul, and body can make me, and keep me, a truly beautiful woman. Teach me to cultivate a gentle and quiet spirit. I know that's of great worth in your sight. Forgive me for the times when I've been so focused on my outward appearance that I've neglected the inward reality. Forgive me, too, for those times when I've neglected both.

Thank you for the example of godly women throughout the Bible. And thank you for revealing that many of them, including Sarah, did possess outward beauty. I'm glad it's okay to be beautiful because it's one of the desires of my heart. Lord, make me beautiful. Amen.

Personal

You can read the character of a man on the countenance of his wife. I'm not sure where I first heard that, but the older I get, the more I'm convinced it's true. A woman's countenance tells the world what kind of man she has in her life. When I see a married woman who looks beat down and discouraged or who looks stressed-out and overwhelmed, I draw some very specific conclusions about her husband. Having once been in an abusive relationship myself, I can quickly identify a woman who is being abused. I can also tell when a woman feels precious and honored.

There are some women whose countenance reflects the love and care they receive, not from an earthly husband but a heavenly one. These are women who know deep down in their spirit that they are precious and honored in God's sight. These are women who derive their primary identity from their relationship with God rather than their relationship with any human being.

Although we are all profoundly impacted by our human relationships, it is possible for a woman to transcend the treatment she receives. I didn't say it is easy, but it is possible. Even if you are in a less-than-ideal marriage, God can give you the grace to reflect him as your heavenly Husband.

A countenance that radiates a gentle and quiet spirit grows out of God-confidence. A contentious spirit (the opposite of gentle and quiet) is rooted in insecurity and a lack of self-confidence. Today's passage goes on to cite Sarah as a positive example of a beautiful woman who possessed a gentle and quiet spirit and reminds us, "You are her daughters if you do what is right and do not give way to fear" (1 Peter 3:6). Let's think about that for a minute. When was Sarah most tempted to give in to fear? Probably when she ended up in Pharaoh's harem, because of her husband's foolish decisions. Imagine how frightening it would be, day after day, being prepared to go into this strange man to have sex with him for one night, knowing you were just one woman among hundreds he slept with. For one thing, she probably would have walked away with a venereal disease, which was rampant in the harems.

But the Bible says she didn't give in to fear—not because she had any confidence in her husband, for he had gotten her into this mess. She certainly didn't have confidence in herself; she was powerless to escape. No, Sarah kept a gentle and quiet spirit, even in the worst of circumstances, because she had confidence in God.

Self-confidence is based on your level of trust in your own ability and resources. Your level of self-confidence is derived from your own interpretation of things, including who your parents were; what kind of family life you had; what schools you went to; which side of the tracks you grew up on; how long you've been a Christian; how well you perform certain Christian rituals, such as praying, reading your Bible, attending Sunday school; the condition of your marriage and family life; your status in the church and community; how others treat you; how you judge your own personal appearance; your past successes and failures; plus dozens of other personal and cultural criteria.

By contrast, with God-confidence you trust completely that God has a purpose for your life and that he is more than capable of seeing it fulfilled despite all evidence to the contrary. You trust that God is the greatest Husband in the world and he will take care of you even if your earthly husband won't.

Self-confidence looks inward; God-confidence looks upward. On which one does your life rest? Those who look inward are exhausted and their faces are haggard. But "those who look to him are radiant; their faces are never covered with shame" (Ps. 34:5). When we develop God-confidence, as Sarah did, we become the women God wants us to be. We become more than women who are confident in God; we become women in whom God can place his confidence. That, my dear sisters, is what makes a woman truly beautiful.

Affirmation: A gentle and quiet spirit makes me truly beautiful.

Practical

Evaluate the basis of your confidence. Are you operating on self-confidence or God-confidence? What does your countenance reflect? What does it tell the world about your husband (both earthly and heavenly)?

Day 48

Weekly Checkup

Cumulative Scripture Review

A wife of noble character who can find?
  She is worth far more than rubies.
Her husband has full confidence in her
  and lacks nothing of value.
She brings him good, not harm,
  all the days of her life.
She selects wool and flax
  and works with eager hands.
She is like the merchant ships,
  bringing her food from afar.
She gets up while it is still dark;
  she provides food for her family
  and portions for her servant girls.
She considers a field and buys it;
  out of her earnings she plants a vineyard.
She sets about her work vigorously;
  her arms are strong for her tasks.
She sees that her trading is profitable,
  and her lamp does not go out at night.
In her hand she holds the distaff
  and grasps the spindles with her fingers.
She opens her arms to the poor
  and extends her hands to the needy.
When it snows, she has no fear for her household;
  for all of them are clothed in scarlet.
She makes coverings for her bed;
  she is clothed in fine linen and purple.
Her husband is respected at the city gate,
  where he takes his seat among the elders of the land.

Proverbs 31:10–23

Turn verses 22–23 into a Scripture-based prayer:

_____

_____

_____

Practical

Saturday is your day to review and catch up on any unfinished items. Check to confirm that you have completed the following one-time tasks:

- ☐ I identified my core color.
- ☐ I emptied my closet of anything that doesn't coordinate with my core color.
- ☐ I exchanged, gave away, or consigned all clothing that did not coordinate with my core color.
- ☐ I determined my ideal weight and have a workable plan to achieve it.
- ☐ I removed from my closet all clothing that does not fit me and stored the very best items in a bin.
- ☐ I marked my calendar for one year from now and committed myself to give away the entire "dream clothes" bin contents if I still cannot fit into them at that time.
- ☐ I purged my hair care products, skin care products, makeup, and accessories.
- ☐ I reevaluated my entire wardrobe with modesty in view.
- ☐ I evaluated my countenance honestly.

Check to confirm you are routinely incorporating the following positive changes into your daily routine:

- ☐ I'm using my Personal Notebook.
- ☐ I'm regularly reviewing my Personal Vision Statement.
- ☐ I'm spending time in my prayer place, enjoying TAG.
- ☐ I'm dealing proactively with my secret sins.
- ☐ I'm completing this study every day, practicing the memory verse, and reciting affirmations daily.

- [ ] I'm becoming consciously selective about how I dress and how I use my time and resources.
- [ ] I'm becoming a more serious student of the Bible.
- [ ] I'm practicing the presence of God, being watchful, thankful, and prayerful.
- [ ] I'm following my EVENING ROUTINE and going to bed on time.
- [ ] I'm inviting God to awaken me each morning, saying no to the snooze button, and following a MORNING ROUTINE.
- [ ] I'm exercising control over my eating habits and limiting sugar intake.
- [ ] I'm using smaller plates and controlling food portions.
- [ ] I'm planning ahead for healthier eating.
- [ ] I'm prayer walking three to five days per week.
- [ ] I begin each day with a cleansing drink and consume sixty-four ounces of water every day.
- [ ] I stop eating several hours before bed.
- [ ] I'm using a rebounder to fight gravity and cellulite.
- [ ] I routinely take cleansing baths.
- [ ] I'm using my DAILY PAGE and applying the 80/20 rule.
- [ ] I routinely give away everything I can.
- [ ] I'm tackling items on my TACKLE LIST.
- [ ] I'm tithing.
- [ ] I'm clearing out the rubble of debt and paying with cash.
- [ ] I have my savings and investments on autopilot.
- [ ] I'm wearing fashionable yet modest, correct-color clothing that actually fits and flatters me.

Day 49

Weekly Reflection

Sunday is a great day to devote extra time meditating on the entire Proverbs 31 passage, memorizing your assigned verses, praying, and preparing your heart for the week ahead. Take one day out of every seven to rest and reflect.

Do *not* catch up on assignments you did not complete, but *do* schedule them for the coming week.

Fill in the remainder of Proverbs 31:10–23 from memory:

A _____ ___ _____ _____ who can find?

   She is worth ____ _____ _____ _____.

Her husband _____ ____ _____ ___ ____

   and lacks _____ ___ _____.

She brings him _____, ____ _____,

   all the _____ __ ____ _____.

She selects _____ ____ _____

   and works _____ _____ _____.

She is like ____ _____ _____,

   bringing her _____ _____ ____.

She gets up _____ __ __ _____ _____;

   she provides _____ ____ ____ _____

   and portions ____ ____ _____ _____.

She considers __ _____ ____ _____ ___;

   out of her earnings ____ _____ __ _____.

She sets about ____ _____ _____;

   her arms ____ _____ ____ ____ _____.

She sees that ____ _____ __ _____,

   and her _____ _____ ____ ____ __ _____.

In her hand ____ _____ ____ _____

   and grasps ____ _____ _____ ____ _____.

She opens ____ _____ __ ___ _____

   and extends ____ _____ ___ ____ _____.

When it _____, she ____ ___ _____ ____ ____

   _____;

   for all ___ _____ ___ _____ ___ _____.

She makes _____ ____ ____ ___;

she is _____ ___ _____ _____ _____ _____.

Her husband ____ _____ ___ _____ _____ _____,

where he takes _____ _____ _____ _____ _____ ___

_____ _____.

Weekly Evaluation

1. Am I listening for and hearing God's voice? What is he saying to me?

   _____

   _____

2. Am I increasingly manifesting the fruit of the Spirit: love, joy, peace, patience, kindness, goodness, faithfulness, gentleness, and self-control (Gal. 5:22–23)? What areas look encouraging? What needs prayer?

   _____

   _____

3. What did God teach me during my TAG?

   _____

   _____

4. Which priorities did I live by? Which goals did I pursue?

   _____

   _____

5. Which priorities or goals did I neglect?

   _____

   _____

6. What new thing did I learn—about life, God, my family, and the people around me?

_____

_____

7. What are my specific priorities/goals for the coming week?

_____

_____

Take out your notebook and schedule your priorities or goals for the coming week.

WEEK EIGHT
HOME ENTERPRISES

Day 50

Work from Home

Scripture to Memorize

She makes linen garments and sells them,
and supplies the merchants with sashes.
She is clothed with strength and dignity;
she can laugh at the days to come.

Proverbs 31:24–25

Passage to Read

Make it your ambition to lead a quiet life, to mind your own business and to work with your hands, just as we told you, so that your daily life may win the respect of outsiders and so that you will not be dependent on anybody.

1 Thessalonians 4:11–12

Guided Prayer

Dear heavenly Father, I have made it my ambition to lead a quiet life. I pray you will give me the wisdom and insight required to mind my own business and work with my own hands to help provide for the financial needs of my family. Lord, I want my daily life to win the respect of outsiders. I want them to see that I am not idle, but busy at home, and that, although my home is the center of my life, it is not my entire life. I am a capable, productive member of society. Lord, I do not want to be dependent on anybody as my provider. I want to look to you alone as my Jehovah Jireh, my provider. I know you will lead me as I seek to begin (or expand) my home enterprise. I ask you to establish the work of my hands for the sake of your kingdom. Amen.

Personal

Today's passage from 1 Thessalonians was my inspiration almost twenty years ago when I walked away from a steady paycheck and decided to explore what it meant to mind my own business so I would not have to be dependent on anybody. At the time, the work-from-home phenomenon had not yet begun. In fact "working from home" meant you were unemployed, unstable, or otherwise dysfunctional.

But I was one of countless women who had gotten fed up with the corporate greed of the 1980s. I had no desire to spend my life bumping up against glass ceilings, exhausting myself to make someone else rich. I also experienced corporate downsizing firsthand. In 1989 my entire investment banking department was eliminated one morning without notice. I vividly remember wandering the streets of downtown Philadelphia—in shock, overwhelmed with helplessness. I never wanted to feel so dependent on anybody again. So I made a decision, somewhere between my former office and the train ride home, to launch out on my own.

My first business was marketing communications: writing press releases, brochures, and ad campaigns. It was hard to get people to take me seriously as I tried to compete with the big-city advertising agencies. But I had a talent for writing and fresh motivation in the form of my first daughter, Leah, born in March 1990. I landed my largest client when I walked into his office wearing a dark pinstriped business suit, pushing my newborn in her stroller. He said he was impressed with my determination and touched by my priorities.

There was just one small problem, and it didn't take me long to notice it. I was paid, of course, only when I worked. And there are just so many hours a day one woman can work. I had not yet discovered the joy of residual income—but I was about to. (We'll look at residual income beginning tomorrow.)

While still pregnant with Leah, I had come in contact with Larry Weeden, an acquisitions editor at Focus on the Family. He was intrigued by my conviction that I had a viable *and biblical* solution to the dilemma so many Christian women faced: how to balance the needs of family and the demands of the family budget. The answer, I told him, was found in 1 Thessalonians 4:11–12 and modeled by the Proverbs 31 woman, who was clearly a home-based businesswoman. We set to work on a project almost immediately (thank you, Larry, Keith Wall, and Janet Kobobel Grant).

Two years later my first book hit the Christian bookstores. It was titled *Homemade Business: A Woman's Step-by-Step Guide to Earning Money at Home.* I was featured on Focus on the Family's radio broadcast, and the book became an overnight sensation, sometimes selling as many as three thousand copies a day. (To put that in perspective, 93 percent of books don't sell more than a thousand copies in an entire year[1]). The Focus on the Family staff told me it was one of the largest responses they had ever had to a radio broadcast. I knew I was in the middle of a God-thing. God was calling his women to rediscover home as a place of productivity. Today 53 percent of all U.S. small businesses are home based, and the rate of growth is booming. What is more, women start twice as many businesses as men and are far more likely to succeed.[2]

Almost twenty years later, I remain convinced that God intended the home to be the *center* of our lives, not just the place we come to *recover* from our lives. The Proverbs 31 woman was *busy* at home. She was *productive*. Maintaining her home wasn't an end in itself. A smooth-functioning home was a means to an end. It created an environment that fostered creativity and launched a broad range of income-generating activities. Clearly, she manufactured and sold goods she made at home. It says, "She makes linen garments and sells them, and supplies the merchants with sashes." And she wasn't just playing at business; she was in it to make money. The Proverbs 31 woman made sure her trading was *profitable*.

I often chuckle when I hear people interpret these Scripture passages with an emphasis on the words *at home*. They completely ignore the context. First of all, the Bible was written *before* the Industrial Revolution. Of course these women were *at home*—there weren't any corporations or factories even if a woman wanted to go land a job outside of her home. The emphasis was not on *being* at home; it was on being *busy* at home.

Clearly the Thessalonians had a problem with idleness, since 2 Thessalonians devotes an entire segment to the topic. Paul writes: "We hear that some among you are idle. They are not busy; they are busybodies. Such people we command and urge in the Lord Jesus Christ to settle down and earn the bread they eat" (2 Thess. 3:11–12). My guess is that this problem existed in the days of the Proverbs 31 woman because it says *she* does not eat the bread of idleness. The implication is: *unlike many women who do.*

Now don't jump off the page and smack me for saying this, because someone has to. We have the same problem today among some Christian women. They are at home, true, but they are not *busy* at home. They are on the phone gossiping, watching soaps, reading romance novels, and surfing the Internet. At the very least, they are not setting an example of productivity.

Obviously, you are not one of those women or you wouldn't have made it to Day 50. However, there may be women in your life who need the inspiration of your positive example so they can learn what it means to be busy at home. The Proverbs 31 woman stayed busy at home, generating income to support her family and to alleviate some of the financial burden that was on her husband's shoulders. No wonder he praised her!

As a joke, a friend recently gave me an absolutely ridiculous book about *how to get your husband to make more money so you can stay home.* And do what? Having been at it for twenty years, I'm here to tell you *any* woman can make extra money from home if she is willing to work. God's ideal wife, the Proverbs 31 woman, used her home to generate income. It is unwise to rely solely on one income source in today's unstable economy. My husband, a very talented architect, lost his job several months ago. It was completely unexpected. I thank God that I have multiple streams of income. And while I'm busy thanking God, my husband is thanking me for being willing to colabor with him.

Some would argue: "I'm too busy training my children." Hello! Don't you think it just makes sense to include your children *in your business* so they learn to be entrepreneurial and self-sufficient under God's sufficiency? Don't you think training them to run their own business might prove more significant than running them around to various after-school activities?

Fortunately, neither of my daughters has the mindset that some corporation is going to give her a paycheck and job security for the rest of her life. That is an absolute delusion. We need to train our children for the real world, where the wisest people use the gifts God has given them to mind their own business. Both of my daughters, aged seventeen and eleven, have already had *many money-making businesses.* They've done everything from making bookmarks and jewelry to running my book table and processing credit card orders from my website. When my oldest daughter was fifteen, she organized a teen missions conference that attracted seven hundred people. I had very little involvement. How did she know how to do that? She's been working at Christian conferences since she was two years old!

If I can brag a little more, just so you know being busy at home has rewards, Leah (my older daughter) is currently in Egypt, where she is spending her entire summer serving at the largest orphanage—and as far as I know, the only *Christian* orphanage—in the Middle East. This is her third mission trip. She hopes to go to Mongolia next year, which will mean that, by the age of eighteen, she will have served the Lord on five continents: North America, South America, Europe, Africa, and Asia. Her little sister, Tara, just returned from Wisconsin where her team placed eighth in the National Bible Quiz competition. She had sixty dollars of her own hard-earned money in her pocketbook when she left. My guess is most of the other kids had their hands out to mom and dad for spending money. Think about it.

Having your own business offers tremendous rewards, both personal and financial, not the least of which is significant tax write-offs. Once again, my purpose is to jumpstart your thinking. Keep an open mind in the coming days as we explore some additional home enterprise opportunities.

Affirmation: I stay busy at home.

Practical

Prayerfully consider whether or not you should explore ways to generate additional family income through your own home-based business. For further suggestions, visit www.donnapartow.com/homemadebusiness.

Day 51

Develop Multiple Streams of Income

Scripture to Memorize

She makes linen garments and sells them,
  and supplies the merchants with sashes.
She is clothed with strength and dignity;
  she can laugh at the days to come.

Proverbs 31:24–25

Passage to Read

She considers a field and buys it;
  out of her earnings she plants a vineyard.
She sets about her work vigorously;
  her arms are strong for her tasks.
She sees that her trading is profitable,
  and her lamp does not go out at night.
In her hand she holds the distaff
  and grasps the spindle with her fingers. . . .
She makes linen garments and sells them,
  and supplies the merchants with sashes.

Proverbs 31:16–19, 24

Guided Prayer

Dear heavenly Father, I marvel at the accomplishments of your ideal woman. Sometimes I'm also a bit intimidated. I'm not sure I could manage all the various enterprises that she did. Thank you for reminding me, even now, that I don't have to compare myself to anyone else—not even the Proverbs 31 woman. Lord, I know you said you've included all of these examples throughout the Bible as an encouragement, not to make me feel bad about myself. I know I don't have to do everything all at once, but I can do something at once. So show me today and in the coming days

189

what you would have me do to become a smarter businesswoman. Remind me that I have the mind of Christ and I can do all things through Christ who strengthens me. I can invest in real estate; I can work hard and turn a profit in my own home business enterprise; I do have creative gifts that people might very well be willing to pay me for. Lord, show me the talents you've placed within me. I don't want to keep them hidden. I want to recognize the financial potential in each of my gifts and use them for the benefit of my family and your kingdom. I'm excited about the adventure ahead. Lead on. Amen.

Personal

Every once in a while, you read a book that changes your viewpoint entirely. For me one such book was Robert Allen's *Multiple Streams of Income*. (He has similar material in a more recent book, *The One Minute Millionaire*.)[3] In it, he points out the foolishness of relying on a paycheck, or even a single income source, to provide current financial security and a solid foundation for your retirement years.

Of course the Proverbs 31 woman had multiple streams of income long before Mr. Allen wrote his book. She operated various manufacturing and direct-selling enterprises: "She makes linen garments and sells them, and supplies the merchants with sashes." She invested in real estate: "She considers a field and buys it." What's even more significant is that she *reinvested the profits* into yet another income-generating business: "Out of her earnings she plants a vineyard."

Rather than expanding her manufacturing business or simply reinvesting everything into real estate, she diversified her income streams. If we are wise, we will do the same. Here are some possible ways to develop multiple streams of income:

- interest from savings
- dividends from investments
- rents from properties you own
- profits from the sale of investment properties
- profits from your own business

- residual income from network marketing
- passive income from the Internet (affiliate marketing and "infopreneuring")
- royalties from intellectual property you create (books, music, inventions, and so on)

The key to financial success is moving from employment or even self-employment to business ownership and investment. Business owners and investors are *not limited* to earning money only when they are working. Instead, they enjoy passive and residual income. In other words, they earn money while they sleep, either because other people are busy working for them or because they've put *their money* to work for them. Do you remember that I mentioned discovering the major pitfall of operating a one-woman marketing communications firm: *no* residual income?

The wise woman develops multiple streams of *residual income* by leveraging other people's time and money and profiting from it. Here are the criteria for evaluating if a particular business is a wise investment:

1. Leverage: Can I train other people to work for me, so I can earn money while they are working, not just when I, personally, am working?
2. Control: Do I have a protected system that belongs to me?
3. Creativity: Will the business allow me to be creative and develop my own personal style and talents?
4. Expandability: Can my business grow indefinitely?
5. Predictability: Is my income predictable if I do what is expected of me? If I am successful, and keep expanding my business, will my income increase with my success and hard work?

Now you know how to evaluate the viability of any potential business.[4]

During Week 6, we explored two streams of income—interest and dividends from your automatic savings and investment. (You *did* set those up, right?) For the remainder of this week, we'll explore the remaining options.

Affirmation: I see that my trading is profitable.

191

Practical

Begin to investigate the option of developing multiple streams of income.

Day 52

Try Direct Marketing

Scripture to Memorize

> She makes linen garments and sells them,
>   and supplies the merchants with sashes.
> She is clothed with strength and dignity;
>   she can laugh at the days to come.

> Proverbs 31:24–25

Passage to Read

And it is a good thing to receive wealth from God and the good health to enjoy it. To enjoy your work and accept your lot in life—this is indeed a gift from God.

Ecclesiastes 5:19 NLT

Guided Prayer

Dear Lord, thank you for all you've given to me. You are a wonderful God. You are El Shaddai, the God of more than enough. It is a good thing to receive wealth from you and the good health to enjoy it. Holy Spirit, give me enough wisdom not to sacrifice my health to get wealth; otherwise I'll end up spending all that wealth to regain my health! I want to be wiser than that. Grant me the serenity to accept the things I cannot change and courage to change the things I can, so that I can enjoy my work and accept my lot in life. I know this is a gift from you. In fact every good and perfect gift is from you. Thank you, Lord. Amen.

Personal

The Proverbs 31 woman was a saleswoman. She made linen garments and sold them, so she was a manufacturer. But she also supplied sashes to the merchants, which may imply that she was also a distributor for other manufacturers. Many Christian women develop valuable business skills with direct selling companies like Mary Kay, Pampered Chef, and Creative Memories. These companies offer great opportunities for women to earn money from home while doing something they love, whether it's makeovers, cooking, or scrapbooking. Perhaps even more important, they provide on-the-job training and professional development. I have friends who've earned a steady income with a direct sales business for twenty, thirty, and even forty years.

The best part about joining forces with an existing business is that you don't have to start from scratch. They've already researched and developed the products. They've already created all the promotional material you will need and, in some cases, will even provide you with your own website for a very reasonable fee. Personally, I think it's a fabulous way to go. The Direct Selling Association includes hundreds of business opportunities, one of which is bound to reflect an area that might interest you. You can check out their website at www.dsa.org.

In direct selling companies, the person who does the work earns the money. You are rewarded for your hard work in direct proportion to your accomplishments without regard to gender, race, education, or any other consideration. Mary Kay has more than four hundred women who earn a six-figure income each year and many of them do not even have a college degree.

Whichever direct sales company you choose, remember the 80/20 rule applies here as it does everywhere else. The top 20 percent of salespeople earn 80 percent of the money. That's true in *every corporation*. Your first question, then, is, *Can I make it to the top 20 percent?* Maybe, maybe not. So the second question is even more important: *Is the business successful enough that the remaining 80 percent can earn a decent income?* If it's a billion-dollar corporation, which many of these companies are, then ordinary 80 percent–types can earn a nice stream of income. Not enough to buy a yacht or retire in Tahiti, but even if you earn just a few hundred extra dollars a month, isn't it worth it? That's a few hundred dollars you can *invest*. Just $250 per month, beginning at age forty, will yield $330,000 for your retirement. The fact is almost *anyone* can earn $250 per month with a reputable direct sales or network marketing company. And many people do much, much better.

The Proverbs 31 woman was active in product sales. You might want to seriously consider following her example. Even if you work only one night per week, you can surely earn some extra money for the family, and it will force you to develop your skills as a businesswoman so you can ensure that your trading is profitable.

Affirmation: I enjoy my work.

Practical

Explore the possibility of investing some of your time and energy in building a direct sales business.

Day 53

Consider Real Estate Investing

Scripture to Memorize

> She makes linen garments and sells them,
>   and supplies the merchants with sashes.
> She is clothed with strength and dignity;
>   she can laugh at the days to come.
>
> Proverbs 31:24–25

Passage to Read

> Wisdom, like an inheritance, is a good thing
>   and benefits those who see the sun.
> Wisdom is a shelter
>   as money is a shelter,

but the advantage of knowledge is this:
that wisdom preserves the life of its possessor.

Ecclesiastes 7:11–12

Guided Prayer

Dear Lord, thank you for the gift of wisdom. As long as I am alive to see the sun each day, I need to grow in wisdom. I know it can shelter me from tough times. Your Word says wisdom is like an inheritance. It's something I can pass on to my children and grandchildren. Help me to learn something new every day so I will be able to impart valuable insights to the people I care about. Your Word acknowledges that money is a shelter, and I want to develop a financial shelter for my future. But wisdom is even more important, so help me to make that a priority. Money cannot preserve my life, but I know wisdom can. Help me to keep all of life in balance. Amen.

Personal

The Proverbs 31 woman earned money in real estate. She considered a field, bought it, and earned a profit on it. It's a smart move that the smartest people still make today. More than 80 percent of wealthy people earned their wealth through real estate. And it's something a woman at home can pursue in her spare time, using her computer and the Internet and doing some driving around. One of my best friends earned one hundred thousand dollars last year on the sale of just one house (which she had purchased the previous year as an investment property). Of course she was fortunate to "get in on" the red hot Phoenix market at just the right time. But earning money in real estate also means knowing when to sell. One day, we were praying and I said, "I believe God is telling you to sell that property." She did so immediately and within two months, the bubble burst in the Phoenix market. So she took my husband and me on a Caribbean cruise to thank me.

I met Tamera Aragon and Michelle Burgad of iSPIproperties while speaking at a women's retreat in Northern California. We formed an immediate friendship. When I learned that these women had been personally mentored by Robert Allen and had successfully developed a multimillion-dollar real estate business, they had my full attention. I asked Tamera to share her thoughts on how the modern woman can follow in the Proverbs 31 woman's footsteps. Here is her story in her own words:

"I was not born with a silver spoon in my mouth. I had to work for most everything I have ever called my own. At age thirty-two, after owning a multimillion-dollar business, putting my all into it for eleven years, I couldn't believe I was on my way to losing everything—divorce, bankruptcy—everything gone. I thought this was the worst thing that could ever happen to me, until my mother died of cancer. Then, when I thought it couldn't get worse, I was seriously injured in a car accident, bringing me chronic pain. When you reach this point, there is nowhere to look but up. I was as low as a person could get.

"I reached out for answers and was directed to study the book of Romans. It was at this time I found God in a way I had never known before. I had pushed him away for so many years, yet he had been right with me the entire time. He was just waiting for me to lean on him instead of my own understanding. He had been nudging me all along. I just wasn't listening. I am so thankful today that I asked Jesus to come into my life. He took my life and turned it around. He pulled me out of the muck I was in and has blessed me with his presence and guidance ever since.

"Now I am extremely financially secure, healthy, and content. I have been happily married for ten years with two children. God has blessed me with the wisdom to know where to go to find these things—only from him.

"So how did I go from having no money to the prosperity I enjoy today? It started with a book that I feel God brought to me called *One Minute Millionaire* by Mark Victor Hansen and Robert G. Allen. This book showed me I could really have the kind of lifestyle God wanted for me, if I would diversify my income, while at the same time making wise investments. I studied the philosophy on money found in this book as well as in others like it. Then I did something many are too afraid to do—I put what I learned to work in my life.

"Where I invest varies depending on the location of the investment as well as market timing. My investment choices change as often as the market does. Currently I divide my income into various investment strategies, such as real estate, stocks, business ownership, savings, Money Market, IRAs, inventions, and more.

"Since 80 percent of the wealthy made their money in real estate, I have chosen to place a large percentage of my investments here. What type of real estate? This varies about every six months, depending on the market. I enjoy doing real estate investing with my friend and partner, Michelle Burgad. I have found that having a second set of eyes to evaluate a property before investing has been vital to our success in real estate. Together we also bring in our 'power team' of experts so we have all the correct data to consider. We have a lot of fun investing and working together. We have a saying: 'If it's not fun, we're done.'

"And more important, God says, 'And it is a good thing to receive wealth from God and the good health to enjoy it. To enjoy your work and accept your lot in life—this is indeed a gift from God' (Eccles. 5:19 NLT).

"We have successfully profited from foreclosures, rentals, rehabbing, property management, and more. We are now focusing on an Internet support hub for real estate investors. Via this website, we are brought new investment strategies every day to evaluate and share with others. We take our research for real estate investment tools and properties and put our findings out for others. Through this website, we have been blessed with the opportunity to meet and provide mutual support to other investors like us.

"In summary, there is no hard-and-fast rule that applies to all investing—except one: to profit from your investments, we have found it is vital always to diversify them. I do as the Bible advises in Ecclesiastes 11:2: 'Divide your means seven ways, or even eight, for you do not know what disaster may happen on earth' (NRSV).

"There are two ways for investors to make money in real estate: appreciation and cash flow. Income through appreciation is available only when you sell or refinance the house. Income from cash flow rolls in month after month, as long as you own the property. You can earn plenty of money either way. The question is: do you want to buy and sell (appreciation) or buy and hold (cash flow).

"So where do you start? Since real estate investing encompasses so many types of investment properties, it's essential to classify them and pick those you are most passionate about. The following are some of the most popular real estate investment strategies with their advantages and disadvantages.

Cash flow/rental properties. These types of investment properties are the ones that generate rental income. You can start by purchasing a small starter home and renting it out to a couple who cannot yet afford to purchase a home. Eventually, you can grow into purchasing apartment buildings.

Advantages: A small rental property is one of the easier ways to get started. Rental properties produce monthly income and are likely to be a good long-term investment as they appreciate in value.

Disadvantages: You run the risk of not renting the property, leaving you with the mortgage payment and no income. Property management can be a challenge (collecting rent, fixing leaky toilets, evicting difficult tenants, and so on). Typically you will wait a while to sell your property, so payoff is slow.

Lease Option. This is when you buy a property, then find someone who wants a rent-to-own arrangement.

Advantages: You can get higher rent and the buyer is usually responsible for maintenance. Cash flow can be good.

Disadvantages: Most rent-to-own buyers don't complete the purchase. This can actually be an advantage in the long run, but it does mean more work for you. Bookkeeping must be done properly.

Fixer-uppers. You buy a place in ugly condition that needs renovation. You fix it up and quickly resell it.

Advantages: You can receive a quick return on your investment. You usually buy below market value, so you have instant equity and can use a home equity loan to finance the renovation.

Disadvantages: Higher risk. Many unpredictable expenses come up in construction. You have no guarantee about how long it will take to sell or what price you'll receive. You get taxed heavily on the gain if you resell in less than a year.

Vacant land. You can buy land and just hold it while it appreciates or you can buy and subdivide for resale.

Advantages: History has shown that land always appreciates in value. It's the buildings on the land that go down. It is simpler than most real estate investments with the possibility of great profits.

Disadvantages: It can take a long time for land to increase in value. You have expenses but no cash flow while you wait.

Forced Appreciation. Buy property in the path of growth and hold it until values rise. For instance, buy a vacant lot in a residential development prior to roads being completed. When the roads go in, the price goes up, and you sell at a profit.

Advantages: This can yield large profits.

Disadvantages: Future price is not predictable. You have expenses but no income while you're waiting for the price to rise.

Preconstruction. Buy directly from a developer before the construction or renovation is completed when prices are low.

Advantages: You may have to put up only a small amount of money to tie up the property while it's being built. If purchased in appreciating markets, you make money in equity at closing and can instantly resell at a profit.

Disadvantages: You can't always predict what a market is going to do. If market depreciates, you have lost money. You'll also get hit hard at tax time if you sell in less than a year.

Foreclosures. These types of investment properties are the ones you buy from sellers who are behind in their payments and may lose their property to the bank via foreclosure.

Advantages: You have opportunities to buy properties at below value pricing, creating instant equity. Then you can turn around and sell the property for a substantial profit.

Disadvantages: Legal liabilities are higher. Finding these properties requires a lot of research and footwork to find a deal that works. You can do all the work and still not have a deal with enough equity to profit after expenses (taxes, Realtors)."

You can consider a field and buy it, using any one of these strategies. Just pick the one that most appeals to you, then *do your homework*. You'll also need a team of advisors (Realtors, lenders, bankers, attorneys, home inspectors, and others). It's especially helpful to have a mentor to discuss a deal before buying, so you can avoid having to attend your own "school of hard knocks." Tamera says she never would have made it without the love and support of her business partner, Michelle.

You can learn about real estate through classes, CDs, DVDs, seminars, and books. Tamera and Michelle host free online webcasts and are offering my readers a free report containing a list of questions you will want to ask before buying any investment property. Visit www.donnapartow. com/realestate for details on Tamera and Michelle's offering, along with links to other helpful resources.

Again, our purpose in the 90-Day Jumpstart is just to get you thinking about the possibilities. The Proverbs 31 woman *considered* the field before she bought it; she didn't jump in mindlessly. Nevertheless, there are very few better ways to make a significant chunk of money than real estate. So be like the Proverbs 31 woman and at least consider it.

Affirmation: I consider a field and buy it.

Practical

Consider what type of real estate investing might appeal to you. Do your homework, then consider a field and buy it.

Day 54

Explore the World of Internet Marketing

Scripture to Memorize

She makes linen garments and sells them,
   and supplies the merchants with sashes.
She is clothed with strength and dignity;
   she can laugh at the days to come.

Proverbs 31:24–25

Passage to Read

Be very careful, then, how you live—not as unwise but as wise, making the most of every opportunity, because the days are evil.

Ephesians 5:15–16

Guided Prayer

Dear Lord, I want to be very careful how I live. I confess that I have not always lived carefully. Sometimes I have been unwise and failed to make the most of the opportunities that came my way. Holy Spirit, help me to grow in wisdom. Train me to hear your voice and to quiet my mind so I can perceive opportunities when they arise. That's especially important because the days are evil. As a follower of Jesus, I have an obligation to shine the light of truth into every life I touch. Help me to redeem the time so I can live each day to the fullest. Amen.

Personal

The Proverbs 31 woman's lamp did not go out at night (v. 18)—are we *sure* she wasn't surfing the Internet? Isn't that what keeps most of us awake at night? Of course the Internet is a new technology. In fact I'm pretty sure I can say I was there the day Internet marketing was born. No kidding. In

1996 an editor I had worked with from *Home Office Computing* magazine called to tell me she was leaving the magazine to work for an Internet content developer. *I had no clue what she was talking about.* Neither did 99.9 percent of people on the planet. She invited me, and a handful of others, to join her in this new venture called ivillage.com. My mission, should I choose to accept it, was to develop content—articles, self-tests, tidbits of information—that programmers would "put up" on the Internet. It made little sense to me, but since they offered to pay and I needed the money, I agreed.

I was appointed the resident work-from-home guru and began writing mini-articles about working from home, balancing family and career, that sort of thing. I would send them via email—something I had done *for the first time* just a few months earlier—to the computer geeks who would post them out in cyberspace where, hopefully, someone, somehow, would find them and read them. My head literally *hurt* as I tried to wrap my little brain around what we were doing.

Then it happened. One day I went to my little corner of cyberspace and there it was: a brown box with the letters UPS on it. Immediately I called my supervisor to ask what on earth was going on? She exclaimed: "We have our first advertiser: UPS."

My immediate response: "Advertiser? Why on earth would someone advertise on the Internet? *No one's going to buy anything on the Internet!*" Yes, my friends, those were my exact words. So much for my brilliant, prophetic insight! Today ivillage.com is the largest content provider on the Internet. Alas, I quit shortly after the mysterious appearance of the little brown box, firm in my conviction that *no one would ever buy anything on the Internet.*

But buy they do. As of this writing, Internet sales were conservatively estimated to be around two hundred billion dollars annually,[5] and that number grows by the nanosecond. The simplest way to become involved with Internet marketing is selling on eBay and Craigslist. Forget the hassle of a local garage sale and join the world's biggest online flea market! Thousands of people buy and sell on eBay and Craigslist every day—even people who are not computer whizzes. These online stores are so easy to operate, my ten-year-old set up one for herself in less than an hour.

With eBay, users must enter their name, address, telephone number, and credit card number to begin bidding and selling products. The site charges a small fee for each ad you post. As a general rule, you should list items worth more than fifteen dollars to justify the advertising expense. On the other hand, Craigslist is free, which explains its growing popularity. It's estimated to have five billion page views per month.

All you need to get started is stuff to sell, a camera, a PayPal account (which is free and takes less than five minutes to set up), and a little creativity. Here are ten tips for selling online:

1. *Write a great headline.* You've got to grab the buyer's attention.
2. *Post quality product images.* Eighty-three percent of eBay shoppers skip listings without images. Always put a product image right by the headline. You may need to post multiple photos from various angles.
3. *Accept PayPal.* PayPal is the currency of choice on eBay and Craigslist. Eventually you might consider setting up a merchant account to accept credit cards, but PayPal is good enough to get you started. Forget expecting people to send you a check or money order. They'll buy from someone else.
4. *Write an interesting advertisement.* Make it a reflection of your personality, using wit and humor when appropriate.
5. *Price to sell.* The competition online is stiff. Hunt around to see what others are charging for similar products and cut your price 10 percent. For bidding purposes, determine what you hope the final selling price will be and start the bid at 60 percent off. If you're willing to accept a price that's around or below where it's selling elsewhere on eBay, list that price as the "Buy It Now" price.
6. *Offer a great deal and tell them why.* Say you are simplifying your life and everything must go! Or your cat is threatening to move out if you don't clear out the place.
7. *Be honest.* Tell buyers up front about any defects, so they can tell you are an honest person.
8. *Free shipping.* This is a great selling point, but make sure you are still making a profit.
9. *Be reasonable about shipping.* If you are not offering free shipping, don't try to make a profit by overcharging for shipping. Be fair

with your customers or they may strike back and cost you future business.

10. *Have a star rating above 99 percent.* If you follow the first nine tips, this shouldn't be a problem. Make sure you deliver what you say you will, when and how you say you'll do it.

If selling on eBay and Craigslist doesn't interest you, or if you grow beyond those enterprises and want to launch out into the deep, you can easily create your own website using free user-friendly software through companies like Yahoo, Site Build It, 1ShoppingCart, and others. Of course, there is a monthly fee to have these companies host your site, but it's worth it. The various fees for my website and other online marketing tools cost me about seventy-five dollars per month but typically generate five hundred to one thousand dollars per month in additional income. You can hire a webmaster to create a site for you—just be *sure* to check his or her references. View the sites the person has created and talk with the site owners to find out how happy they were with the service they received. These days, it should cost around five hundred dollars to have a simple webpage created.

Just keep in mind a few simple tips:

1. *Your website must capture prospects' names and email addresses.* The easiest way to do this is to offer them a free report (related to your product or service) or some other valuable information *free.* They must provide their name and email address as a ticket to the freebie. These contacts become your prospects for the sale of your products and services.

2. *Share testimonials on your website.* Since people won't be able to meet you face-to-face, this lends credibility. You can have written testimonials or, better still, short video testimonials.

3. *Make sure your webhost provides a shopping cart feature,* so that people can purchase what you are offering using a credit card or PayPal. No one wants to mail you a check!

4. *Your website must recruit affiliates.* In other words, you must make it easy for other website owners to recommend your product and service. Enable them to link to your page; then send them a small

commission every time one of their referrals buys from you. Providers like 1ShoppingCart and SiteSell do this automatically.

It's easy to get involved with Internet marketing, even without developing your own product or service, by specializing in affiliate marketing. Affiliate marketers don't sell their *own* products or services. Instead, they serve as informal representatives for a wide variety of *other* web-based marketers. You could be sound asleep and someone in China clicks a button and stumbles on your website, clicks a button that takes him or her to a website offering products you recommend, clicks another button to buy the product. Three clicks and *you* are getting paid. The most obvious example is Amazon.com. You can create an informative website about a topic of interest to you—say, for example, cooking. Then you provide a list of recommended cookbooks and a direct link to Amazon. Amazon stocks the books, ships the books, bills the customer, and *you* get paid by Amazon. That's what residual income is all about. Earning money while you sleep. Of course affiliate marketers have to provide links to lots of websites if they hope to make significant income.

Yes, you can earn money on the Internet. The options are numerous and the opportunities are limitless, because, contrary to my prophecy of long ago, almost *everyone* buys something on the Internet—even Proverbs 31 women, whose lamps do not go out at night!

Affirmation: My lamp doesn't go out at night.

Practical

Investigate Internet marketing as an additional stream of income. Visit www.donnapartow.com/internet for more information.

Day 55

Weekly Checkup

Cumulative Scripture Review

A wife of noble character who can find?
    She is worth far more than rubies.
Her husband has full confidence in her
    and lacks nothing of value.
She brings him good, not harm,
    all the days of her life.
She selects wool and flax
    and works with eager hands.
She is like the merchant ships,
    bringing her food from afar.
She gets up while it is still dark;
    she provides food for her family
    and portions for her servant girls.
She considers a field and buys it;
    out of her earnings she plants a vineyard.
She sets about her work vigorously;
    her arms are strong for her tasks.
She sees that her trading is profitable,
    and her lamp does not go out at night.
In her hand she holds the distaff
    and grasps the spindles with her fingers.
She opens her arms to the poor
    and extends her hands to the needy.
When it snows, she has no fear for her household;
    for all of them are clothed in scarlet.
She makes coverings for her bed;
    she is clothed in fine linen and purple.
Her husband is respected at the city gate,
    where he takes his seat among the elders of the land.
She makes linen garments and sells them,
    and supplies the merchants with sashes.

She is clothed with strength and dignity;
she can laugh at the days to come.

Proverbs 31:10–25

Turn verses 24–25 into a Scripture-based prayer:

_____

_____

_____

Practical

Saturday is your day to review and catch up on any unfinished items. Check to confirm that you have completed the following one-time tasks:

☐ I began exploring various options for developing multiple streams of income through home enterprise.

Check to confirm you are routinely incorporating the following positive changes into your daily routine:

☐ I'm using my Personal Notebook.
☐ I'm reviewing regularly my Personal Vision Statement.
☐ I'm spending time in my prayer place, enjoying TAG.
☐ I'm dealing proactively with my secret sins.
☐ I'm completing this study every day, practicing the memory verse, and reciting affirmations daily.
☐ I'm becoming consciously selective about how I dress and how I use my time and resources.
☐ I'm becoming a more serious student of the Bible.
☐ I'm practicing the presence of God, being watchful, thankful, and prayerful.
☐ I'm following my EVENING ROUTINE and going to bed on time.
☐ I'm inviting God to awaken me each morning, saying no to the snooze button, and following a MORNING ROUTINE.
☐ I'm exercising control over my eating habits and limiting sugar intake.

- ☐ I'm using smaller plates and controlling food portions.
- ☐ I'm planning ahead for healthier eating.
- ☐ I'm prayer walking three to five days per week.
- ☐ I begin each day with a cleansing drink and consume sixty-four ounces of water every day.
- ☐ I stop eating several hours before bed.
- ☐ I'm using a rebounder to fight gravity and cellulite.
- ☐ I routinely take cleansing baths.
- ☐ I'm using my DAILY PAGE and applying the 80/20 rule.
- ☐ I routinely give away everything I can.
- ☐ I'm tackling items on my TACKLE LIST.
- ☐ I'm tithing.
- ☐ I'm clearing out the rubble of debt and paying with cash.
- ☐ I have my savings and investments on autopilot.
- ☐ I'm wearing fashionable yet modest, correct-color clothing that actually fits and flatters me.
- ☐ I'm developing multiple streams of income through home enterprise.

Day 56

Weekly Reflection

Sunday is a great day to devote extra time meditating on the entire Proverbs 31 passage, memorizing your assigned verses, praying, and preparing your heart for the week ahead. Take one day out of every seven to rest and reflect. Do *not* catch up on assignments you did not complete, but *do* schedule them for the coming week.

Fill in the remainder of Proverbs 31:10–25 from memory:

A _____ ___ _____ _____ who can find?

She is worth ____ _____ _____ _____.

Her husband ____ ____ _____ ___ ____

and lacks _____ ___ _____.

She brings him _____, ____ _____,

    all the _____ ___ ____ _____.

She selects _____ ____ _____

    and works _____ _____ _____.

She is like ____ _____ _____,

    bringing her _____ _____ _____.

She gets up _____ ___ ___ _____ _____;

    she provides _____ ____ ____ _____

    and portions ____ ____ _____ _____.

She considers __ _____ ____ _____ __;

    out of her earnings ____ _____ __ _____.

She sets about ____ _____ _____;

    her arms ____ _____ ____ ____ _____.

She sees that ____ _____ __ _____,

    and her _____ ____ ___ __ ___ __ _____.

In her hand ____ _____ ____ _____

    and grasps ____ _____ _____ ____ _____.

She opens ____ _____ __ ____ _____

    and extends ____ _____ __ ____ _____.

When it _____, she ____ ___ _____ ____ ____

    _____;

    for all ___ _____ ____ _____ __ _____.

She makes _____ ____ ____ ____;

    she is _____ __ ____ _____ _____.

Her husband ___ _____ __ ___ ____ _____,

    where he takes ____ _____ _____ ____ _____ __

    ____ _____.

She makes _____ _____ ____ _____ _____,

  and supplies ____ _____ _____ _____.

She is clothed _____ _____ ____ _____;

  she can _____ ___ ____ _____ ___ _____.

Weekly Evaluation

1. Am I listening for and hearing God's voice? What is he saying to me?

_____

_____

2. Am I increasingly manifesting the fruit of the Spirit: love, joy, peace, patience, kindness, goodness, faithfulness, gentleness, and self-control (Gal. 5:22–23)? What areas look encouraging? What needs prayer?

_____

3. What did God teach me during my TAG?

_____

_____

4. Which priorities did I live by? Which goals did I pursue?

_____

_____

5. Which priorities or goals did I neglect?

_____

_____

6. What new thing did I learn—about life, God, my family, and the people around me?

_____

_____

7. What are my specific priorities/goals for the coming week?

_____

_____

Take out your notebook and schedule your priorities or goals for the coming week.

HOUSEHOLD MANAGEMENT

Identify Household Trouble Spots

Scripture to Memorize

She speaks with wisdom,
and faithful instruction is on her tongue.
She watches over the affairs of her household
and does not eat the bread of idleness.

Proverbs 31:26–27

Passage to Read

She sets about her work vigorously;
her arms are strong for her tasks. . . .
She watches over the affairs of her household
and does not eat the bread of idleness.
Her children arise and call her blessed;
her husband also, and he praises her:
"Many women do noble things,
but you surpass them all."

Proverbs 31:17, 27–29

Guided Prayer

Dear Lord, I'm humbled as I read about the virtuous woman in Proverbs 31. It's hard enough when I'm tempted to compare myself to women around me and end up feeling inferior. Sometimes when I read this passage and compare myself to an ideal, I fear I'll never measure up. But I know there's not a passage in the Bible written to make me feel bad about myself. Instead, everything that was written is there for my encouragement. You have not set an unattainable goal, nor are any of your commands burdensome. It is possible for me to become the kind of woman in today's passage—it won't be easy, but nothing worthwhile ever is.

Help me to set about my work vigorously. I know this means I need to become stronger—physically, spiritually, and emotionally. Holy Spirit, guide me each day as I watch over the affairs of my household. I can't possibly do it all, so I need your help to discern the things that are most important.

Forgive me for those times when I've eaten the bread of idleness, when I've given in to the temptations to gossip on the phone, watch television, or surf the Internet rather than work vigorously. Help me see areas in my life where I should put forth more effort.

Thank you so much for the words of encouragement I receive from my family. I want to be a blessing to my husband and children, knowing that even though they may not thank me now, someday they will appreciate those things I do to keep our family life operating smoothly. And on those days when my family isn't exactly appreciative, help me to listen for your voice. Jesus, you set the example by laying down your life for us; and you said that the greatest love of all is laying down my life for others. Help me to not become resentful about the mundane tasks of motherhood, but to go about my tasks vigorously, doing all things as unto you. Amen.

Personal

The Proverbs 31 woman watches over the affairs of her household and does not eat the bread of idleness. So this week, we return our focus to the important task of managing your home. You will recall the management principle introduced in Week 5: the 80/20 rule. Twenty percent of your house probably creates 80 percent of your problems. These are your danger zones. For me it's the laundry room and the kitchen counters. For you it might be something else. We all have places in our home that are just ripe for disaster. Identify and deal with yours and you will have solved 80 percent of household disorder.

No matter how many rooms you have, divide your entire house into ten zones (so you may need to combine a couple rooms or divide one room into two sections) and list them below:

1. _____   6. _____

2. _____   7. _____

3. _____   8. _____

4. _____   9. _____

5. _____   10. _____

Now place a star next to the two zones that tend to be the messiest. You do not need an organizational system for every square inch of your house (unless of course you want to go that far). Just focus on these two zones. Analyze what, exactly, is causing the problem and begin to envision a solution. For inspiration, visit a home organization store. Don't let your mind go crazy trying to figure out how to organize your entire house. You'll get 80 percent return if you can master these two zones. Focus!

Affirmation: I bring order to my home, because God is not a God of disorder.

Practical

Identify the two messiest zones in your home and develop a strategy for managing them. Visit a home organization website or store to obtain the tools you need to conquer the chaos.

Notebook: Create a "Zones" page in the Household section of your Personal Notebook. Use this page to jot down ideas you gather along with your organizational strategy.

Day 58

De-clutter

Scripture to Memorize

She speaks with wisdom,
and faithful instruction is on her tongue.
She watches over the affairs of her household
and does not eat the bread of idleness.

Proverbs 31:26–27

Passage to Read

There is a time for everything,
and a season for every activity under heaven:
a time to be born and a time to die,
a time to plant and a time to uproot,
a time to kill and a time to heal,
a time to tear down and a time to build,
a time to weep and a time to laugh,
a time to mourn and a time to dance,
a time to scatter stones and a time to gather them,
a time to embrace and a time to refrain,
a time to search and a time to give up,
a time to keep and a time to throw away,
a time to tear and a time to mend,
a time to be silent and a time to speak.

Ecclesiastes 3:1–7

Guided Prayer

Dear Lord, thank you for reminding me that life happens in seasons. I'm so glad. If everything happened at once, it would overwhelm me. There's a time for everything: birth and death, weeping and dancing, scattering and gathering, embracing, searching, and surrendering, a time to speak and a time to keep silent. There's even a time to keep—and a time to throw away. Lord, as I continue on this journey, grant me wisdom to know what time it is. I confess my inclination is always toward building, gathering, and keeping. Your Word makes it clear that sometimes I need to tear down, scatter, and throw away.

Since you've brought this book into my life, it's safe to assume that I'm in a season of purging. Holy Spirit, help me to trust this process. Part of me is resisting, but I know that if I yield to your leadership, I'll find rest for my soul. Grant me wisdom to know what else needs to go and the courage to tear down and throw away. I want to embrace simplicity, but it scares me, too. I fear that letting go means losing. I know that's not true. Your Word says that only in losing our lives can we truly find them. Make my arms strong for the task and my heart eager to obey. I trust you, Lord. Amen.

Personal

The Proverbs 31 woman watched over the affairs of her household and that's our job, too. But remember this: the less you accumulate and cling to, the less you have to watch over and the easier your job becomes. When it comes to clutter, there should be no doubt in your mind that less is more. Nevertheless, people hang on to all kinds of junk. Have you ever said these words: "Don't throw that out. I might need it someday!" If so, you might be carrying around some excess emotional weight in the form of clutter. Almost all of us have clutter in our homes, on our desks, maybe even in our cars. What we don't realize is that these visual reminders of unfinished work can be a real energy drain and source of unneeded stress.

Here are just a few good reasons to minimize clutter:

1. *Clutter wastes time.* How much time do you spend looking for lost items buried in unorganized stacks and boxes? If you spend just fifteen minutes a day looking for stuff, you waste ninety hours a year, which is more than enough time to read the entire Bible.
2. *Clutter wastes money.* If something you need is lost in a mess, you are likely to go to the store and purchase a replacement. These unnecessary expenses add up quickly. How many of us have five pairs of scissors—somewhere?

3. *Clutter is dangerous.* Have you ever tripped on a pile of paper or clothes or "stuff"? I sure have! Plus, all those boxes in your basement are a breeding ground for mold and bugs. Cardboard and paper clutter is also a possible fire hazard.

Don't kid yourself into saving things because you might need them someday. You won't be able to find them when you need them anyway! From someone who recently lost a parent, let me offer a word of caution: don't keep anything based on the rationale that your children will want it. If they are grown, ask them if they want it. If they do, give it to them now. Otherwise, get rid of it. If your children are still very young, here's what you can do. Create a bin for each child in your storage area and allow yourself to fill it with keepsakes you want to pass down. The trick is, if you decide you want to add something else you are certain they will treasure for all eternity, then you have to throw something else out to make room. (I am not talking here about furniture or other high-ticket items; I'm referring to knickknacks and other clutter creators.)

If you've stuck with the program this far, you've already done quite a bit to de-clutter your house. Today we're going to go even further by attacking the paper monster. First, get rid of every outdated magazine, newsletter, and newspaper in your house. Every drop of information recorded by any reputable organization on the planet is now archived on the Internet. *Throw out* the periodicals you have collected. And don't save them as *memorabilia.* They're not; they're junk. *Throw them out.*

Sort the mail *before* you go into the house. Stand by your outdoor trash can and toss the junk mail directly into it. You can also opt out of many junk mail lists using the Direct Marketing Association's Mail Preference Service. Visit www.dmaconsumers.org/cgi/offmailing. There's a one-dollar fee but it's worth it. You can even stop telemarketing calls by contacting the Federal Trade Commission's National Do Not Call Registry at www.donotcall.gov or by phone at 1-888-382-1222.

Now go through your files. Once again, I'm not going to give you an elaborate filing system to follow. Stick with the system you've been using, or, when you've finished this 90-Day Jumpstart, read a book on paper management and set up a system (for instance, *The Messies Manual* and *Smart Organizing* by Sandra Felton). For now, *quickly* go through paper piles wherever you find them. Make fast decisions. If you can find the information on the Internet (which you can 99.9 percent of the time), *throw it out.* Keep only what you absolutely need. If you are unsure, put it in a bin labeled IMPORTANT PAPERS. Once a year, go through the bin and throw out anything that's more than five years old.

Lose the emotional weight: de-clutter!

Affirmation: There's a time to keep and a time to throw away.

Practical

Spend fifteen minutes a day de-cluttering. One great trick is to de-clutter while you're on the phone. It's an easy way to multitask.

Day 59

Get Equipped for a Clean House

Scripture to Memorize

> She speaks with wisdom,
> and faithful instruction is on her tongue.
> She watches over the affairs of her household
> and does not eat the bread of idleness.
>
> Proverbs 31:26–27

Passage to Read

> Where no oxen are, the manger is clean,
> But much revenue comes by the strength of the ox.
>
> Proverbs 14:4 NASB

Guided Prayer

Dear Lord, my household can be such a challenge some days. It's tempting to think my life would be so much better if I didn't have anyone around here making a mess! But I know that's not true. It's the people and the critters that make this house a home. And yes, the more living beings I allow into my home, the more mess there is to clean up. But life is worth living, so messes are worth cleaning. Forgive me for all the times I've complained about the mess; a mess is just proof that I have enough blessings to make messes! Holy Spirit, I invite you to bring your loving correction when I lose perspective. Remind me: this is what a lived-in, loved-in home *should* be like. Grant me wisdom to manage all that goes on within these four walls. I need your grace to make it. Amen.

Personal

I know a surefire way to keep your house spotlessly clean. Never be there. Seriously, this works! The less time you spend at home, the neater your house will stay. Of course it's not a strategy I want to adopt. Actually I like the truth of today's Scripture: "Where no oxen are, the manger is clean, but much revenue comes by the strength of the ox." We really *live* in our house. It is in constant use and it shows. I run a full-time ministry from a spare bedroom—complete with a huge inventory of books that spills over into the garage. I also homeschool, so we have schoolbooks and supplies, not to mention school project messes to contend with. We used to have farm animals. That really made life interesting, especially since the goats thought *they* belonged in the house and would just barge right in.

My house would be a whole lot cleaner if I went to work at an office and both my children attended school outside the home. But there's much to be gained from homeschooling, working from home, and just plain *living* at home.

Because I firmly believe the home should be our central headquarters, I was alarmed when I learned that women who stay at home have a 54 percent higher death rate from cancer than women who work outside of the home, according to a seventeen-year study conducted by the Environmental Protection Agency.[1] Poor indoor air quality in American homes

221

is a serious issue, and I believe the constant exposure to toxic household cleaning chemicals is a far more serious issue than most women realize.

As you watch over the affairs of your household, don't overlook the importance of creating a healthy home. Keep windows cracked open all year-round—yes, even in extreme weather and especially at night. Don't "seal" your house to save a few dollars. Your health is more important. You are sealing out fresh air and sealing in germs and household pollutants. When all those medical bills come due, you'll realize you were penny-wise and pound-foolish. Whenever weather permits, air out your entire house. Throw open doors and windows (you can swat any bugs that sneak in). And change the filters in your furnace and air conditioning unit. I've marked my calendar the first day of every month: change air filters.

One key to keeping a clean, healthy home is making it as easy to maintain as possible. That's the reason I've urged you to give away everything you can and keep clutter to a minimum. There's more you can do. For example, we replaced all the wall-to-wall carpeting on our first floor with hardwood flooring. When we have the funds available, we intend to do the same on the second floor. Wood is much easier to keep clean and is more conducive to a healthy home environment. If you don't believe me, rent a carpet shampoo machine and take a good hard look at the dirt it brings up. That's what your kids have been rolling around on for the last X number of months. Gross! The next time your carpet needs to be replaced, consider replacing it with wood.

Dust mites are a major source of allergens, especially in children. Keep your home free from dust by making sure you vacuum upholstery and under beds. Use washable mattress and pillow covers. Wash linens weekly.

Now I want you to go through your house and gather up every household cleaning item. This might be quite a scavenger hunt for some of us! Read the labels. If they include bleach, ammonia, or any aerosol propellant, throw them out. Forget how much they cost you and think about how much they *are costing you* in terms of your health. Which matters more? In fact I would encourage you to discard *all* conventional cleaning products and purchase nature-based, nontoxic alternatives. You can visit my website if you'd like more information on the brands I use.

This is especially important if you have children in your home, because accidental poisoning in the home is the second leading cause of death in children under the age of five. Your home should be a haven not a hazard. Be sure it is not only clean but safely so.

Next, purchase three cleaning caddies, one for each of three distinct cleaning tasks: general purpose, bathroom, and kitchen. Fill each caddy with everything you need to clean each type of room safely. Yes, this will cost a little extra money, but it is well worth it for the increased efficiency you'll experience. Here's how to stock your three caddies:

General purpose: living room, dining room, and bedroom
- furniture polish
- glass cleaner
- rags
- paper towels

Bathroom
- glass cleaner
- tub and tile cleaner
- toilet cleaner
- paper towels
- gloves
- scrub brush

Kitchen
- glass cleaner
- appliance cleaner
- furniture polish (if wood cabinets)
- rags
- paper towels

Now stash each cleaning caddy in the room where it will be used most frequently. Tomorrow you'll discover a very good reason for having more than one cleaning caddy. (Hint: it's because you should have more than one cleaning person!)

Affirmation: I maintain a safe, healthy home environment.

Practical

Purchase three cleaning caddies, stock them with nontoxic cleaning supplies, and store them where they are easily accessible. Consider implementing other suggestions from the day's reading.

Notebook: Mark your calendar for the first of every month: "Change air filters."

Day 60

Practice Shared Servanthood

Scripture to Memorize

> She speaks with wisdom,
> and faithful instruction is on her tongue.
> She watches over the affairs of her household
> and does not eat the bread of idleness.

Proverbs 31:26–27

Passage to Read

But if serving the LORD seems undesirable to you, then choose for yourselves this day whom you will serve, whether the gods your forefathers served beyond the River, or the gods of the Amorites, in whose land you are living. But as for me and my household, we will serve the LORD.

Joshua 24:15

Guided Prayer

Dear Lord, serving you is desirable to me. I choose this day to serve you. Help me to set such a powerful example of a life spent following you that my children can't imagine choosing any other path. Holy Spirit, give me wisdom and spiritual discernment whenever I'm tempted—even unknowingly—to serve the gods of this land. As for me and my household, we will serve the Lord. Amen.

Personal

I don't serve my children. Some moms do and I think it's a huge mistake. When we wait on our children hand and foot, we teach them that they are on the earth to be served—wrong message. Notice what Joshua says: "As for me and my household, *we* will serve the Lord." That's what we need to teach our children. Together, we serve the Lord. The Proverbs 31 woman watched over the affairs of her household; it doesn't say she did all the work. Quite the contrary: it's obvious that she was a capable delegator.

One way to cultivate a servant-hearted attitude in your children is to train them to serve one another. Mom isn't the household servant. We *all* serve God and each other. Part of the "faithful instruction" that needs to be on our tongue is teaching our kids how to run a household so they'll know what to do when they leave home.

Researcher Marty Rossman, at the University of Minnesota, studied a group of young adults from the time they were young children. The startling results of the study were that the young adults who had participated in household chores when they were ages three and four were more successful as adults than those who hadn't had household jobs to do. Specifically, these young adults were more likely to complete their education, get a good start on a career, develop adult relationships, and avoid the use of drugs. The early participation in household chores was deemed more important in their success than any other factor, including IQ.[2]

Yesterday you created three cleaning caddies. Today you can introduce the cleaning caddies to the rest of the family. Point out that there's more than one cleaning caddie because there's more than one person who can clean the house. Remember the premise of *The Greatest Management Principle in the World*, a book written by my good friend Dr. Michael LeBoeuf: Behavior that gets rewarded gets repeated. Add to that principle this one: people don't do what you expect; they do what you *inspect*.

So reward your kids in whatever way seems agreeable to you and your husband and be sure to *inspect* your children's work. You and your husband can also negotiate special rewards for his cooperation! Remember, as a

Proverbs 31 woman-in-the-making, your job is to "watch over" the affairs of your household, not to do all the work yourself. Put on some music and send everyone off in three different directions, each crew equipped with their own cleaning caddy suited to either general bathroom or kitchen cleaning.

Sit down with your family and negotiate a strategy for shared servanthood. If you've been doing all the work yourself, *apologize* to your family. Tell them, "I need to ask your forgiveness. I've been doing all the work around here and robbing every one of you of the opportunity to discover the joy of serving. From now on, *we* will serve the Lord by serving each other." Tell your kids you'd rather apologize to them now instead of having to apologize to their frustrated spouses later on.

Everyone lives in and enjoys the house, so everyone needs to be part of maintaining it. Your future sons- and daughters-in-law will rise up and call you blessed for teaching your kids shared servanthood.

Affirmation: My household serves the Lord.

Practical

Call a family meeting and create a strategy for shared servanthood.

Day 61

Purify Your House Spiritually

Scripture to Memorize

> She speaks with wisdom,
>   and faithful instruction is on her tongue.
> She watches over the affairs of her household
>   and does not eat the bread of idleness.
>
> Proverbs 31:26–27

Passage to Read

Here I learned about the evil thing Eliashib had done in providing Tobiah a room in the courts of the house of God. I was greatly displeased and threw all Tobiah's household goods out of the room. I gave orders to purify the rooms, and then I put back into them the equipment of the house of God, with the grain offerings and the incense.

Nehemiah 13:7–9

Guided Prayer

Dear Lord, thank you for the example of Nehemiah's life. Thank you for showing me (through him) that it's okay to be greatly displeased by things in my household that don't belong there. My home is your home and if there's anything in it that displeases you, I want to remove it and purify my home. Holy Spirit, guide me in this process. Give me wisdom as I seek to make my home a holy sanctuary. Amen.

Personal

The Proverbs 31 woman spoke with wisdom as she watched over the affairs of her household. But the voice of wisdom isn't always speaking words everyone longs to hear; sometimes the voice of wisdom needs to speak out for truth and take a firm stand against ungodly influences in the home.

If you are unfamiliar with the story of Tobiah (from today's Passage to Read), let me briefly recap. Tobiah was one of the sworn enemies of the Israelites. He did everything he could to oppose the rebuilding of the walls that protected God's people. Then Eliashib, who was supposed to be *protecting* the house of the Lord, invited one of God's sworn enemies to move in. When Nehemiah learned about it, he pitched a fit. We might think he overreacted when he took everything out of Tobiah's room and gave orders to have it purified. But it wasn't an overreaction. It was an appropriate response.

Part of watching over the affairs of our household is carefully guarding what we allow to come into the rooms of our house. This applies even to those rooms that belong to someone else, as long as that someone else is under our authority.

227

Today I want you to move from room to room in your house. Go in a spirit of prayer. Ask the Holy Spirit if there is *anything* offensive. In particular, take a long, hard look at every book, painting, plaque, print, periodical, DVD, CD, and the like. Some of these may be Trojan horses that bring the forces of darkness into your home.

If you've traveled to other countries, be particularly alert to the fact that some items sold as tourist trinkets are actually foreign idols. Cartoon characters, action figures, computer and electronic games also warrant special scrutiny. I know, I know, some of you are thinking, *Donna's going a bit overboard today.* Fine. This is between you and God. Listen to his voice, not mine. Tempted though I am to give more specific direction, I'm going to trust this process to the Holy Spirit.

Let me share an example from my own life. The level of conflict in our home had been escalating dramatically. My then sixteen-year-old daughter, Leah, who had been homeschooled most of her life, had begun attending the local high school. I found her newfound interests and attitudes intolerable; she found my continuing efforts to control her every thought and action equally intolerable. A war of the wills was underway—and my teenager was winning decisively. For some reason, all of our knock-down, drag-out fights occurred in one particular room. One day I was sitting in there and Leah said, "I don't know how you can stand to sit in the screaming room. All we ever do is fight in here."

The screaming room.

I was crushed to think my children would grow up remembering there was a room in our house devoted to screaming. That's when I decided to change the dynamic completely. I took almost everything out of that room and either threw it out, gave it away, or moved it elsewhere in the house. Then I moved every sacred object (crosses, Scripture verse plaques, mission-trip artifacts) from elsewhere in the house into that one room. When I had completely re-created the room, and spent an entire night praying aloud in it, we celebrated with our first family communion.

Now this room is our family prayer chapel. And guess what? Ever since we've instituted our weekly gatherings, the level of conflict has plummeted. Yes, we still have our challenges but there has definitely been a shift in the atmosphere. And the perception of that room has turned 180 degrees. Now it's the most peaceful room in the house. I believe the peace we are fostering in this room is permeating the rest of the house. Peace has a powerful way of spreading.

If you have a teenager, particularly a troubled teenager, I *urge* you to consider prayerfully a Nehemiah purge of your house. First, approach the child and invite his or her participation. If the child is not open, you may have even greater cause for concern. This is very delicate. People have different convictions about personal privacy and invasion of space. Let the Holy Spirit and wisdom guide you. But remember, this is *your* home and *you* are in authority. Nehemiah didn't hesitate to invade a complete stranger's room because it was defiling everyone else.

Again, I'm going to be completely open with you. I am not one to see a demon under every rock, and my husband is quite conservative theologically and levelheaded to the extreme. With that said, we were going through an extremely difficult time with one of my daughters, and I decided to pray over her room. My husband sat in our family prayer chapel, praying aloud, while I went upstairs. When I returned, he reported that he had distinctly felt something evil come down the stairs and go out the front door.

You can choose to believe this or not, but we can both assure you it's true. And *this* occurred in a Christian, homeschooling household. Do not deceive yourself into thinking the Enemy hasn't managed to sneak anything in through something you thought was completely harmless.

Your assignment for today is a spiritual one. Please include your husband if you possibly can; invite your children, too; go from room to room, purifying your house.

After Nehemiah emptied out the room of anything offensive to God, he purified the room and brought in items that were suitable for the house of the Lord. You might consider doing the same. Although I previously advocated keeping collections to a minimum, I'll admit I do have one: crosses. The walls in my house are covered with crosses from around the world. You may want to invite your pastor, priest, or church elder over to your home to anoint it with oil, sprinkle it with holy water, or bless it in whatever manner seems most appropriate, based on your spiritual convictions. We invited a spiritual leader from our church to come in and pray over every area of our home.

Affirmation: I purify my home.

Practical

Rid your house of anything that might be offensive to God or anything that might serve as a foothold for the Enemy. Consider replacing the items with Scripture plaques, crosses, or other sacred items. Pray over and spiritually purify your home. Invite a spiritual leader to bless your house, if you desire.

Day 62

Weekly Checkup

Cumulative Scripture Review

> A wife of noble character who can find?
>   She is worth far more than rubies.
> Her husband has full confidence in her
>   and lacks nothing of value.
> She brings him good, not harm,
>   all the days of her life.
> She selects wool and flax
>   and works with eager hands.
> She is like the merchant ships,
>   bringing her food from afar.
> She gets up while it is still dark;
>   she provides food for her family
>   and portions for her servant girls.
> She considers a field and buys it;
>   out of her earnings she plants a vineyard.
> She sets about her work vigorously;
>   her arms are strong for her tasks.
> She sees that her trading is profitable,
>   and her lamp does not go out at night.
> In her hand she holds the distaff
>   and grasps the spindles with her fingers.
> She opens her arms to the poor

and extends her hands to the needy.
When it snows, she has no fear for her household;
    for all of them are clothed in scarlet.
She makes coverings for her bed;
    she is clothed in fine linen and purple.
Her husband is respected at the city gate,
    where he takes his seat among the elders of the land.
She makes linen garments and sells them,
    and supplies the merchants with sashes.
She is clothed with strength and dignity;
    she can laugh at the days to come.
She speaks with wisdom,
    and faithful instruction is on her tongue.
She watches over the affairs of her household
    and does not eat the bread of idleness.

Proverbs 31:10–27

Turn verses 26–27 into a Scripture-based prayer:

_____

_____

_____

Practical

Saturday is your day to review and catch up on any unfinished items. Check to confirm that you have completed the following one-time tasks:

- ☐ I identified the two messiest zones in my household and developed a strategy for conquering them.
- ☐ I gathered up toxic chemical cleaners and removed them from my house.
- ☐ I replaced the toxic cleaners (or am in the process of replacing them) with nontoxic alternatives.
- ☐ I aired out my entire house (weather permitting).
- ☐ I have cracked open a window or two in my house.
- ☐ I changed the air filter. I added to my calendar a reminder to change the air filter the first day of each month.

231

- [ ] I am exploring replacing the carpet with wood flooring.
- [ ] I created three cleaning caddies.
- [ ] My family worked together to create a shared servanthood strategy.
- [ ] I purified my house spiritually.
- [ ] I invited a spiritual leader to come and pray through my house (optional).

Check to confirm you are routinely incorporating the following positive changes into your daily routine:

- [ ] I'm using my Personal Notebook.
- [ ] I'm regularly reviewing my Personal Vision Statement.
- [ ] I'm spending time in my prayer place, enjoying TAG.
- [ ] I'm dealing proactively with my secret sins.
- [ ] I'm completing this study every day, practicing the memory verse, and reciting affirmations daily.
- [ ] I'm becoming consciously selective about how I dress and how I use my time and resources.
- [ ] I'm becoming a more serious student of the Bible.
- [ ] I'm practicing the presence of God, being watchful, thankful, and prayerful.
- [ ] I'm following my EVENING ROUTINE and going to bed on time.
- [ ] I'm inviting God to awaken me each morning, saying no to the snooze button, and following a MORNING ROUTINE.
- [ ] I'm exercising control over my eating habits and limiting sugar intake.
- [ ] I'm using smaller plates and controlling food portions.
- [ ] I'm planning ahead for healthier eating.
- [ ] I'm prayer walking three to five days per week.
- [ ] I begin each day with a cleansing drink and consume sixty-four ounces of water every day.
- [ ] I stop eating several hours before bed.
- [ ] I'm using a rebounder to fight gravity and cellulite.
- [ ] I routinely take cleansing baths.
- [ ] I'm using my DAILY PAGE and applying the 80/20 rule.
- [ ] I routinely give away everything I can.
- [ ] I'm tackling items on my TACKLE LIST.
- [ ] I'm tithing.
- [ ] I'm clearing out the rubble of debt and paying with cash.
- [ ] I have my savings and investments on autopilot.

☐ I'm wearing fashionable yet modest, correct-color clothing that actually fits and flatters me.

☐ I'm developing multiple streams of income through home enterprise.

☐ My family is maintaining our home using the shared servanthood strategy.

☐ I spend fifteen minutes a day de-cluttering.

Day 63

Weekly Reflection

Sunday is a great day to devote extra time meditating on the entire Proverbs 31 passage, memorizing your assigned verses, praying, and preparing your heart for the week ahead. Take one day out of every seven to rest and reflect. Do *not* catch up on assignments you did not complete, but *do* schedule them for the coming week.

Fill in the remainder of Proverbs 31:10–27 from memory:

A _____ ___ _____ _____ who can find?

    She is worth _____ _____ _____ _____.

Her husband _____ ____ _____ ___ _____

    and lacks _____ ___ _____.

She brings him _____, _____ _____,

    all the _____ ___ ____ _____.

She selects _____ _____ _____

    and works _____ _____ _____.

She is like _____ _____ _____,

    bringing her _____ _____ _____.

She gets up _____ ___ ___ _____ _____;

    she provides _____ ____ ____ _____

and portions _____ _____ _____ _____.

She considers __ _____ ____ _____ ___;

out of her earnings _____ _____ __ _____.

She sets about _____ _____ _____;

her arms _____ _____ ____ ____ _____.

She sees that _____ _____ ___ _____,

and her _____ _____ ____ __ ____ __ _____.

In her hand _____ _____ ____ _____

and grasps _____ _____ _____ ____ _____.

She opens _____ _____ ___ ____ _____

and extends _____ _____ ___ ____ _____.

When it _____, she _____ ____ _____ ____ ____

_____;

for all ___ _____ ____ _____ ___ _____.

She makes _____ ____ ____ ____;

she is _____ ___ _____ _____ ____ _____.

Her husband ___ _____ ___ ____ _____ _____,

where he takes _____ _____ _____ ____ _____ ___

_____ _____.

She makes _____ _____ ____ _____ _____,

and supplies _____ _____ _____ _____.

She is clothed _____ _____ ____ _____;

she can _____ ___ ____ _____ ___ _____.

She speaks _____ _____,

and faithful _____ ___ __ ____ _____.

She watches _____ ____ _____ ___ __ _____

and does not _____ ____ _____ ___ _____.

Weekly Evaluation

1. Am I listening for and hearing God's voice? What is he saying to me?

_____

_____

2. Am I increasingly manifesting the fruit of the Spirit: love, joy, peace, patience, kindness, goodness, faithfulness, gentleness, and self-control (Gal. 5:22–23)? What areas look encouraging? What needs prayer?

_____

_____

3. What did God teach me during my TAG?

_____

_____

4. Which priorities did I live by? Which goals did I pursue?

_____

_____

5. Which priorities or goals did I neglect?

_____

_____

6. What new thing did I learn—about life, God, my family, and the people around me?

_____

_____

7. What are my specific priorities/goals for the coming week?

_____

_____

Take out your notebook and schedule your priorities or goals for the coming week.

Week Ten
Family Relationships

Day 64

Love Your Husband

Scripture to Memorize

Her children arise and call her blessed;
    her husband also, and he praises her:
"Many women do noble things,
    but you surpass them all."

Proverbs 31:28–29

Passage to Read

The same goes for you wives: Be good wives to your husbands, responsive to their needs. There are husbands who, indifferent as they are to any words about God, will be captivated by your life of holy beauty. What matters is not your outer appearance—the styling of your hair, the jewelry you wear, the cut of your clothes—but your inner disposition.

1 Peter 3:1–4 Message

Guided Prayer

Dear Lord, I want to be a good wife to my husband. I want to be responsive to his needs. Lord, you know I've nagged, complained, and preached until his ears about fell off! Forgive me, Lord. The time for words is over. It's time for me to become the woman *you* are calling me to be. Lord, I pray that my husband would be captivated by my life of holy beauty. I want him to be madly in love with me, inside and out. I know what matters most is not my outer appearance (although my husband does care about that, so help me to look my best), but my inner disposition. Holy Spirit, transform me into a woman with a beautiful disposition. I want to be pleasant to be around, a constant source of joy to my husband. Thank you for giving me the supernatural power of God. I know that, with your help, I can become a wife of noble character. Amen.

Personal

Is there a job on earth harder than being a good wife? If there is, I *don't* want to apply! I think it's the hardest job in the world, harder even than being a good mother. But if you're going to be a wife, it's best to be the wife of a happy husband. The Proverbs 31 woman clearly had a happy husband. The passage tells us he called her blessed and offered her the highest praise, saying, "Many women do noble things, but you surpass them all." There's something very special about knowing your husband thinks you are the greatest, even if you're not.

My mother had that privilege for nearly sixty years. She and my father met shortly after he returned from World War II, and he instantly fell head over heels in love with her. Not long before he died, he walked into the house carrying a single rose. My mother asked, "What on earth is that for?" He seemed surprised by her surprise: "Isn't it obvious? It's a beautiful flower for a beautiful lady." No special occasion. He just wanted to honor her. And yes, my mother is still beautiful at nearly eighty years old, even though she uses a scooter and an oxygen tank. As far as my dad was concerned, she was the most beautiful woman on the planet, oxygen or not. He never saw anything but good and beauty in her. It's a gift few men bestow on their wives, and to be honest, I almost envied her for it.

We cannot all be blessed with a man who simply adores us with or without cause. But we can all do our best to be the best wife we can be. Some time ago I picked up a book by Dr. Laura Schlessinger titled *The Proper Care and Feeding of Husbands*. Inspired by what I was reading, I made two lists: what all men like in a wife and what all men dislike in a wife. Yes, these are generalizations, but having observed men for nearly fifty years now, I think these are a very accurate reflection of what most men want in a wife. Here goes:

Almost all men like:

- to come home each day to a well-organized home
- to live in a nurturing environment, where people feel loved and accepted
- to be respected
- to feel appreciated
- to enjoy a healthy physical relationship
- to receive encouragement
- a cheerful wife
- to hear gratitude expressed
- to have children who are well cared for
- the security of a regular family routine, so they know what to expect

Almost all men dislike:

- to feel disrespected
- listening to complaints
- the sound of nagging
- a woman who uses hurt as a weapon
- being verbally abused
- putting up with mood swings
- a woman who talks subjects to death
- a woman who constantly needs validation
- a woman who takes things too personally
- a wife who is unable to forgive and forget

Reread these lists several times. Pray over them. Ask the Holy Spirit to speak the truth to you about how difficult or easy it is to live with you. Put an asterisk next to items in the first category that you are doing right. Then put an *X* next to the items in the second category that you struggle with. Now for the real challenge: go to your husband. Yes, my sister, go! Ask *him* how well he thinks you're doing. Pray about your attitude before going to your husband. You may feel defensive when he points out things he would like changed. Don't argue about what he says! This may be very difficult for some women. But God will help you face the truth and make necessary changes.

Again, you can apply the 80/20 rule. Ask your husband which two items in the "Like" list would mean the most to him if you were to make improvements. Then ask him which two items in the "Dislike" list would have the most positive impact if you were to make improvements. Focus on the 20 percent (the things he mentions) that will yield 80 percent return. (Once you've mastered those areas, he can pick another two!)

Of course God knew what men like and dislike about women long before Dr. Laura did her research. That's the reason he inspired King Lemuel to write the description of the ideal woman in Proverbs 31. Even if you didn't ace this test, be encouraged by the realization that you are now participating in a 90-Day Jumpstart to become the woman God wants you to be. And that is sure to be very much in alignment with the woman your husband wants you to be, too. Stay with it, don't give up, and someday, perhaps very soon, your husband will arise and call you blessed, praising you and declaring, "Many women do noble things, but you surpass them all."

Affirmation: I am becoming the wife God wants me to be.

Practical

Prayerfully evaluate how well you are doing in terms of what men like and dislike about wives. Ask your husband to evaluate you, too. Then, most important, ask the Holy Spirit to help you close the gap between where you are now and where God is calling you to be.

Day 65

Cherish Your Children

Scripture to Memorize

Her children arise and call her blessed;
  her husband also, and he praises her:
"Many women do noble things,
  but you surpass them all."

Proverbs 31:28–29

Passage to Read

Sons are a heritage from the LORD,
  children a reward from him.
Like arrows in the hands of a warrior
  are sons born in one's youth.
Blessed is the man
  whose quiver is full of them.
They will not be put to shame
  when they contend with their enemies in the gate.

Psalm 127:3–5

Guided Prayer

Dear Lord, thank you for giving me my children. I know they are a heritage and a reward from you. Forgive me for those times when I have acted as though children were an inconvenience rather than a gift. My children are like arrows in the hands of a warrior, so help me (and my husband) to point them in the right direction. We are blessed by the children you have provided, so we will not be put to shame, even when we have to contend with our enemies.

Holy Spirit, give me wisdom to be the mother my children need. Help me to stay focused on the eternal significance of motherhood, especially in the moments when my work feels so insignificant. Thank you for empowering me to build a godly heritage that will last for generations to come. Amen.

Personal

The Proverbs 31 woman's children arose and called her blessed. I'm not sure they arose off their potty-chair to do so; my guess is that it was sometime after college graduation. Or more likely, it happened some time after they had children of their own. That's when most of us finally wake up and realize that our mother did a pretty fantastic job of it.

Our children provide the greatest opportunity for us to impact the future. When we are dead and gone; when all our possessions are broken, obsolete, sold at yard sales, or thrown away; when the memories of our accomplishments have long been forgotten and our trophies are collecting dust in the attic, what will remain? When the money and houses and property we leave as an inheritance to our children are spent, worn out, or worthless, what will remain? If we live our lives the way God is calling us to, our godly heritage will remain.

In the late 1700s an English woman named Susanna Wesley had nineteen children (eleven survived to adulthood). She spent thirty minutes of one-on-one time with each of them every week. She taught them to read the Bible, beginning in Genesis. When she needed time alone with God, she simply pulled her apron over her head. Two of her sons, Charles and John, were key leaders in the Great Awakening of the eighteenth century. We still sing hymns that Charles wrote: "O for a Thousand Tongues to Sing," "Hark! the Herald Angels Sing," and many more. John Wesley is the father of both the Methodist and Wesleyan denominations.

Many historians believe that the Great Awakening was the primary reason England was spared a bloody revolution like the one that occurred in France. Susanna Wesley's children literally changed the course of a nation and impacted the eternal destiny of countless thousands.

Among the men John Wesley led to the Lord was John Taylor. John Taylor heard John Wesley preach on the morning he was to be married and was so moved by what he heard that he ended up late for his own wedding. He was in his barn praying that God would bless his home. John Taylor became a lay Methodist preacher. He was zealous for the Lord and raised up several sons who also became lay Methodist preachers. Those sons had several sons who became—you guessed it—lay Methodist preachers.

One of those men had a little boy who used to listen to his daddy pray every day: "O Lord, please send missionaries to China." When that little boy was six years old, he said, "God, I will go to China." His name was Hudson Taylor. Sound familiar? J. Hudson Taylor grew up to become the founder of the China Inland Mission and the father of the modern faith mission movement.

Ruth Tucker, in her history of Christian missions, writes: "No other missionary in the nineteen centuries since the apostle Paul has had a wider vision and has carried out a more systematic plan of evangelism across a broader geographic area than Hudson Taylor. In his lifetime, the missionary force under him totaled more than eight hundred and continued to grow in the decades after he died."[1]

As of this writing, there are nine generations of preachers in the Taylor family—and one of those men is right now a missionary to Thailand. That's a godly dynasty. And it all started with Susanna Wesley—one woman who had a vision that mothering could make a difference for eternity, one woman with an apron over her head!

Another man impacted by Susanna Wesley's children was Jonathan Edwards, a minister and evangelist who lived in the United States 150 years ago. He and his wife had ten children. They passed on to those children a godly heritage. The state of New York did a study on five generations of the Edwards family and found that of their 729 descendants, 300 were preachers, 65 became college professors, 13 were university presidents, 60 were authors, 3 were congressmen, and 1 became vice president of the United States. All were from one family who determined to raise godly children, one family who built a godly dynasty.[2]

I want my great-great-great-great-great-great-grandchildren to say, "Thank God, Grandma Donna finally got her priorities straight. Thank God, she decided to invest time attending to the small stuff that adds up over time. Thank God, she poured her energy, creativity, and ambition into the lives of her children and, as a result, changed the course of her family history."

Perhaps you didn't inherit a godly dynasty. No matter where you came from, it can start with you.

Affirmation: My children are my heritage; they are a gift from the Lord.

Practical

Spend time getting to know your children. Plan when and how you will spend thirty minutes of one-on-one time with each child every week. Mark it on your monthly calendar so you never miss it.

Notebook: Note your one-on-one meetings with each family member on your monthly calendar.

Day 66

Establish Family Traditions

Scripture to Memorize

> Her children arise and call her blessed;
>   her husband also, and he praises her:
> "Many women do noble things,
>   but you surpass them all."
>
> Proverbs 31:28–29

Passage to Read

When you enter the land that the LORD will give you as he promised, observe this ceremony. And when your children ask you, "What does this ceremony mean to you?" then tell them, "It is the Passover sacrifice to the LORD, who passed over the houses of the Israelites in Egypt and spared our homes when he struck down the Egyptians."

Exodus 12:25–27

Guided Prayer

Dear Lord, thank you for bringing me into the promised land of life lived to the fullest. Holy Spirit, help me to live with such fullness that my children want to know more about my faith. Grant me wisdom so I'll be able to answer their questions in a way that's both biblical and relevant to their stage of development. I thank you, Jesus, for offering yourself as the ultimate Passover Lamb so that the Father's righteous judgments might pass over all those who put their faith in you. I pray for each of my children, right now, that they will trust in the Lamb that was slain for their sins. I pray, too, that they will fully understand the magnitude of the cross and discover its meaning for themselves, rather than living off borrowed faith from their parents.

Father, throughout the Old Testament, you provided traditions to help your people remember important spiritual truths. Even in the New Testament, Jesus established communion as a routine reminder of his sacrifice and the call for us to pick up our cross and follow after him. Help me establish meaningful traditions for my family, traditions that draw us closer to you and to one another. Amen.

Personal

The children of the Proverbs 31 woman arose and called her blessed. One of the greatest blessings we can give our children is a strong sense of family identity. Children long for it. That's the reason two of the most powerful words in any child's vocabulary are "we always." It means they have a sense of family identity. There's security and confidence in knowing that certain things can be counted on. *We always* have breakfast together. *We always* go to Sunday school and church. *We always* pick apples at the orchard in the fall. *We always* decorate for Christmas the day after Thanksgiving. *We always* watch *The Rosa Parks Story* on Martin Luther King Day. *We always* make Irish potatoes on St. Patrick's Day. *We always . . .*

Children show their need for "we always" at an early age. Every child has a favorite bedtime story they want to hear, night after night. And just *try* changing one line. They will go absolutely nuts because that's not what the story *always says*. They want it to be predictable. They want to know that they know what's going to happen next.

Life is unpredictable. Unexpected things happen and there's nothing we can do about that. But what we can do is make sure that in the midst of all the unpredictability, we inject some predictability. We arrange for some "we always" opportunities.

My mother was the absolute master of "we always." With eight children, she needed to inject as much predictability as she could. We always had the coolest scarecrow sitting in our front yard every fall. We always picked apples and peaches, and my mom always baked the most amazing fruit pies. We always had the best Christmas window decorations on the block. On the Fourth of July, we always had fireworks my dad smuggled from South Carolina into New Jersey. (Oops, maybe I shouldn't have admitted that one!) No one in the world could make a holiday special like my mother—but I'm trying.

If you can cook, one of the easiest ways to make a holiday special is to have specific foods for certain occasions. My husband, Jeff, has a favorite "we always" from his early childhood. Every Sunday his family always had a spaghetti dinner at his grandmother's house. In fact, to this day, he still calls her "Spaghetti Grandma." We think children want variety. They *don't*. They like tradition.

Since I can't cook, I have had to rely on decorations. The secret: the day *after* the holiday, go to the store and purchase everything you can find. Immediately stow it for next year in your holiday bin. I always buy holiday paper plates, cups, and napkins on clearance. It's a quick, cheap way to create a festive feeling.

Even if you aren't a culinary artist, you can surely find one recipe— like a Fourth of July American flag cake—and make it the centerpiece. I purchased a heart-shaped cake pan that gets put to use every Valentine's Day. If only I could find a shamrock-shaped cake pan, we'd be in business. Well, you get the idea.

Bring some predictability into your life with "we always." You'll be amazed at the joy and peace it brings. And it might just be one of the primary reasons some day that your children arise and called you blessed.

Affirmation: My children arise and call me blessed.

Practical

Make a list of your existing "we always" traditions. Use your calendar and your children to jog your memory. Ask: "Is there anything *we always* do in January? February?" Start with what you are already doing and think about how you can strengthen it. Also look at all the holidays—even the obscure ones—and invent creative ways to make them fun and memorable. Keep your eyes open for post-holiday sales.

Notebook: In the HOUSEHOLD section, create a page entitled FAMILY TRADITIONS. Jot down what you're already doing along with ideas for what you plan to do in the future to create "we always" traditions. Before each holiday, be sure to review your list so you always do your "we always" activities.

Day 67

Honor the Sabbath

Scripture to Memorize

> Her children arise and call her blessed;
>   her husband also, and he praises her:
> "Many women do noble things,
>   but you surpass them all."

Proverbs 31:28–29

Passage to Read

There remains, then, a Sabbath-rest for the people of God; for anyone who enters God's rest also rests from his own work, just as God did from his. Let us, therefore, make every effort to enter that rest.

Hebrews 4:9–11

Guided Prayer

Dear Lord, thank you for creating the Sabbath as a gift for your people. Left to our own devices, we'd exhaust ourselves mentally and emotionally. We'd run our bodies right into the ground in the frantic pursuit of *stuff*. But you created us and you know what we need. We need time to rest and reflect. Holy Spirit, help me to understand that the Sabbath was created *for me*. It's not something you demand *from me*. I confess that I've sometimes viewed it as a religious requirement or an inconvenience. I need a fresh perspective. You weren't punishing yourself when you rested from your work, neither is it a punishment when you ask me to rest. It's for my good and the good of my family. Therefore, with your grace enabling, I will make every effort to enter that rest. Amen.

Personal

Today's Passage to Read commands us to make every effort to enter rest. It sounds contradictory. Yet I've found it to be true in my own life that rest takes deliberate effort, while restlessness seems to come naturally. Throughout this 90-Day Jumpstart you've been, well, jumping! But taking time *not to* jump, taking time to rest is just as important. Honoring the Sabbath is our way of saying: "Heavenly Father, I believe your grace is more powerful than my work. I trust your love more than I trust my own self-effort."

We are not under law but under grace. God isn't coming down from heaven to hit you over the head with a hammer if you work on Sunday. We don't honor the Sabbath to earn points with God. We honor the Sabbath to regain our strength and put life back into perspective. Again, I'm not going to give you a specific prescription, but I'll give two simple guidelines for the Sabbath: If it's work-related or stressful, don't do it. If it's restful, do it.

Yesterday I mentioned my husband's fond memories of Sundays spent at Spaghetti Grandma's house. We have a tradition, at least once a month, of having the whole extended family over for Sunday supper. My husband always does the cooking and it's either a big pot of chili or, you guessed it, spaghetti. Part of me would like to host a dinner every Sunday, but I don't think my life will be calm enough for that to be *relaxing* until I'm the grandma!

The highlight of our Sabbath rest is always our family communion time. It is, without question, the most effective means we have ever discovered for experiencing God's power to transform our family. Sometime around 7 p.m. I'll put on soft praise music. Then I'll set out crackers and pour grape juice. We gather together in our family prayer chapel (formerly dining room/school room) and talk casually about the previous week. Then we read a Scripture passage and share a brief teaching. We take turns confessing our sins and offering a word of encouragement to each person. We have two very simple rules. We can confess *our own* sins and point out what everyone else did right. We cannot brag about or defend ourselves and point out what someone else did wrong. These rules apply to everyone and have proven 100 percent effective in ensuring that communion is always a powerful, spiritually uplifting time for each of us.

We partake quietly of communion, keeping in mind the Scripture that says: "A man ought to examine himself before he eats of the bread and drinks of the cup. For anyone who eats and drinks without recognizing the body of the Lord eats and drinks judgment on himself" (1 Cor. 11:28–29). It is always a holy time.

Your Sabbath celebration may be very different from ours. The important thing is to decide what will be restful and meaningful for your family. Put some thought, prayer, and preparation into it and let the Holy Spirit be your guide. I believe one of the greatest blessings you can give to your children is the tradition of honoring the Sabbath.

Affirmation: I honor the Sabbath.

Practical

Prayerfully consider ways you can make the Sabbath special. Decide when, where, and how you can incorporate family communion. If you feel only a pastor or priest can lead communion, you will want to partake of the elements only when a spiritual leader is available.

Day 68

Live in Peace

Scripture to Memorize

Her children arise and call her blessed;
   her husband also, and he praises her:
"Many women do noble things,
   but you surpass them all."

Proverbs 31:28–29

Passage to Read

Do not repay anyone evil for evil. Be careful to do what is right in the eyes of everybody. If it is possible, as far as it depends on you, live at peace with everyone. Do not take revenge, my friends, but leave room for God's wrath, for it is written: "It is mine to avenge; I will repay," says the Lord.

Romans 12:17–19

Guided Prayer

Dear Lord, just reading this passage brings me to my knees before you. Forgive me, Father, for I have sinned. I have repaid evil for evil. I have failed to do what's right in the eyes of everybody. I have lived in strife, not peace. I have sought revenge. I have lashed out with my tongue when I was offended. I have sought justice when I was wronged. Forgive me.

Prince of Peace, I need you to be the center of my life and my relationships. I need the power of the Holy Spirit and the peaceable fruit of righteousness he brings. Strengthen me in my inner being, enabling me to stand firm under life's hurts and injustices. It is my earnest desire to resist the ever-present temptation to return evil for evil. I want to do what is right in the eyes of everyone and to live at peace, but I need your grace to live out this commitment. Teach me, dear Lord, to trust you as the righteous Judge. Let me learn to do what Jesus did: entrust myself to the one who judges justly. Right now, by faith, I release every person from whom I feel entitled to demand justice. I release: _____.

I give all of these people over to you. I lay them down at the foot of the cross. Even if your verdict is that they should receive the same mercy I have received, I will be content, knowing your judgments are always right. I trust you to be just. I trust you with my life. Amen.

Personal

We interrupt this wonderful week on family togetherness, traditions, and spiritual inheritances to face a hard reality. Many of our families have been profoundly affected by divorce. No matter how hard we work to create our ideal family life, we find that less-than-ideal circumstances intrude. As a result, many of us fear our children will arise and call us just about everything in the book *other than* blessed. But you do not have to live in fear and defeat. Your family *can* be blessed, even if you've suffered the pain of a broken family.

First, the obvious. You can't change your ex-husband. If you had the power to change that man, you'd still be married to him. You certainly can't change your husband's ex-wife. *He* couldn't change her, and the two of them were probably madly in love at one point in time. What do you think your chances are? Exactly nonexistent.

What you can do is make the best of a bad situation. The Bible tells us how: if possible, as far as it depends on *you*, live at peace with everyone. No matter what awful, terrible things someone's "ex" might do, don't repay evil for evil. Even if someone is "talking trash" about you, don't fight back by "talking trash" about him or her. It is not appropriate for you to criticize or demean any adult authority figure in your children's life. If the person is doing something illegal, that's a matter for the courts. But even in that case, *you* are not the judge and jury. The judge and jury will be provided by the state.

You may think that your ex or your spouse's ex is the most horrible person on the planet. If you can't find something nice to say about him or her, don't say anything at all. Eventually, your children will figure it out for themselves. You don't need to give them an earful about how you are right and wonderful, while the other parent is wrong and awful. Remember, that parent is part of your child. When you tear that parent down, you tear down part of your child, as well. You may not realize that every time you put the other person down, you also put yourself down. You stoop down to his or her level. Don't do it.

I know how tempting it is to lash out, but the Bible says no temptation has seized you except what is common to man and to ex-wives. Fortunately, the Bible has also provided a way of escape for you:

1. Don't repay evil for evil.
2. Be careful to do what is right in the eyes of everybody.
3. Live at peace, if possible, and as far as it depends on you.
4. Do not take revenge.
5. Leave justice in the hands of the one who judges justly.

The same five peacekeeping steps apply to your in-laws, your ex–in-laws, your next-door neighbor, and your co-workers. Set a godly example for your children by endeavoring to live at peace with everyone, if possible.

Notice that it says "if possible." Even the God of the impossible knows it's not possible to get along with some people. Do the best you can and leave the rest to God. Don't let the pain of divorce rob your children of a blessing and, in the future, they will bless you for it.

Affirmation: As far as it depends on me, I live at peace with everyone.

Practical

Make and keep peace with everyone, especially your relatives.

Take time to truly release every person concerning whom you feel entitled to demand justice. You cannot pursue justice for others and receive mercy for yourself.

Day 69

Weekly Checkup

Cumulative Scripture Review

A wife of noble character who can find?
  She is worth far more than rubies.
Her husband has full confidence in her
  and lacks nothing of value.
She brings him good, not harm,
  all the days of her life.
She selects wool and flax
  and works with eager hands.
She is like the merchant ships,
  bringing her food from afar.
She gets up while it is still dark;
  she provides food for her family
  and portions for her servant girls.
She considers a field and buys it;
  out of her earnings she plants a vineyard.
She sets about her work vigorously;
  her arms are strong for her tasks.
She sees that her trading is profitable,
  and her lamp does not go out at night.
In her hand she holds the distaff
  and grasps the spindles with her fingers.
She opens her arms to the poor
  and extends her hands to the needy.
When it snows, she has no fear for her household;
  for all of them are clothed in scarlet.
She makes coverings for her bed;
  she is clothed in fine linen and purple.
Her husband is respected at the city gate,
  where he takes his seat among the elders of the land.
She makes linen garments and sells them,
  and supplies the merchants with sashes.
She is clothed with strength and dignity;
  she can laugh at the days to come.
She speaks with wisdom,

and faithful instruction is on her tongue.
She watches over the affairs of her household
and does not eat the bread of idleness.
Her children arise and call her blessed;
her husband also, and he praises her:
"Many women do noble things,
but you surpass them all."

Proverbs 31:10–29

Turn verses 28–29 into a Scripture-based prayer:

_____

_____

_____

Practical

Saturday is your day to review and catch up on any unfinished items. Check to confirm that you have completed the following one-time tasks:

- ☐ I completed a self-evaluation of how well I'm doing as a wife.
- ☐ I courageously asked my husband for his feedback.
- ☐ I've developed a plan to implement positive changes in the areas my husband indicated would have the most impact.
- ☐ I planned one-on-one time with each of my children and wrote the times on my calendar.
- ☐ I made a list of family traditions (existing and proposed). I sought input from my family concerning what they would like to "always" do.
- ☐ We, as a family, developed a plan to honor the Sabbath.
- ☐ I've made a firm decision to live in peace with everyone, including exes, in-laws, and any troublesome people.

Check to confirm you are routinely incorporating the following positive changes into your daily routine:

- ☐ I'm using my Personal Notebook.
- ☐ I'm regularly reviewing my Personal Vision Statement.

- ☐ I'm spending time in my prayer place, enjoying TAG.
- ☐ I'm dealing proactively with my secret sins.
- ☐ I'm completing this study every day, practicing the memory verse, and reciting affirmations daily.
- ☐ I'm becoming consciously selective about how I dress and how I use my time and resources.
- ☐ I'm becoming a more serious student of the Bible.
- ☐ I'm practicing the presence of God, being watchful, thankful, and prayerful.
- ☐ I'm following my EVENING ROUTINE and going to bed on time.
- ☐ I'm inviting God to awaken me each morning, saying no to the snooze button, and following a MORNING ROUTINE.
- ☐ I'm exercising control over my eating habits and limiting sugar intake.
- ☐ I'm using smaller plates and controlling food portions.
- ☐ I'm planning ahead for healthier eating.
- ☐ I'm prayer walking three to five days per week.
- ☐ I begin each day with a cleansing drink and consume sixty-four ounces of water every day.
- ☐ I stop eating several hours before bed.
- ☐ I'm using a rebounder to fight gravity and cellulite.
- ☐ I routinely take cleansing baths.
- ☐ I'm using my DAILY PAGE and applying the 80/20 rule.
- ☐ I routinely give away everything I can.
- ☐ I'm tackling items on my TACKLE LIST.
- ☐ I'm tithing.
- ☐ I'm clearing out the rubble of debt and paying with cash.
- ☐ I have my savings and investments on autopilot.
- ☐ I'm wearing fashionable yet modest, correct-color clothing that actually fits and flatters me.
- ☐ I'm developing multiple streams of income through home enterprise.
- ☐ My family is maintaining our home using the shared servanthood strategy.
- ☐ I'm focusing on being a better wife, mother, and general family member.
- ☐ My family is developing "we always" traditions, including honoring the Sabbath.
- ☐ As far as it depends on me, I am at peace with all people.

Day 70

Weekly Reflection

Sunday is a great day to devote extra time meditating on the entire Proverbs 31 passage, memorizing your assigned verses, praying, and preparing your heart for the week ahead. Take one day out of every seven to rest and reflect. Do *not* catch up on assignments you did not complete, but *do* schedule them for the coming week.

Fill in the remainder of Proverbs 31:10–29 from memory:

A _____ ___ _____ _____ who can find?

   She is worth ____ _____ _____ _____.

Her husband ____ ____ _____ ___ ____

   and lacks _____ ___ _____.

She brings him _____, ____ _____,

   all the _____ ___ ____ _____.

She selects _____ ____ _____

   and works _____ _____ _____.

She is like _____ _____ _____,

   bringing her _____ _____ _____.

She gets up _____ ___ ___ _____ _____;

   she provides _____ ____ ____ _____

   and portions ____ ____ _____ _____.

She considers _ _____ ____ _____ ___;

   out of her earnings ____ _____ __ _____.

She sets about ____ _____ _____;

   her arms ____ _____ _____ ____ _____.

She sees that ____ _____ __ _____,

   and her _____ _____ ____ ____ ___ _____.

In her hand _____ _____ ____ _____

   and grasps _____ _____ _____ ____ _____.

She opens _____ _____ ___ ____ _____

   and extends _____ _____ ___ ____ _____.

When it _____, she _____ ___ _____ ____ ____

   _____;

   for all ___ _____ ____ _____ ___ _____.

She makes _____ ____ ____ ____;

   she is _____ ___ _____ _____ ____ _____.

Her husband ___ _____ ___ ____ _____ _____,

   where he takes _____ _____ _____ ____ _____ ___

   _____ _____.

She makes _____ _____ ____ _____ _____,

   and supplies _____ _____ _____ _____.

She is clothed _____ _____ ____ _____;

   she can _____ ___ ____ _____ ___ _____.

She speaks _____ _____,

   and faithful _____ ___ ___ ____ _____.

She watches _____ ____ _____ ___ __ _____

   and does not ____ ____ _____ ___ _____.

Her children _____ ____ _____ ____ _____;

   her husband _____, and ___ _____ ____:

"Many women ___ _____ _____,

   but you _____ _____ ____."

258

Weekly Evaluation

1. Am I listening for and hearing God's voice? What is he saying to me?

_____

_____

_____

2. Am I increasingly manifesting the fruit of the Spirit: love, joy, peace, patience, kindness, goodness, faithfulness, gentleness, and self-control (Gal. 5:22–23)? What areas look encouraging? What needs prayer?

_____

_____

3. What did God teach me during my TAG?

_____

_____

4. Which priorities did I live by? Which goals did I pursue?

_____

_____

5. Which priorities or goals did I neglect?

_____

_____

6. What new thing did I learn—about life, God, my family, and the people around me?

_____

_____

7. What are my specific priorities/goals for the coming week?

_____

_____

Take out your notebook and schedule your priorities or goals for the coming week.

The Ministry of the Home

Day 71

The Ministry of Family Meals

Scripture to Memorize

Charm is deceptive, and beauty is fleeting;
> but a woman who fears the LORD is to be praised.

Proverbs 31:30

Passage to Read

This is what the LORD says:
"Stand at the crossroads and look;
> ask for the ancient paths,
ask where the good way is, and walk in it,
> and you will find rest for your souls."

Jeremiah 6:16

Guided Prayer

Dear Lord, I want to take time today to stand at the crossroads and look at my life. I confess that I haven't always followed the ancient or wise path, but have rushed headlong with the maddening crowd that's going nowhere in a hurry. Holy Spirit, teach me to slow down. Show me the ancient paths, the good way to follow. I want to walk in it. More than anything, I long to find rest for my soul. Then I'll be able to guide my family down the path that will restore their souls as well. Be with me as I make changes in our lifestyle. Help me to use wisdom and to be considerate of my family members as we travel along. Amen.

Personal

Whatever happened to the family dinner hour? I was the youngest of eight children, and every night we had dinner together. Occasionally one of us would miss dinner for a sporting event or after-school activity, but if we did, our dinner plate was prepared and ready for us to heat up when we got home. I *remember* the times we had McDonald's. It was so rare, it was memorable! I *remember* going to IHOP on several occasions precisely because each time was a big occasion. Things have changed.

According to several surveys, 30–40 percent of families do not eat dinner together five to seven nights a week, and families with older teenagers eat fewer dinners together than those with younger children.[1] This is a disturbing trend when you consider the research that has shown the significance of family meals. For example, a 2004 study of 4,746 children eleven to eighteen years old, published in the *Archives of Pediatrics and Adolescent Medicine*, found that frequent family meals were associated with a lower risk of smoking, drinking, and using marijuana; with a lower incidence of depressive symptoms and suicidal thoughts; and with better grades.[2]

Another study surveyed twelve- to seventeen-year-olds and found that teenagers who reported eating two or fewer dinners a week with family members were more than one and a half times more likely to smoke, drink, or use illegal substances than were teenagers who ate five to seven family dinners per week. "We also noticed that the more often teens had dinner with their parents, the less likely they were to have sexually active friends, less likely girls were to have boyfriends two years older, and the less time teens spent with boyfriends or girlfriends," said Joseph A. Califano Jr., the chairman and president of the National Center on Addiction and Substance Abuse.[3]

A recent study from the University of Minnesota found that adolescent girls who reported having more frequent family meals and a positive atmosphere during those meals were less likely to have eating disorders. A Harvard University study of sixteen thousand nine-year-olds found that those who ate dinner at home with their parents regularly are more likely to have higher intakes of essential nutrients and vitamins.[4]

Clearly, family meals are extremely significant, but no one has time to cook anymore! What's the answer? Here's my proposal: the family breakfast half hour. Get everyone together *before* they scatter to the four winds. This has proven to be a much more realistic approach for our family. It doesn't have to be elaborate. A protein shake and fresh fruit are sufficient. There are many breakfast casserole recipes you can prepare the night before. Put one in the oven when you awake for your TAG and it will be ready in time for breakfast. Once in a while, you can surprise everyone with a more elaborate meal of flapjacks, eggs, and hash browns.

If you want to make the meal extra special, you can set a beautiful table the night before, complete with china, napkins, and so on. Whatever works for you and your family is fine. Put some praise music on to create an uplifting atmosphere. Share a Scripture, prayer, or word of encouragement from your own TAG time. Have your Personal Notebook handy to bring everyone up to speed on important happenings for the day and jot down anything a family member needs from you. If you want to be supermom of the year, during your TAG time, jot down a Scripture or one-sentence encouragement on an index card, and give it to a family member you know really needs it before he or she goes out into the big, cruel world.

Though I have proclaimed the virtues of the family breakfast half hour, I don't think you should give up all hope of ever having dinner together as a family. It probably won't happen every night. In my family, my ten-year-old is at gymnastics three nights a week during what would normally be dinnertime, so she eats two minimeals: one before and another after her lessons.

My teenager is often running here and there, and my husband, who is in the process of starting his own business, keeps erratic hours. My guess is this sounds a lot like your household. You can still make nutritious food available, rather than running to fast-food restaurants, sending out for pizza, or picking up Chinese food. The average American family spends more than two thousand dollars a year on dinners away from home, and 10 percent of those dinners come from McDonald's.[5] God's people can do better.

If you haven't already implemented my suggestions on Day 19 (concerning Crock-Pots and meal assembly kitchens), you should prayerfully reconsider doing so. Anything you can do to make it more likely that your family can share a meal together is well worth the time and effort. And something that actually makes this possible while *saving you* time, effort, and money is priceless.

Affirmation: I make mealtimes special.

Practical

Have one sit-down-at-home meal every day. Try instituting a family breakfast half hour.

Day 72

Dress Your Family for Spiritual Success

Scripture to Memorize

Charm is deceptive, and beauty is fleeting;
but a woman who fears the LORD is to be praised.

Proverbs 31:30

Passage to Read

Finally, be strong in the Lord and in his mighty power. Put on the full armor of God so that you can take your stand against the devil's schemes. For our struggle is not against flesh and blood, but against the rulers, against the authorities, against the powers of this dark world and against the spiritual forces of evil in the heavenly realms.

Ephesians 6:10–12

Guided Prayer

Dear heavenly Father, I want to be strong in you and in your mighty power. Today I put on the full armor of God so that I can take my stand against the Enemy's schemes, for my struggle is not against flesh and blood, but against the rulers, against the authorities, against the powers of this dark world, and against the spiritual forces of evil in heavenly realms. Lord, help me to arm myself for battle and to never forget that my family, friends, and foes are not the enemy. The enemy is spiritual. Holy Spirit, equip me for the spiritual battles I will face today and every day. Teach me that I might teach my children how to wage war and win decisively for the kingdom's sake. Amen.

Personal

Just as you wouldn't send your family out into the world undressed physically, you shouldn't send them out undressed spiritually. The armor of God (see Eph. 6:14–18) includes:

Truth—knowing what's right

Righteousness—doing what's right

Peace—being in right relationship with God, yourself, and the world around you

Faith—believing God will turn everything out right

Salvation—trusting that you are right with God because of what Jesus accomplished on the cross

The Word of God—giving us the wisdom we need to understand truth, righteousness, peace, faith, and salvation

Prayer—inviting the power of God into our lives, enabling us to live right

As you gather at the family breakfast table, take a few moments to ensure that everyone is dressed and ready to face the day. Talk about any scheduled events and apply God's truth to the situation. Invite your children to be open about areas of temptation, whether it's the temptation to hold a grudge against the class bully or the temptation to follow the crowd. Discuss the rewards of right living and the consequences when we refuse to do what's right. Remind them how important it is to do right even when no one else is watching.

Breakfast is also a great time to pray together, asking the Holy Spirit to bring to light any issues that need to be resolved so that the family can face the day at peace with God and one another. Bolster your children's faith with stories of God's past faithfulness—both from the Word of God and from your own life experience. Encourage them to believe that God's Word is true and that *all things*—even the hard things—work together for good for those who love God and have been called according to his purpose. Thank God for the amazing gift of salvation and ask him to bring people across your path who need to experience it for themselves.

As suggested yesterday, you might even share some truths God gave you during TAG or give one or more family members a Scripture verse to carry with them into their day.

You're never fully dressed until you are clothed in the full armor of God. Be sure to dress for spiritual success and help your family do the same.

Affirmation: I dress for spiritual success.

Practical

Use your family breakfast to ensure that everyone is dressed for spiritual success.

Day 73

Practice Hospitality

Scripture to Memorize

Charm is deceptive, and beauty is fleeting;
    but a woman who fears the LORD is to be praised.

Proverbs 31:30

Passage to Read

Be joyful in hope, patient in affliction, faithful in prayer. Share with God's people who are in need. Practice hospitality.

Bless those who persecute you; bless and do not curse.

Romans 12:12–14

Guided Prayer

Dear heavenly Father, thank you for sending me the Holy Spirit to empower me to live the way you've called me to live. I know that, by myself, I could never become the woman you want me to be. Apart from you, I can do nothing. But with your power at work in my life, I can be joyful in hope, patient in affliction, and faithful in prayer. Change my heart, O God, that I might earnestly desire to share with your people in need. Teach me how and when to practice hospitality. Grant me strength to bless those who persecute me and to resist the temptation to curse them or speak unkind words about them. I know there's a connection between showing hospitality and choosing to not curse those who have hurt me. Hospitality is not the time to sit around talking about all the people who have done me wrong and hurt my feelings or what I don't like about the church. Hospitality is a time to reach out to others with love and caring. It's time to be a blessing and a vessel of healing within the body of Christ. Lord, make my home a hospital! Teach me to practice hospital-ity for your kingdom's sake. Amen.

Personal

Throughout the Bible, hospitality is both demonstrated and commended. Today's passage includes the injunction to "practice hospitality" right alongside prayer and blessing those who persecute us. Paul commends Gaius "whose hospitality I and the whole church here enjoy" (Rom. 16:23) and instructs Timothy that "no widow may be put on the list of widows unless she is over sixty, has been faithful to her husband, and is well known for her good deeds, such as bringing up children, showing hospitality, washing the feet of the saints, helping those in trouble and devoting herself to all kinds of good deeds" (1 Tim. 5:9–10).

Paul wasn't the only New Testament writer to emphasize the importance of hospitality. Peter instructs us to "offer hospitality to one another without grumbling" (1 Peter 4:9); and John says, "We ought therefore to show hospitality to such men so that we may work together for the truth" (3 John 8). Hospitality is not a low-priority option for Martha Stewart wannabes. Obviously it's something on which God places a high value and every Christian should practice in her own way.

Today I want to introduce you to a contemporary Proverbs 31 woman who happens to be the loveliest hostess on the planet. I met Deb Lovett while speaking at a conference in Ohio. Shortly thereafter, she became the director of women's ministry at her church and invited me to do a women's conference in her hometown. Having become acquainted by phone, she invited me to stay in her home rather than a hotel. Let me tell you, not even the seven-star hotel in Dubai could hold a candle to the royal treatment Deb extended to me. Then, several years later, Deb hosted my entire family for Thanksgiving, and truly it was like stepping into the pages of *Town and Country* magazine! I have never felt like such a princess. For years afterward, my youngest daughter would ask if we could move to Ohio to be near Mrs. Lovett. No kidding!

So I asked Deb to share what God has shown her about how to create a home environment that ministers to the spirit, soul, and body of her guests. Here are her thoughts.

"Everything good that we have belongs to God and is to be used for his glory. He is the owner of all good things, and we are the property managers. So many times we are looking for some 'ministry' out there—on the stage, in front of lots of people, when our ministry is right under our noses. You have heard that church is a hospital for sinners. Well, hospitality turns your home and property into ministry for people in the name of Jesus when you open your heart and hands to him.

"Hospitality doesn't have to mean the perfect dinner, but a beautiful presentation combined with the presence of the Lord through an attitude of love. Now after many years of planning parties, Bible studies, women's conferences, and memorable family times, I can happily rejoice in the fact that my home is a haven of rest to all, no matter what is going on. The Lord has blessed my obedience in this area to serve and has expanded my horizons. We are now building a larger lodge on-site to accommodate more people for hospitality!

"I would now like to share with you some 'props' that I consider essentials to hospitality:

"*Gifts:* Always have on hand a boutique of gifts available for an assortment of ages and sexes to give at a moment's notice, things like unusual soaps, stationery, baby bibs, books, CDs, grooming kits. Have a standard wedding gift handy for those times you just can't find time to shop. I keep these in unused dresser drawers and always provide my guest with a little something to show him or her my appreciation—usually before dinner.

"*Paper:* Always have white wrapping paper on hand. White paper can wrap any occasion and can be decorated with stamps, different colored ribbons and bows. My daughter loves to use felt-tip markers to write cool sayings on them to celebrate the holiday. Gift bags are great as well. While we are on the subject of paper, I suggest spending the extra couple of bucks it takes to put some squeezably soft toilet tissue out for guests, and have on hand the rectangular hand napkins rather than a cloth towel that can spread germs.

"*Candles:* Create an atmosphere that says, 'Aha, time to relax,' by using candles. Use them all over, but be wise and keep tabs on them throughout your event. I have a drawer that holds only candles: all types, sizes, scents, and colors. Oh, and don't forget a lighter or matches!

"*Flowers:* Know where your local flower warehouse is. This is where I go to buy my flowers wholesale. Literally I can have flowers strewn throughout my home for twenty dollars or less. Flowers wake up the soul with their aroma and colors. Give an arrangement to your guests on their way out if you really want to bless them.

"*Food:* If you have time to fix a dinner, that's great. Most of the time, however, I have my meals catered for less than I would spend if I cooked, when I count up the hours I spend shopping, preparing, and cleaning up. Check out the places that have a monthly menu and order a few dinners for the freezer that can be pulled out at a moment's notice.

"*Prayer:* Last but not least. You can go to all the trouble you want, but without the Holy Spirit's presence and anointing, it is just another party. I stand at my front door and pray, 'Holy Spirit, I invite you into my home and heart for this time with friends. I ask you to guide all of our conversations so that they bring glory to the Father and to show me how I can bless each one who enters here in a loving way that represents Jesus. Bring your peace that surpasses all understanding now in the name of Jesus to this place. Amen.'

"Hospitality is the best way I know of turning our homes into hospitals for the tired, harassed, and weary travelers on this road we call earth; but even more than that, it also honors God by 'loving your neighbor' on the road to heaven!"

Charm is deceptive and beauty is fleeting, but a woman who turns her home into a hospital for the weary by showing hospitality is to be praised. Having been to Deb's hospital more than once, I can tell you hospitality truly is a powerful and important ministry. Especially in today's society, with people running here and there, grabbing fast food and never taking time to truly connect, the opportunity to relax around a table is a welcome relief.

We have dear friends who put on a pot of soup every Sunday morning and ask the Lord during the service, "Whom should we invite home with us today?" Then they gather around the soup, with some salad, and talk about what they learned from the pastor's sermon, what God is teaching them, how he is working in their lives, and other topics that actually *matter*.

Why not consider how you can use your home as a way of reaching out? It can be elaborate, as Deb's gatherings sometimes are, or as simple as soup and salad. The important thing is to have a heart that wants to bless others and ears to hear whom God is directing you toward.

Affirmation: I practice hospitality.

Practical

Pray about how you can use your home to extend hospitality.

Day 74

Open Your Home for Ministry

Scripture to Memorize

Charm is deceptive, and beauty is fleeting;
  but a woman who fears the LORD is to be praised.

Proverbs 31:30

Passage to Read

On the Sabbath we went outside the city gate to the river, where we expected to find a place of prayer. We sat down and began to speak to the women who had gathered there. One of those listening was a woman named Lydia, a dealer in purple cloth from the city of Thyatira, who was a worshiper of God. The Lord opened her heart to respond to Paul's message. When she and the members of her household were baptized, she invited us to her home. "If you consider me a believer in the Lord," she said, "come and stay at my house." And she persuaded us. . . .

After Paul and Silas came out of the prison, they went to Lydia's house, where they met with the brothers and encouraged them.

Acts 16:13–15, 40

Guided Prayer

Dear Lord, thank you for the example of Lydia. May you find me, as Paul found her, in a place of prayer. Help me to find a group of faithful prayer warriors I can gather with on a regular basis. I confess that I have sometimes neglected the gathering together of your saints and at other times we have gathered for every purpose under the sun other than prayer.

Holy Spirit, keep my heart open to the people you will send into my life in response to my prayers, even as you sent Paul in response to Lydia's prayers. I pray that I'll be known as a worshiper of God. I also want to open my home to your workers and show hospitality to your people. Make my home, like hers, a center of your activity in my community. Amen.

Personal

Lydia is a tremendous role model of a first-century Proverbs 31 woman. Like the Old Testament example, she was a businesswoman who sold high-end fabric. In other words, she worked in the fashion industry. Yet she was known not just as a businesswoman but also as a worshiper of God and a woman who feared the Lord. She was able to balance her financial and spiritual life in a healthy way.

Lydia was almost certainly a hard worker, but she wasn't a workaholic. I know that because she had a routine habit of honoring the Sabbath, gathering with other godly women to pray and fellowship. When God's man for her city showed up, she was on her knees praying. My guess is that she was praying, "God, send someone to help us reach this city." So when God sent an answer, she recognized it. She was watching and praying.

I notice, too, that she immediately opens her home. This tells me it was probably in good order—do *you* invite people home when the place is in chaos? Probably not! She had positioned herself and her home to be ready for God's use at a moment's notice.

Sisters, the reason we've worked so hard to get our homes in order is not to congratulate ourselves on what wonderful housekeepers we are. The purpose, above all else, is that our homes can become a center for God's work in our community. Lydia was willing to open her home as a place of *outreach*. She and her friends were the first Christians in all of Europe, so it's not likely that she was inviting over the women from the church missionary society. They were all either seekers or brand-new believers. But she didn't hesitate to invite them all over. Think about that!

Now here's something that didn't hit me until recently, even though I've studied the Bible for almost thirty years. When Paul and Silas got out of prison, they went to Lydia's little house church and greeted—who? The sisters? The sewing circle? The ladies' Bible study? No, it says they met "the brothers." Paul had spoken to Lydia and a group of women. We don't know how the other women responded; we only know that Lydia and her household believed. Paul and Silas were the only known male believers on the entire European continent and *they were in jail*. Yet when they were released from jail, it appears that a thriving house church was meeting in Lydia's home.

How do you suppose that came about?

I suspect some very powerful ministry was taking place in Lydia's home. How about your home? Is it a place of ministry? Or is it just a place for amusement and self-gratification? Yes, it's important to have a place to kick off your shoes and be yourself, and home should be that place. But home can be more than that. Your home can become central to the work of God in your neighborhood. It will mean keeping the place in reasonable enough order that you can say, "Come home with me" at a moment's notice. It means having systems in place so your household runs smoothly enough for you to host routine gatherings of believers without disrupting the household. It means creating an atmosphere of prayer and blessing that immediately grabs the attention of everyone who walks through your front door.

Recently I visited such a home in Bogotá, Colombia. Twenty years ago, God spoke to a beautiful, gifted woman named Inga Suarez and instructed her to open her home for a weekly Bible study. Once a week, they have to remove all furniture from the first floor so they can bring in three hundred chairs to accommodate all the people who want to hear Inga teach. Inga is now the head of women's ministries for the National Association of Evangelical Churches in Colombia and, for the record, every piece of clothing she wears is custom designed by her daughter-in-law and hand-tailored just for her. She is one of the most elegant women I've ever met. She looks just like how I picture Lydia: an irresistible blend of godliness and sophistication. No wonder she has now been invited to speak in twenty-six countries around the world! And it all began in her living room.

God only knows what he can do through one woman on her knees who is willing to say, "Come to my house. Let's learn about God together." God only knows, but wouldn't you like to find out? One thing we know for sure: a woman who fears the Lord is to be praised.

Affirmation: I open my home to the work of God.

Practical

Pray and seek God's direction. What does *he* want to do with your home? How can *your home* serve the kingdom of God? Consider hosting a small-group Bible study, youth group meeting, or some other gathering.

Day 75

Host God's Servants

Scripture to Memorize

Charm is deceptive, and beauty is fleeting;
but a woman who fears the LORD is to be praised.

Proverbs 31:30

Passage to Read

Delight yourself in the LORD
and he will give you the desires of your heart.
Commit your way to the LORD;
trust in him and he will do this:
He will make your righteousness shine like the dawn,
the justice of your cause like the noonday sun.

Psalm 37:4–6

Guided Prayer

Dear Lord, I delight myself in you. Thank you for giving me the desires of my heart in so many areas of my life. I can truly say I've been richly blessed. At the same time I want to find increasing delight in those things that delight you most; I want my heart to be filled with your desires so I live by your priorities. It amazes me how my desires have changed over the years, how things I once thought were vitally important now seem insignificant, and how things that never even crossed my mind, like the needs of oppressed people around the world, have become increasingly important to me. Lord, let me, more and more, allow my heart to be broken by the things that break your heart.

Today I commit my way to you. Both the "big picture" of my lifetime and the most mundane chore on my schedule. It's all for you. Holy Spirit, empower me to do everything wholeheartedly. I trust you, Lord. I trust that you'll make my righteousness shine—you'll make me a light in this dark world. Help me to shine wherever I go and to shine the brightest right here in my own home, in the midst of my ordinary routine, where it's most difficult.

Thanks for reminding me that I don't need to serve as my own advocate anymore. I don't need to demand my rights—my right to have the last say or get my own way. When my cause is just, you'll make it blindingly obvious. Meanwhile, I entrust myself, my life, and this day to you, with all my heart. I delight in you. May I live my life in such a way that you can delight in me, too. Amen.

Personal

I thought my teenager was going to burst with excitement. She and two friends had spent Friday evening and Saturday working the book table for Tina Marie, a former Hollywood actress who now speaks to teens around the country about personal purity. I had met Tina Marie on a mission trip to Peru; I had met her husband's brother on a trip to Papua New Guinea even before I met her or her husband!

Tina Marie was in town speaking at a local church, so we offered to let her and her husband stay in our home, volunteered to help at the conference, and were on our way to take the couple out to dinner before their 9 p.m. flight home to begin their training with New Tribes Mission. The real excitement unfolded when my phone rang and it was Hector Torres, a Latin American pastor whom my daughter considers her greatest hero. Hector and his wife also happened to be in town and had just agreed to join all of us for dinner.

My daughter was breathless as she tried to explain to her friends the magnitude of this moment. "It's almost like having dinner with Billy Graham and your favorite movie star at the same time!" As I looked up at my daughter during the course of the meal, her eyes sparkled and I knew she would remember this night forever.

Why not play host to the servants of the Lord? Read the Bible from Genesis to Revelation and you will see believers holding those who serve the Lord in the highest esteem. Previously we talked about hospitality in the sense of sharing meals with fellow Christians—and that's important—but

I want to encourage you to go a step farther, to deliberately seek out opportunities to host Christian servants—those who are in full-time ministry, especially missionaries—in your home. The fact is, almost all missionaries have to travel around the country to raise awareness and funds to support their ministry. These people have amazing stories to tell and can make a tremendous impact on the lives of your children.

By creating opportunities to serve those who serve the Lord, you are not only blessing the Lord, you are opening the door for him to bless your family. My children have met amazing people who serve God all over the world. As a result, they are genuine world Christians who have the big picture in view. My daughter Tara went on her first mission trip at age ten. Together, we went to Mexico for an outreach to kids that included games, food, music, and a gospel presentation. Tara practiced her Spanish for weeks, learning songs and basic greetings. As mentioned previously, Leah and I have been on two mission trips—to Panama and Peru—and she went to Egypt with Teen Missions for her first solo trip.

I do not believe my children would have such a heart for the world if I hadn't deliberately created opportunities for them to meet missionaries up close and personal. Why not talk to the missions coordinator at your church or denominational headquarters and find out what your family can do to host missionaries? If your church doesn't have a missions coordinator, volunteer your family to fill the role.

Affirmation: I welcome God's servants into my home.

Practical

Contact your church or denominational missions coordinator and find out how you can host a missionary.

Day 76

Weekly Checkup

Cumulative Scripture Review

A wife of noble character who can find?
  She is worth far more than rubies.
Her husband has full confidence in her
  and lacks nothing of value.
She brings him good, not harm,
  all the days of her life.
She selects wool and flax
  and works with eager hands.
She is like the merchant ships,
  bringing her food from afar.
She gets up while it is still dark;
    she provides food for her family
    and portions for her servant girls.
She considers a field and buys it;
    out of her earnings she plants a vineyard.
She sets about her work vigorously;
    her arms are strong for her tasks.
She sees that her trading is profitable,
    and her lamp does not go out at night.
In her hand she holds the distaff
    and grasps the spindles with her fingers.
She opens her arms to the poor
    and extends her hands to the needy.
When it snows, she has no fear for her household;
    for all of them are clothed in scarlet.
She makes coverings for her bed;
    she is clothed in fine linen and purple.
Her husband is respected at the city gate,
    where he takes his seat among the elders of the land.
She makes linen garments and sells them,
    and supplies the merchants with sashes.

She is clothed with strength and dignity;
    she can laugh at the days to come.
She speaks with wisdom,
    and faithful instruction is on her tongue.
She watches over the affairs of her household
    and does not eat the bread of idleness.
Her children arise and call her blessed;
    her husband also, and he praises her:
"Many women do noble things,
    but you surpass them all."
Charm is deceptive, and beauty is fleeting;
    but a woman who fears the LORD is to be praised.

Proverbs 31:10–30

Turn verse 30 into a Scripture-based prayer:

_____

_____

_____

Practical

Saturday is your day to review and catch up on any unfinished items. Check to confirm that you have completed the following one-time tasks:

- ☐ I instituted the family breakfast half hour.
- ☐ I began dressing my family for spiritual success before they leave the house in the morning.
- ☐ I made a commitment to practice hospitality and am taking steps toward hosting my first guest.
- ☐ I have prayed about opening my home for ministry.
- ☐ I contacted the missions coordinator for my church or denomination to find out how I can host a missionary.

Check to confirm you are routinely incorporating the following positive changes into your daily routine:

- ☐ I'm using my Personal Notebook.
- ☐ I'm regularly reviewing my Personal Vision Statement.
- ☐ I'm spending time in my prayer place, enjoying TAG.
- ☐ I'm dealing proactively with my secret sins.
- ☐ I'm completing this study every day, practicing the memory verse, and reciting affirmations daily.
- ☐ I'm becoming consciously selective about how I dress and how I use my time and resources.
- ☐ I'm becoming a more serious student of the Bible.
- ☐ I'm practicing the presence of God, being watchful, thankful, and prayerful.
- ☐ I'm following my EVENING ROUTINE and going to bed on time.
- ☐ I'm inviting God to awaken me each morning, saying no to the snooze button, and following a MORNING ROUTINE.
- ☐ I'm exercising control over my eating habits and limiting sugar intake.
- ☐ I'm using smaller plates and controlling food portions.
- ☐ I'm planning ahead for healthier eating.
- ☐ I'm prayer walking three to five days per week.
- ☐ I begin each day with a cleansing drink and consume sixty-four ounces of water every day.
- ☐ I stop eating several hours before bed.
- ☐ I'm using a rebounder to fight gravity and cellulite.
- ☐ I routinely take cleansing baths.
- ☐ I'm using my DAILY PAGE and applying the 80/20 rule.
- ☐ I routinely give away everything I can.
- ☐ I'm tackling items on my TACKLE LIST.
- ☐ I'm tithing.
- ☐ I'm clearing out the rubble of debt and paying with cash.
- ☐ I have my savings and investments on autopilot.
- ☐ I'm wearing fashionable yet modest, correct-color clothing that actually fits and flatters me.
- ☐ I'm developing multiple streams of income through home enterprise.
- ☐ My family is maintaining our home using the shared servanthood strategy.
- ☐ I'm focusing on being a better wife, mother, and general family member.
- ☐ My family is developing "we always" traditions, including honoring the Sabbath.
- ☐ As far as it depends on me, I am at peace with all people.

☐ I'm taking every opportunity to share meals with my family, beginning with breakfast each morning.

☐ I'm practicing hospitality, opening my home to the workers and the work of the Lord.

Day 77

Weekly Reflection

Sunday is a great day to devote extra time meditating on the entire Proverbs 31 passage, memorizing your assigned verses, praying, and preparing your heart for the week ahead. Take one day out of every seven to rest and reflect. Do *not* catch up on assignments you did not complete, but *do* schedule them for the coming week.

Fill in the remainder of Proverbs 31:10–30 from memory:

A _____ ___ _____ _____ who can find?

   She is worth _____ _____ _____ _____.

Her husband _____ ____ _____ ___ ____

   and lacks _____ ___ _____.

She brings him _____, ____ _____,

   all the _____ ___ ____ _____.

She selects _____ ____ _____

   and works _____ _____ _____.

She is like _____ _____ _____,

   bringing her _____ _____ ____.

She gets up _____ ___ ___ _____ _____;

   she provides _____ ____ ___ _____

and portions _____ _____ _____ _____.

She considers _ _____ ____ _____ ___;

out of her earnings _____ _____ __ _____.

She sets about _____ _____ _____;

her arms _____ _____ ____ ____ _____.

She sees that _____ _____ ___ _____

and her _____ _____ ____ __ ____ ___ _____.

In her hand _____ _____ ____ _____

and grasps _____ _____ _____ ____ _____.

She opens _____ _____ __ ____ _____

and extends _____ _____ __ ____ _____.

When it _____, she _____ ___ _____ ____ ____

_____;

for all ___ _____ ____ _____ __ _____.

She makes _____ ____ ____ ____;

she is _____ __, _____ _____ ____ _____.

Her husband ___ _____ ___ ____ _____ _____,

where he takes ____ _____ _____ ____ _____ __

_____ _____.

She makes _____ _____ ____ _____ _____,

and supplies _____ _____ _____ _____.

She is clothed _____ _____ ____ _____;

she can _____ ____ _____ __ ____ _____.

She speaks _____ _____,

and faithful _____ ___ ___ ____ _____.

She watches _____ ____ _____ ___ ___ _____

and does not ____ ____ _____ ___ _____.

Her children _____ ____ _____ ____ _____;

her husband _____, and ___ _____ ____:

"Many women ___ _____ _____,

but you _____ _____ ____."

Charm is _____, and _____ ___ _____;

but a woman ____ _____ ____ _____ __ __ __

_____.

Weekly Evaluation

1. Am I listening for and hearing God's voice? What is he saying to me?

   _____

   _____

2. Am I increasingly manifesting the fruit of the Spirit: love, joy, peace, patience, kindness, goodness, faithfulness, gentleness, and self-control (Gal. 5:22–23)? What areas look encouraging? What needs prayer?

   _____

   _____

3. What did God teach me during my TAG?

   _____

   _____

4. Which priorities did I live by? Which goals did I pursue?

_____

_____

5. Which priorities or goals did I neglect?

_____

_____

6. What new thing did I learn—about life, God, my family, and the people around me?

_____

_____

7. What are my specific priorities/goals for the coming week?

_____

Take out your notebook and schedule your priorities or goals for the coming week.

WEEK TWELVE
RETIREMENT PLANNING

Get a Reality Check

Scripture to Memorize

Give her the reward she has earned,
and let her works bring her praise at the city gate.

Proverbs 31:31

Passage to Read

For God is not a God of disorder but of peace.

1 Corinthians 14:33

Guided Prayer

Dear Jesus, I praise you because you are such an awesome God. Thank you for all you have done in my life, especially for being my Prince of Peace. The price you paid on the cross bought me the right to have peace with the Father. That's a debt I can never repay. Just as you've given me peace in my spirit—and as I'm learning to experience your peace in my mind, will, and emotions—I ask you to bring peace into my physical world. Thank you for telling me plainly that you are not a God of disorder but of peace. That helps me understand that any area of my life that is *out of order* has not yet come under your lordship. I want the peace of God to rule over every area of my life. Holy Spirit, I can't do this without you and the power you alone can impart. Lead me on the path of peace. Amen.

Personal

When my father passed away in June 2006, it hit me much harder than I thought it would. I'm writing this exactly one year later and still struggling to regain my equilibrium. Thankfully, I was with my father when he went home to heaven. The room was enveloped with the peace of God, and I've never had a doubt about where my father will spend eternity. The funeral was unforgettable, as those who loved him came out to honor his memory—giving him the reward he had earned and publicly praising his virtues.

Someday I'll receive the rewards I've earned—both earthly and heavenly. Someday a funeral will be held, and my life's work will receive the praise it is due—whether that honor is minimal or significant, whether that praise is lavish or sparing, is really up to me.

As I have reflected on my life, I have had peace about many things, but there is one area where I know the rewards will be few and the praise hollow—and that's the area of personal finance. The reality that my children will one day say good-bye to me and have to cope with the aftermath of my life choices hit me like a ton of bricks. As I'll share later in the week, I've made many foolish financial decisions, which I must now work to reverse *for my children's sake.*

Now I'm on a mission to *wake up* as many people as I can to the reality and the financial responsibility involved with our inevitable aging and death. Here are some facts we need to face:

- There are 78 million American baby boomers.
- Many have already entered retirement. Over the next two decades, the rest will follow.
- Life expectancy is now 77.9 years in the United States.[1]
- People who are 85 years of age or older constitute the single most rapidly growing group in our population.[2]
- The number of Americans over 100 years old is also growing exponentially.

Think about the implications of these numbers. It means there are millions of aging people, many of whom will not contribute to the economy or the financial well-being of their families—unless they've planned ahead.

It means millions of people will require vast financial resources, including funding for health care. Have you considered *what you will live on* if God grants you one hundred years or more? Will you be able to *live on* your investments or will you have to *live off* your children and grandchildren?

Previously, I mentioned my husband's great-grandfather, Mike "The Chief" Nasco, age 104. At his recent birthday celebration, he was on his feet the entire time, greeting relatives and even granting an interview to the local television station. He was so busy, the restaurant staff finally *brought the cake to him* and he blew out the candles *while standing*. The Chief is independent today because he exercised financial wisdom yesterday. He developed multiple streams of income, including operating his own business and various real estate investments. He's actively enjoying his long life because he was financially prepared for it.

Are *you* prepared? You need to be. Kim Kiyosaki, author of *Rich Woman*, shares the following startling statistics:[3]

- 47 percent of women over 50 are single.
- Approximately 7 out of 10 women will, at some time, live in poverty. For most of them, it will be during their retirement years.
- 80 percent of widows now living in poverty were not poor before the death of their husband.
- Women's retirement income (social security, pensions, 401(k)s) will be lessened because, on average, a woman is away from the work force 14.7 years as compared to 1.6 years for men.

Have you thought about what will happen to you when your husband dies? You *do know* that wives almost always outlive their husbands. Will you end up a poverty statistic? When my father died, my mother's Social Security check was immediately cut in half to $1,200 a month. Her rent alone was $850, leaving her less than $100 a week to live on. Her insurance and medical expenses are far more than that. She is fortunate to have children who are willing and able to care for her, but what if she didn't? What would have happened to her? If that doesn't wake you up, I don't know what will.

Here's another thing you don't want to think about, but you need to. More than 50 percent of marriages end in divorce, after which, on average, a woman's standard of living drops 73 percent.[4] Have you thought about what would happen to you financially if your marriage ended? I know this is a difficult subject, particularly for Christian women. We don't want to even *think* that it could happen to us. However, the statistics indicate otherwise. The divorce rate among American evangelical Christians is actually *higher* than the divorce rate in the population at large.[5]

When we read these statistics and this information, we can respond one of two ways: like a victor or a victim. A victim thinks, *Wow, that could happen to me. That's so unfair. Someone really ought to do something about that. They should pass a law! I sure hope my kids are ready to step up to the plate and pay me back after* all *I've done for them.*

A victor thinks, *Now I know what I'm up against. I'm going to study and learn all I can about personal finance. I'm going to start a part-time business on the side to begin earning residual and investment income. I'm not going to rely on my employer or the government or anyone else. God has given me a good mind. I will apply my mind to making wise financial choices for my future. The Bible says the virtuous woman is entitled to the rewards she has earned; it doesn't say the world owes her a comfortable retirement.*

The Proverbs 31 woman could laugh at the days to come because she *prepared* for them. I want you to be able to laugh at the days to come. So let's get you prepared. Your children will definitely arise and call you blessed when they find out you are financially able to care for yourself until God calls you home.

Affirmation: I can laugh at the days to come because I am financially prepared for them.

Practical

Prayerfully consider the startling statistics shared today.

Calculate what your financial resources would be if you lost your husband. If you are already single, take a closer look at your financial reality. Check out the retirement planning tools available on the following websites:

Charles Schwab at www.schwab.com

Vanguard at www.vanguard.com

Fidelity at www.fidelity.com

Day 79

Prepay Your Mortgage

Scripture to Memorize

> Give her the reward she has earned,
> and let her works bring her praise at the city gate.

Proverbs 31:31

Passage to Read

Suppose one of you wants to build a tower. Will he not first sit down and estimate the cost to see if he has enough money to complete it? For if he lays the foundation and is not able to finish it, everyone who sees it will ridicule him, saying, "This fellow began to build and was not able to finish."

Luke 14:28–30

Guided Prayer

Dear Lord, I want to build a tower. I want to build a secure financial future for my family and me. Thank you for the wisdom of your Word. Thanks for reminding me that, before I do anything, I need to sit down and estimate the cost to see what my financial reality is. I want to have enough money to complete this race of life without becoming a burden on anyone else. I know you can give me the financial wisdom I need to make that happen. Help me to lay a firm foundation based on sound financial principles so I will be able to finish. Holy Spirit, don't leave me open to the charge of being unable to finish what I've begun building. Lead me every step of the way. I know I can count on you. I want you to be able to count on me, too. Amen.

Personal

It's obvious that the Proverbs 31 woman was smart with money. You can be, too. You don't need an MBA from Harvard to position yourself to receive the rewards you have earned for planning ahead. You just have to be determined to gain some basic financial literacy and then do the smart thing. Often it's not the big things that make a difference; it's the little things. Today we'll explore a little thing you can do that will have a dramatic impact on your financial future.

This little thing assumes you've done a big thing: bought your own home. If you have not done so, and you are still renting, you need to become a homeowner immediately. Ask around to obtain a recommendation for a reputable Realtor in your neighborhood. Find a place *within your financial reach* by having the Realtor "crunch the numbers" to ensure that your monthly mortgage payment will be in the range of your current rent. Do this *before* you start looking at houses. There's nothing worse than touring ten homes you can't afford. You'll end up feeling discontent with the homes that are within your price range. If you're not convinced home ownership is the right choice or you need practical help working out the financial details, read *The Automatic Millionaire Homeowner* by David Bach. It's easy to read and implement his ideas.[6]

Let's assume you already own a home. For most Americans, our home is our financial fortress. We put everything into it. Then when we retire, we can sell it, move to a smaller place, and maybe even buy an RV with the excess cash. But what if you could pay off your mortgage *seven years early* and save a fortune in interest payments while you're at it? You can, and it's not hard to do. Simply calculate 10 percent of your mortgage and add that much as *an additional payment against principal* each month. Let's say you pay $1,500 per month. For just 10 percent extra, or $150, you can pay off a 30-year mortgage seven years early. Take a look at your monthly mortgage statement. It probably has a line that says "Additional principal payment." *If so, simply write in the amount there—and make sure you do it every month.* If there isn't a space for additional principal payments, contact your lender. Do not assume your extra payments will automatically go against the principal. They may apply them to the interest. That's not what you want.

The other way to pay down your mortgage in less time is with a biweekly mortgage. So rather than paying your $1,500 once a month, you pay $750 every two weeks. Your checking account basically looks the same, but your mortgage balance will be dramatically reduced because you end up making the equivalent of 13 monthly payments rather than 12. You will have to contact your mortgage lender to make arrangements for a biweekly mortgage. There may be a fee involved, but it's worth it. You can save tens of thousands of dollars with this simple technique.

Personally, I've found it easier just to add 10 percent to each monthly payment. But if you are not disciplined enough to stick with it, make it automatic.

Your home is probably your largest financial investment. You can make it an even better investment by paying off the mortgage *years* ahead of schedule. The financial reward you'll receive will have you laughing all the way to the bank, while your family sings your praises.

Affirmation: I prepay my mortgage.

Practical

If you're not a homeowner, get yourself on the pathway to becoming one. If you are a homeowner, make your investment even smarter by paying a little extra on your mortgage or arranging a biweekly mortgage.

Day 80

Live within Your Means

Scripture to Memorize

Give her the reward she has earned,
and let her works bring her praise at the city gate.

Proverbs 31:31

Passage to Read

But godliness with contentment is great gain. For we brought nothing into the world, and we can take nothing out of it. But if we have food and clothing, we will be content with that. People who want to get rich fall into temptation and a trap and into many foolish and harmful desires that plunge men into ruin and destruction. For the love of money is the root of all kinds of evil. Some people, eager for money, have wandered from the faith and pierced themselves with many griefs.

1 Timothy 6:6–10

Guided Prayer

Dear Lord, thank you for holding out the truth before me. Sometimes I don't want to face the fact that I brought nothing into this world and I will take nothing out of it. I confess that I have *not* been content but instead have chased after riches and fallen into various temptations. I know the love of money is the root of all kinds of evil, and I ask you, Lord Jesus, to deliver me from it. I don't want to wander from the faith and pierce myself with grief. I want to live my life pursuing godliness with contentment, for I know that is great gain. Holy Spirit, help me to fix my eyes on what is unseen, not on what is seen. Help me to live within my means, not only for my sake but for the sake of my descendants. I want to leave them more than boxes full of accumulated stuff. I want to leave them an example of a life lived wholly devoted to you. Amen.

Personal

The Proverbs 31 woman joyously received the rewards her wisdom had earned. Some of us are not content with that; we want the reward without the sacrifice. Life doesn't work that way. Perhaps you've read the previous financial assignments in this 90-Day Jumpstart and mumbled: *Wait one minute! Where's the fun in all of this? If I give God 10 percent and save 10 percent and make an extra payment against my mortgage, what will I have left to live on?*

Do you want to know what you'll have left? Your means.

Your lifelong assignment is learning to live within your means. If you are not willing to tithe, save, and prepare for your retirement by doing what you can to pay your mortgage off early (and save a fortune in the process), what you're really saying is: "I'm not willing to live within my means."

Today's passage says godliness with contentment is great gain. The godly person doesn't try to obtain extra *stuff* by robbing God or her children. Yes, robbing your children. If you refuse to live within your means, the people who will suffer the most are the people you love the most: your children and grandchildren. They are the ones who will have to sacrifice to provide for you in retirement because you weren't willing to exercise wisdom and self-control. I don't mean to be harsh, but sometimes love must be tough.

People in Western cultures are living longer and longer. It's your responsibility to plan responsibly for your prolonged retirement years rather than expecting your descendants to provide for you.

There are four very simple things you can do to show your family that you truly care:

1. Give God what belongs to God, so your life is a life of blessing.
2. Get out of debt and stay out. Is your *stuff* more important than your family's future?
3. Save and invest for your retirement so you don't become a financial burden.
4. Pay off your mortgage early and *invest* the tens of thousands of dollars you otherwise would have squandered on interest.

Put more simply: make the commitment to live within your means. Choose to be content with the funds that remain *after* you've fulfilled your obligations. When you are content with what you have and cease pursuing stuff, you can put all of your efforts into pursuing God. Then you can leave your descendants a godly inheritance rather than boxes full of junk to sort through.

The Proverbs 31 woman spoke with wisdom, and faithful instruction was on her tongue (v. 26). I have no doubt part of the wisdom she imparted to her children was sound financial principles. The Bible, particularly the book of Proverbs, is filled with them. Part of our obligation as godly women and mothers is to study what God's Word has to say about money, then line up our finances accordingly.

If you are like most people, no one taught you about managing your money, and you are worse off because of it. Some have even been destroyed for their lack of knowledge. Let's take the initiative to pursue financial wisdom, so we can impart it to our children and spare them some of the foolish financial decisions we made. If you teach your children nothing more than the handful of principles contained in this 90-Day Jumpstart, and they put them into practice, they will enjoy financial peace throughout their lifetime. What an incredible gift to be able to impart! When your children finally realize the value of what you've given (it may take a few years), they are sure to arise and call you blessed in gratitude.

Affirmation: I believe godliness with contentment is great gain.

Practical

Get on your knees before God and face your future. Repent of any selfishness you've exhibited or disregard for your family's financial future. Make a firm commitment to live within your means.

Day 81

Avoid Financial Folly

Scripture to Memorize

Give her the reward she has earned,
and let her works bring her praise at the city gate.

Proverbs 31:31

Passage to Read

The man who had received the five talents brought the other five. "Master," he said, "you entrusted me with five talents. See, I have gained five more."

His master replied, "Well done, good and faithful servant! You have been faithful with a few things; I will put you in charge of many things. Come and share your master's happiness!"

The man with the two talents also came. "Master," he said, "you entrusted me with two talents; see, I have gained two more."

His master replied, "Well done, good and faithful servant! You have been faithful with a few things; I will put you in charge of many things. Come and share your master's happiness!"

Then the man who had received the one talent came. "Master," he said, "I knew that you are a hard man, harvesting where you have not sown and gathering where you have not scattered seed. So I was afraid and went out and hid your talent in the ground. See, here is what belongs to you."

His master replied, "You wicked, lazy servant! So you knew that I harvest where I have not sown and gather where I have not scattered seed? Well then, you should have put my money on deposit with the bankers, so that when I returned I would have received it back with interest.

"Take the talent from him and give it to the one who has the ten talents. For everyone who has will be given more, and he will have an abundance. Whoever does not have, even what he has will be taken from him. And throw that worthless servant outside, into the darkness, where there will be weeping and gnashing of teeth."

Matthew 25:20–30

Guided Prayer

Dear Lord, this passage containing the parable of the talents challenges me. My natural inclination is to see someone who doesn't have many financial resources and *give* to that person. I don't always stop and think: maybe that person doesn't have financial resources because he or she has been foolish with money or unwilling to do the hard work it takes to make wise investments.

It amazes me that Jesus didn't express compassion toward the servant who didn't invest his money. He rebuked him sharply and called him lazy. Forgive me, Lord, if I have been lazy in any way about investments or financial management. I realize you take money management as seriously as you take any other area of my life. Please help me to become a better investor. Holy Spirit, I invite you to be my financial planning tutor. I want to be an A student to the glory of God. I want to invest every penny for maximum return so I can do the most good for the kingdom. I need your help to do that and thank you in advance for all the exciting lessons I'm going to learn and for the profit I'm going to earn! Amen.

Personal

The Proverbs 31 woman opened and extended her hand to the poor and needy (v. 20). I read that verse out of context and went wild with it. We can and should be generous with our money, but everything we do—including our giving—must be guided by wisdom. Wisdom, after all, is the overriding subject of the entire book of Proverbs. Wisdom wasn't thrown out the window to make room for this one sentence. If only I had realized that a little sooner, my husband and kids would be singing my praises a whole lot louder.

This 90-Day Jumpstart isn't long enough for me to chronicle how foolish I've been with money. And the sad thing is I thought my foolishness was actually spiritual. In the early 1990s the Lord blessed me with a series of bestselling books that generated significant income, which could have, and should have, been wisely invested for my retirement. Instead, I entrusted the funds to a professing Christian who claimed to have my best interests at heart. Several people tried to warn me that this person was untrustworthy, but I thought being a Christian required blind trust. *I lost a small fortune.*

Yet another time I took out a second mortgage to help a couple who were supposedly in desperate need of a home. All they wanted was a second chance at life, and I knew God had sent me to their rescue. (You can laugh, cry, or smack me; whichever you choose is perfectly understandable.) As time progressed I realized there was a reason they were in such dire financial straits. They were unwilling to work and lived a self-indulgent lifestyle. They suffered from the entitlement mentality that has crippled so many people in America. Handing them money only worsened their handicap by rewarding their selfish behavior. Not only were they ungrateful for the help I provided, they were resentful when I wouldn't continue financing their laziness.

I won't even tell you about the time I borrowed money to pay $2,500 on a friend's house because her mortgage was about to be foreclosed. I mean, she was desperate and *God told her* to call me for help. How could I refuse? Besides, she was going to pay me back even if all she could afford was $10 at a time. I turned over the money and that was the last I ever heard from her. Although I did hear from a mutual friend that the bank foreclosed on the mortgage less than a year later anyway.

I thought I was being generous but I was just being stupid. There's a huge difference between sowing seed in good soil and throwing good money after bad. Unfortunately for my children, it's taken me forty-five years to figure that out.

Somewhere along the line, I got it in my head that foolishness is next to godliness. It's not. How much better it would have been to wisely invest money when I had it available and refuse to borrow money to "help people." God will *never* ask you to borrow money to help people. If God wants you to help them, he'll provide the funds. If he doesn't provide the funds, guess what? He doesn't want you to help them. Take it from someone who has learned this lesson through extreme heartache. Very often, people have financial difficulties *for a reason.*

Which brings me to this: never, never, never cosign for a loan—for anyone, ever. For better or worse, almost anyone can get a loan these days. You see ads on TV all the time: "Bad credit. No credit. No problem." Some companies even brag they'll lend you money if you are bankrupt! Keep that in mind when your niece, neighbor, or co-worker comes to you, puppy-eyed, and begs you to cosign for a loan. If the person can't get a loan on his or her own, the lender has compelling reasons to believe the person will *not repay* the loan. If a bank has concluded that a person is not reliable, *believe the bank.* That person is not reliable.

The Proverbs 31 woman extends her hand to the poor and needy, but she doesn't become poor and needy in the process. She doesn't eat the bread of idleness herself and she doesn't enable other people to do so. She doesn't pursue wisdom and promote foolishness. Nor does she allow other people's foolishness to rob her of her financial security or steal her children's future. She knows that if she becomes poor and needy, she won't be in a position to help others. That's why she manages her resources well.

I have loaned people money on many occasions and have never once been paid back—not once. Now I won't even call it a loan or pretend to believe the promises of "I'll pay you back." If God lays it on my heart to help someone, I give the person the money outright. Otherwise, I recognize that God is still working to build character in that person's life, and financial challenges are just one of the tools in his box.

The Bible clearly teaches against cosigning: "It's stupid to guarantee someone else's loan" (Prov. 17:18 CEV) and "He who puts up security for another will surely suffer, but whoever refuses to strike hands in pledge is safe" (Prov. 11:15). If you have already cosigned for someone, you should try to find a legal way to extricate yourself from the agreement:

> My son, if you have put up security for your neighbor,
> if you have struck hands in pledge for another,
> if you have been trapped by what you said,
> ensnared by the words of your mouth,
> then do this, my son, to free yourself,
> since you have fallen into your neighbor's hands:
> Go and humble yourself;
> press your plea with your neighbor!
> Allow no sleep to your eyes,
> no slumber to your eyelids.
> Free yourself, like a gazelle from the hand of the hunter,
> like a bird from the snare of the fowler.
>
> Proverbs 6:1–5

God takes this seriously and so should we. Make a firm decision: "I will not, under any circumstances, cosign a loan for anyone (not even my own children). I will be generous when I can and offer wise counsel, but I will not circumvent God's work by giving someone with character issues a way of escape."

Don't confuse ministry with being foolish with your money. I made that mistake for decades and I regret it. Instead, realize that being wise with your money positions you for long-term ministry. And that's what the Proverbs 31 woman is all about—the long-term view. The Bible doesn't say, "Give the reward she has earned to someone else who hasn't worked for it." No, it says we have the right to enjoy the rewards we've earned. There's nothing unspiritual about that. Sow your seed in good soil, bless others out of the surplus, and enjoy your harvest.

Affirmation: I sow my seed in good soil.

Practical

Do not cosign for loans or in any way rescue people from the financial consequences of their own foolishness. If you have done so, seek a legal way out.

Day 82

Get Your Legal and Financial Affairs in Order

Scripture to Memorize

Give her the reward she has earned,
and let her works bring her praise at the city gate.

Proverbs 31:31

Passage to Read

May the LORD bless you from Zion
all the days of your life;
may you see the prosperity of Jerusalem,
and may you live to see your children's children.
Peace be upon Israel.

Psalm 128:5–6

Guided Prayer

Dear Lord, thank you for blessing me. I believe you will bless me all the days of my life and that I will see prosperity. Thank you for granting me the opportunity to live long enough to see my children's children. Help me to be wise in the way I live my life so I can truly enjoy my senior years. I thank you for your blessings and ask you to empower me to be a blessing to others all the days of my life. I pray for the peace and prosperity of my country. Amen.

Personal

Another important way to get ourselves into position to laugh at the days to come is by getting our legal and financial records in order. Once again, I recognize these are not fun topics. Nevertheless, it is critically important if you care about your family.

Start by creating an EMERGENCY CONTACT list in the PERSONAL section of your notebook. Compile a list of key people to call, including relatives, physicians, and lawyers, in case of emergency. Keep this information in your Personal Notebook and *carry it with you at all times*.

Next, photocopy your credit cards, debit cards, driver's license, Social Security card, insurance card, and any other important items you carry in your purse. If you lose your purse or it's stolen, you'll know exactly what's missing and where to go to replace everything. Put the copies in the *front* of a locked fireproof filing cabinet in a folder labeled VITAL INFORMATION or in your safe. If you don't have either of those two things, you need to buy one immediately. Make sure someone knows where the filing cabinet key is and/or where the safe is kept and how to open it. Make a note at the bottom of the EMERGENCY CONTACT page, indicating the existence and location of your VITAL INFORMATION folder. This is also the place to indicate the name and contact information for the person who knows how to open the filing cabinet and/or safe.

Your VITAL INFORMATION folder should also include:

- ☐ *Passport.* Everyone should have a valid passport. You do not know when you might need to go overseas at a moment's notice, to answer God's call (for a last-minute mission trip) or that of a relative, to take a business trip, or to care for some other circumstance. We live in a global community and the world gets smaller every day. Incidentally, check to see if your passport expires soon. If it does, renew it.
- ☐ *Will.* Lawyers constantly marvel at how many highly intelligent people don't have a will, and how many people who do have wills haven't updated them for decades. When someone dies without an up-to-date will, it can have devastating financial and legal consequences for the family. It can also lead to lengthy family feuds, even over seemingly insignificant details. If you want your loved ones, rather than lawyers and the government, to inherit your estate, make sure your will is valid and easy to

locate. Consider giving the original of your will to your lawyer or some other trusted adviser, in addition to the copy in your fireproof cabinet or safe.

☐ *Power of Attorney*. Take the time to make sure you have a well-written power of attorney and pick someone you trust completely. Check with your lawyer to make sure that any power-of-attorney form you sign does precisely what you want it to do. For example, if you want the person holding your power-of-attorney to be able to make gifts of money or other property on your behalf, say so in writing. While state laws may vary, be as precise as possible on this subject.

Remember that a power of attorney isn't just for the elderly. Sudden illness or accidents can strike at any age, making it important that someone be authorized to manage your affairs. Above all, act now while you're healthy. One of the classic mistakes is to wait until you get sick to start thinking about a power of attorney and other tough topics. You may not think as clearly under such circumstances. Be sure to assign the person as your *health care proxy* so he or she can make life and death decisions on your behalf. If you designate your spouse, also designate a backup person in case you *both* die at the same time.

☐ *Insurance policies*. Make sure you have adequate health insurance coverage. If you do not have adequate insurance, you can wipe out your entire retirement savings in a matter of *months* in a care facility. You should also have term life insurance.

☐ *Deeds to property*. The original deed(s) can be kept by you or filed with an attorney. If filed with an attorney, include a photocopy in your file. You should also have a beneficiary deed, which turns the property over to your heirs on your death.

☐ *Social Security summary*. Keep a copy of your most recent benefit statement. Ensure that all personal information is correct and confirm how much monthly income you are projected to receive. If you don't have or can't find your statement, visit www.ss.gov to obtain one.

☐ *Investment overview*. Include a recent statement for each of your investments, along with any stock or bond certificates. You should also create an INVESTMENT OVERVIEW spreadsheet, listing all of your investments with account numbers, contact information, and estimated value. If you organize your finances using a software program, such as Quicken or Microsoft Money, it will create such an overview for you to print out and file.

While you're at it, review your financial and legal documents to make sure your beneficiaries are up-to-date. Be sure to use effective estate planning tools (like trusts or advance gifts) to reduce estate taxes and ensure that your heirs receive the most benefit.

Every woman reading this should aspire to be a wise, well-prepared woman. Are you prepared? Or are you "hoping" that "someone" will take care of you? You should be reading books like *Rich Dad, Poor Dad.* You may not agree with everything the author says, but you will learn. Read other financial experts like Dave Ramsey (who is a Christian) and David Bach, creator of *The Automatic Millionaire* book series.

Yes, it's true that God is our provider. But often he provides by sending someone to bring us a wake-up call. This is your wake-up call.

Wake up!

Affirmation: I prepare for my future with wisdom.

Practical

Wake up! Face your future with wisdom and preparation. Little by little, tackle the items on today's checklist. Obviously, this cannot be done in a day or two, but at least make a beginning. Let today's reading jumpstart you in the right direction.

Notebook: Create an EMERGENCY CONTACT page in the PERSONAL section of your notebook. Include all family members and friends you would want contacted if something happened to you (accident, hospitalization, death). It should also include contact information for your doctor and lawyer; also add details on how to locate your VITAL INFORMATION file folder.

Day 83

Weekly Checkup

Cumulative Scripture Review

A wife of noble character who can find?
  She is worth far more than rubies.
Her husband has full confidence in her
  and lacks nothing of value.
She brings him good, not harm,
  all the days of her life.
She selects wool and flax
  and works with eager hands.
She is like the merchant ships,
  bringing her food from afar.
She gets up while it is still dark;
  she provides food for her family
  and portions for her servant girls.
She considers a field and buys it;
  out of her earnings she plants a vineyard.
She sets about her work vigorously;
  her arms are strong for her tasks.
She sees that her trading is profitable,
  and her lamp does not go out at night.
In her hand she holds the distaff
  and grasps the spindles with her fingers.
She opens her arms to the poor
  and extends her hands to the needy.
When it snows, she has no fear for her household;
  for all of them are clothed in scarlet.
She makes coverings for her bed;
  she is clothed in fine linen and purple.
Her husband is respected at the city gate,
  where he takes his seat among the elders of the land.
She makes linen garments and sells them,
  and supplies the merchants with sashes.
She is clothed with strength and dignity;
  she can laugh at the days to come.
She speaks with wisdom,

and faithful instruction is on her tongue.
She watches over the affairs of her household
and does not eat the bread of idleness.
Her children arise and call her blessed;
her husband also, and he praises her:
"Many women do noble things,
but you surpass them all."
Charm is deceptive, and beauty is fleeting;
but a woman who fears the LORD is to be praised.
Give her the reward she has earned,
and let her works bring her praise at the city gate.

Proverbs 31:10–31

Turn verse 31 into a Scripture-based prayer:

_____

_____

_____

Practical

Saturday is your day to review and catch up on any unfinished items. Check to confirm that you have completed the following one-time tasks:

- ☐ I am developing a plan for my financial survival in case of a significant loss.
- ☐ I added an EMERGENCY CONTACT page to my notebook.
- ☐ I photocopied all important items carried in my purse.
- ☐ I created a VITAL INFORMATION folder.
- ☐ I stored all suggested documents safely in a fireproof file cabinet or safe.
- ☐ I began work on the checklist of items to be included in the VITAL INFORMATION folder.
- ☐ I calculated my financial resources.
- ☐ I committed to prepaying my mortgage.

Check to confirm you are routinely incorporating the following positive changes into your daily routine:

- ☐ I'm using my Personal Notebook.
- ☐ I'm regularly reviewing my Personal Vision Statement.
- ☐ I'm spending time in my prayer place, enjoying TAG.
- ☐ I'm dealing proactively with my secret sins.
- ☐ I'm completing this study every day, practicing the memory verse, and reciting affirmations daily.
- ☐ I'm becoming consciously selective about how I dress and how I use my time and resources.
- ☐ I'm becoming a more serious student of the Bible.
- ☐ I'm practicing the presence of God, being watchful, thankful, and prayerful.
- ☐ I'm following my EVENING ROUTINE and going to bed on time.
- ☐ I'm inviting God to awaken me each morning, saying no to the snooze button, and following a MORNING ROUTINE.
- ☐ I'm exercising control over my eating habits and limiting sugar intake.
- ☐ I'm using smaller plates and controlling food portions.
- ☐ I'm planning ahead for healthier eating.
- ☐ I'm prayer walking three to five days per week.
- ☐ I begin each day with a cleansing drink and consume sixty-four ounces of water every day.
- ☐ I stop eating several hours before bed.
- ☐ I'm using a rebounder to fight gravity and cellulite.
- ☐ I routinely take cleansing baths.
- ☐ I'm using my DAILY PAGE and applying the 80/20 rule.
- ☐ I routinely give away everything I can.
- ☐ I'm tackling items on my TACKLE LIST.
- ☐ I'm tithing.
- ☐ I'm clearing out the rubble of debt and paying with cash.
- ☐ I have my savings and investments on autopilot.
- ☐ I'm wearing fashionable yet modest, correct-color clothing that actually fits and flatters me.
- ☐ I'm developing multiple streams of income through home enterprise.
- ☐ My family is maintaining our home using the shared servanthood strategy.
- ☐ I'm focusing on being a better wife, mother, and general family member.
- ☐ My family is developing "we always" traditions, including honoring the Sabbath.

- ☐ As far as it depends on me, I am at peace with all people.
- ☐ I'm taking every opportunity to share meals with my family, beginning with breakfast each morning.
- ☐ I'm practicing hospitality, opening my home to the workers and the work of the Lord.
- ☐ I live within my means.
- ☐ I sow financial seed in good soil; I don't throw good money after bad.
- ☐ I'm keeping my VITAL INFORMATION folder up to date.

Day 84

Weekly Reflection

Sunday is a great day to devote extra time meditating on the entire Proverbs 31 passage, memorizing your assigned verses, praying, and preparing your heart for the week ahead. Take one day out of every seven to rest and reflect. Do *not* catch up on assignments you did not complete, but *do* schedule them for the coming week.

Fill in the remainder of Proverbs 31:10–31 from memory:

A _____ __ _____ _____ who can find?

    She is worth ____ ____ ____ _____.

Her husband ____ ___ _____ __ ____

    and lacks _____ __ _____.

She brings him _____, ___ _____,

    all the _____ __ ___ ____.

She selects _____ ___ ____

    and works _____ _____ _____.

She is like ____ _____ _____,

    bringing her ____ ____ ____.

She gets up _____ __ __ _____ ____;

    she provides ____ ___ ___ _____

and portions _____ _____ _____ _____.

She considers __ _____ ____ _____ ___;

   out of her earnings _____ _____ __ _____.

She sets about _____ _____ _____;

   her arms _____ _____ ____ ____ _____.

She sees that _____ _____ __ _____,

   and her _____ _____ ____ __ ____ __ _____.

In her hand _____ _____ ____ _____

   and grasps _____ _____ _____ ____ _____.

She opens _____ _____ __ ____ _____

   and extends _____ _____ __ ____ _____.

When it _____, she _____ ___ _____ ____ ____

   _____;

   for all ___ _____ ____ _____ __ _____.

She makes _____ ____ ____ ____;

   she is _____ ___ _____ ____ ____ _____.

Her husband ___ _____ __ ____ _____ _____,

   where he takes _____ _____ _____ ____ _____ __

   _____ _____.

She makes _____ _____ ____ _____ _____,

   and supplies _____ _____ _____ _____.

She is clothed _____ _____ ____ _____;

   she can _____ __ ____ _____ __ _____.

She speaks _____ _____,

   and faithful _____ ___ __ ____ _____.

She watches _____ ____ _____ __ ____ _____

   and does not ____ ____ _____ __ _____.

Her children _____ ____ _____ ____ _____;

   her husband _____, and ___ _____ ____:

"Many women ___ _____ _____,

   but you _____ _____ ____."

Charm is _____ , and _____ ___ _____ ;

but a woman ____ _____ ____ _____ ___ ___ ___

_____ .

Give her ____ _____ ____ ____ _____ ,

and let her _____ _____ ____ _____ ___ ____

_____ _____ .

Weekly Evaluation

1. Am I listening for and hearing God's voice? What is he saying to me?

   _____

   _____

2. Am I increasingly manifesting the fruit of the Spirit: love, joy, peace, patience, kindness, goodness, faithfulness, gentleness, and self-control (Gal. 5:22–23)? What areas look encouraging? What needs prayer?

   _____

   _____

3. What did God teach me during my TAG?

   _____

   _____

4. Which priorities did I live by? Which goals did I pursue?

   _____

   _____

5. Which priorities or goals did I neglect?

_____

_____

6. What new thing did I learn—about life, God, my family, and the people around me?

_____

_____

7. What are my specific priorities/goals for the coming week?

_____

_____

Take out your notebook and schedule your priorities or goals for the coming week.

WEEK THIRTEEN
FINISH STRONG

Day 85

Commit Yourself to Healthy Aging

Scripture to Memorize

Review entire passage—Proverbs 31:10–31.

Passage to Read

The length of our days is seventy years—
   or eighty, if we have the strength;
yet their span is but trouble and sorrow,
   for they quickly pass, and we fly away.

Psalm 90:10

Guided Prayer

Dear Lord, thank you for reminding me that my time on earth is limited. It is very likely that I'll live at least seventy or eighty years. And many people today are living into their nineties and even to one hundred and beyond. Help me to live each day with a healthy awareness of both the potential longevity and brevity of life. I know that I'll have to deal with my share of trouble and sorrow. That's unavoidable. But, Holy Spirit, I know you can give me the power to handle those things with grace and gratitude. I know my life will quickly pass and I'll fly away home. I look forward to that day when I finally see you face-to-face. Meanwhile, help me to make the most of the days I have here on earth. Amen.

Personal

My husband's great-grandmother died last year at 108. I know what you're thinking if you've read this book carefully. Longevity must run in his family. Actually, his two centenarian great-grandparents are on opposite sides of his family tree, so you can't credit good genes. The primary thing they had in common was a love for Italian food and a glass of red wine each day. So I guess the apostle Paul was right when he instructed Timothy to drink a little wine for his health! What are the secrets to living not only a long life but a long, *healthy, happy life*?

Too many people end up saying, "If I had known I was going to live this long, I would have taken better care of myself." Incidentally, that's not just physical. We need to take care of ourselves spiritually, financially, mentally, and even emotionally. We've all met the stereotypical demanding old woman who does nothing but gripe about her aches and pains. As we age, we don't change into a different person. Instead, who we are simply becomes *magnified*. That's why it's so important to become something worth magnifying.

As this book comes to a close, I'd like to tell you a tale of two people coming into the homestretch of life.[1] The first lived life the American way: eating whatever tasted good, doing whatever seemed convenient for the moment. Let's call her Sue. The other lived out many of the principles shared in this book: eating right, exercising, approaching each new day with a sense of adventure. His name is Warren Faidley.

At the age of sixty-seven, Sue struggles just to walk from room to room. Actually, getting out of her chair is her most significant daily challenge. Her energy level is nonexistent. Her typical day starts off with a few cups of coffee (with plenty of cream and sugar) and a donut or two. Around noontime, she has a sandwich of cold cuts, smothered with butter and mayonnaise, and chases it down with some soda or iced tea. Dinner is meat and potatoes, of course. She snacks on cookies and cakes all day long in front of the television set. Her exercise routine consists of clicking the remote control.

Sue has battled diabetes, cancer, and coronary artery disease. She has had blood clots and tumors. She has suffered a heart attack and had quadruple bypass surgery. Truth be told, she has been in and out of the hospital her entire adult life, turning over most of her money to doctors, hospitals, and pharmacies. Footing the bills for her unending health problems has driven her to the brink of bankruptcy. The saddest part of this tale is that *it's so typical*. The American senior citizen who *doesn't* identify with much of Sue's story is the exception.

Most of Sue's adult children are overweight and in poor health. Now her grandchildren are repeating the lifestyle pattern of watching television and munching potato chips. They call it "the good life." It doesn't seem that good to me.

Once I suggested to Sue that perhaps some dietary modifications might be in order. She chuckled and dipped another fudge-covered Oreo into a glass of whole milk. Then brushing off my comments with a wave of her hand, she said, "Hey, I'm going to *enjoy* my life." Enjoy? Maybe I missed something. If that's *enjoying* life, let's all check out right now. Fortunately, I don't believe Sue. I don't believe there's nothing more to this life than indulging our taste buds and resting in our easy chairs.

Warren Faidley is living proof that there's more—much more.

I met Warren when I vacationed at Tanque Verde Ranch in Tucson, Arizona. The first thing that impressed me about Warren was his bright, cheery smile and positive attitude toward life. Then I couldn't help noticing that he was in perfect physical condition. He could put most teenagers—and many professional athletes—to shame. Over breakfast one morning, as Warren ate a plateful of fresh fruit, he told me of his big plans to become a sailor. At the age of sixty-three, after retiring from thirty-four years with the air force, he was in the process of becoming certified as a crew member on sailing cruises. He shared, "My dream is to have my own yacht someday and maybe live on the Sea of Cortez down in Mexico. What I'd really like to do is sail across the Pacific to Australia."

Warren was not always the picture of vim and vigor. "My wife was a southern belle and cooked wonderful feasts, which of course I ate. Then I sat at a desk in front of a computer all day. It wasn't a healthy combination. When my wife died in 1991, of Lou Gehrig's disease, I decided to change my life. I had high blood pressure and cholesterol problems, but I was determined that I wasn't going to shorten my life if I could help it. It took six months of constant hiking here in the mountains near my home before my doctor said I was in the condition I was at seventeen years old. I was hiking thirty-five miles a week on rigorous terrain and even doing some jogging on the trails."

314

Warren also began modifying his rich diet. "I started reading labels and watching my caloric intake. We have to realize, we're not busy like we used to be on farms. We live a sedentary life and we need to adjust our diet accordingly."

Warren is convinced that life can and should be a great adventure—if you're in good enough condition to enjoy it. He certainly is. His retirement lifestyle is anything but retiring.

We can also enjoy long life if we live right. Sally Beare studied various communities known for long, vibrant lives and compiled the results in her book *50 Secrets to the World's Longest Living People*.[2] Here are a few of the fifty secrets:

- Eat smaller portions.
- Drink plenty of water.
- Exercise.
- Get adequate sunshine.
- Have faith.
- Laugh.
- Help others.
- Enjoy a happy marriage.
- Have a pet.
- Maintain good friendships.
- Get the correct amount of sleep (neither too much nor too little).
- Supplement your diet with vitamins.
- Eat at least five servings of fruits and veggies daily.
- Eat the following foods that many long-living people include in their diets: whole grains, brown rice, sprouted wheat bread, eggs, nuts, seeds, garlic, onion, extra-virgin olive oil, sweet potatoes, berries, and yogurt.
- Eat meat as a treat, not a mainstay.
- Have salad every day.
- Drink red wine and green tea.

You probably notice that "Have good genes" is nowhere on the list. That's because study after study indicates that genetics has very little impact on our ability to live a long, healthy, happy life. Instead, lifestyle choices hold the key. And since you make your own choices, you can largely determine your future health.

It's up to you whether you become a burden or a blessing. Do you want your descendants to rise up and call you blessed or slouch down, mumbling about what a burden you are? Of course there are things beyond your control that you can do nothing about. Nevertheless, you can do everything within your power to lead a long, fruitful life.

I picture the Proverbs 31 woman with a crown of glory on her head. Someday, I want to see a true Proverbs 31 woman looking back at me from the mirror. It won't happen by accident. It's up to us to live now what we want to become in our later years.

Affirmation: I enjoy long life.

Practical

Incorporate into your lifestyle as many of the items on the longevity list as you can.

Day 86

Cultivate a Caleb Heart

Scripture to Memorize

Review entire passage—Proverbs 31:10–31.

Passage to Read

[Caleb said,] "I, however, followed the LORD my God wholeheartedly. So on that day Moses swore to me, 'The land on which your feet have walked will be your inheritance and that of your children forever, because you have followed the LORD my God wholeheartedly.'

"Now then, just as the LORD promised, he has kept me alive for forty-five years since the time he said this to Moses, while Israel moved about in the desert. So here I am today, eighty-five years old! I am still as strong today as the day Moses sent me out; I'm just as vigorous to go out to battle now as I was then. Now give me this hill country that the LORD promised me that day. You yourself heard then that the Anakites were there and their cities were large and fortified, but, the LORD helping me, I will drive them out just as he said."

Joshua 14:8–12

Guided Prayer

Dear Lord, thank you for including the life of Caleb in the Bible. What an amazing man of faith! What an inspiration to us all. Lord, I want a Caleb heart. I want to be eighty-five years old and look back at my life knowing I followed you wholeheartedly. I thank you for the personal promises you've given to me, just as you gave them to Caleb. I believe, even as I have completed this study and am taking steps toward becoming the woman you created me to be, that I've been conquering new land, which will be an inheritance for my children forever. I believe there are rewards for those who choose to follow you wholeheartedly. Thank you, Lord. But just as there are rewards, so are there responsibilities. And I believe one of the most significant responsibilities you've set before me as a godly woman is to age well.

As I grow older, let me grow wiser, stronger, braver, and more spiritually alive and powerful. Help me to set an example for other believers and serve as an inspiration to all who meet me. I don't want to be like the world around me, dreading the aging process and clinging to my youth. I want to age with dignity and grace. Holy Spirit, help me to live my life in such a way that I'll be able to honestly say with Caleb, "So here I am today, eighty-five years old! I am still as strong today as the day God sent me out; I'm just as vigorous to go out to battle now as I was then. Now give me this hill country that the Lord promised me that day. The Lord helping me, I will drive them out just as he said."

Make me a mighty conqueror in the spiritual realm. Give me a Caleb heart. Amen.

Personal

Caleb is my hero.

I want to be eighty-five years old, ready for battle. I want to be eighty-five years old and declare, "I'm just as vigorous to go out to battle now as I was when I was forty years old." Can you imagine?

It's not enough to live a long, healthy life. We have to live a long, healthy life *on mission* for the King of Kings. That's what Caleb was all about. He was determined to fight for what God told him rightfully belonged to the people of God.

I am actually looking forward to a head full of gray hair—not this current nonsense of just enough that I have to pull it out so it doesn't look stupid. I mean a crown of glory. And I want everyone in my church and community to know that, even though I may be in my walker, I'm still spiritually fit enough to walk all over the devil! I've known a Caleb or two in my day and let me tell you, it's a beautiful thing to age mightily.

One thing I pray every day, and I hope you'll make it your prayer, too: *Lord, give me a Caleb heart.* I don't want to live my later years consumed with myself. I want to be consumed by the things of God. It's said that Corrie ten Boom led more people to Christ between the ages of eighty and ninety than she did during the entire preceding years of her life. That's a Caleb heart. My friend Dr. William Miller spoke at a Billy Graham Crusade and at Urbana, the college student mission convention, when he was in his late nineties. That's a Caleb heart.

Lord, let me live long and let my heart beat after yours. Make it a Caleb heart!

Affirmation: I have a Caleb heart.

Practical

Read biographies of Christians who lived great lives for God, especially those who served him into their eighties and beyond.

Notebook: Write a vivid description of the woman you want to be at eighty-five.

Day 87

Encourage and Strengthen Yourself

Scripture to Memorize

Review entire passage—Proverbs 31:10–31.

Passage to Read

David was greatly distressed, for the men spoke of stoning him because the souls of them all were bitterly grieved, each man for his sons and daughters. But David encouraged and strengthened himself in the Lord his God.

1 Samuel 30:6 AMP

Guided Prayer

Dear heavenly Father, thank you for making the Bible so real. It helps me to know that even a man after your own heart like David had times when he was greatly distressed. I can't imagine what it must feel like to have people to whom you have devoted your life threatening to stone you. But hurting people hurt people. There have been times in my life when people I dearly love have lashed out in anger, not with stones but with words that hurt almost as much. Yet even in the worst of trials, David was able to reach deep within his spirit to that place where he knew what a faithful God he served. What an example he set for all of us, as he encouraged and strengthened himself in you!

319

Lord, you know I would much prefer to have everything go my way and never be in distress at all. My second choice would be to always have all the love and support I need when times are tough. But that's not reality. I know there will inevitably be times in my life when I am greatly distressed. There will be times when the people I thought I could count on just aren't there for me—they might even turn against me. And it's in those moments, Holy Spirit, when I will need you most. Empower me and teach me how to encourage and strengthen myself in the Lord my God. I know I can always count on you, no matter what else happens. Thank you for being such a faithful God. Amen.

Personal

We all need people in our lives who encourage and strengthen us. But what about those times when even our most trusted friends are nowhere to be found? Has that ever happened to you? It happened to David. At one of the lowest moments of his life, when his wife and children had been kidnapped, no human being could comfort him because they all had "their own stuff" to deal with.

Fortunately, David had learned something all of us must learn: how to encourage and strengthen *himself.* We also need to take proactive steps to strengthen ourselves. You can't always rely on someone else. As motivational speaker Jim Rohn put it, "You can't hire someone else to do your push-ups for you."

By undertaking this study, you have set out on a path to strengthen yourself. You became mindful of your weaknesses and made a determined effort to focus on improving. That's fantastic. Now it must continue.

One thing I do to encourage and strengthen myself is *constantly* listen to good Bible teaching—in my car, in my bathroom as I get dressed in the morning, in my kitchen while I'm preparing meals or cleaning up. I used to spend a small fortune buying tapes and CDs, but these days you can listen to fabulous Bible teaching *free* over the Internet. Lately I've developed the habit of watching my favorite Bible teacher on the Internet while lifting five-pound dumbbells. It's the ideal way to strengthen spirit, soul, and body all at the same time.

Many Bible teachers now offer podcasts and mp3s, so you can download teaching onto your iPod and strengthen yourself while you walk or run errands. Listening to uplifting praise music is another wonderful way to strengthen and encourage your spirit.

Of course listening to great Bible teachers is not a substitute for spending time in the Word of God, so even though your ninety days are nearly over, my prayer is that you'll continue the good habits you've formed over the past thirteen weeks. We are so blessed to live in an era when it's easy to strengthen ourselves with a wide range of resources. Let's make the most of these opportunities so that when the day of great distress comes, we will be able to stand firm in the faith.

Affirmation: I encourage and strengthen myself in the Lord.

Practical

Strengthen yourself spiritually by availing yourself of great Bible teaching, whether through radio, television, audios, CDs, DVDs, or the Internet. Be sure to continue with the positive spiritual disciplines you've developed during our ninety days together, including daily Scripture reading, Scripture memorization, and prayer.

Day 88

Determine to Finish Well

Scripture to Memorize

Review entire passage—Proverbs 31:10–31.

Passage to Read

I will extol the LORD at all times;
    his praise will always be on my lips.
My soul will boast in the LORD;
    let the afflicted hear and rejoice.
Glorify the LORD with me;
    let us exalt his name together.

Psalm 34:1–3

Guided Prayer

Dear Lord, I will extol you at all times. I will celebrate the beauty of all you have created and your goodness to me. Your praise will always be on my lips. Forgive me for those moments when complaints are on my lips. I know that is so offensive to you, because you take such good care of me. My soul will boast in you, Lord. I want people to know that you have healed my mind, will, and emotions. You have transformed me from the inside out. God, I want you to use me in the lives of hurting people. Let the afflicted hear what you've done in my life and rejoice, knowing you can do the same for them. I want to say to everyone I meet: "Glorify the Lord with me, let us exalt his name together." Holy Spirit, lead me to those people who need to hear this message, and give me the boldness to extol the Lord and tell them what I've learned. Amen.

Personal

Extol. It means to admire, worship, and eulogize. It means to celebrate with great enthusiasm.

It's said that you can tell a lot about a culture by looking at whom and what it celebrates. In America we celebrate celebrities. I spent time in a Muslim country shortly after the death of Anna Nicole Smith, a twenty-first-century Marilyn Monroe, whose primary claim to fame was being a loose woman who took off her clothes for money. Viewing the 24/7 American television coverage through Muslim eyes was an eye-opening experience. They couldn't comprehend why anyone (except her immediate family) would care about the life and death of a woman who was so immoral that several men laid claim to fathering her child. It's tragic that she died so young and I feel genuine sorrow for the child she left behind. But what does it say about us, as a culture, that we considered her life worthy of so much media time and attention?

It's sad that pop culture no longer celebrates a woman of noble character. Don't expect television cameras to follow your every move if your highest ambition is serving God and loving your family. As you journey toward becoming the woman God wants you to be, don't expect the world at large to celebrate or consider your life story newsworthy. But remember this: God celebrates you, and the angels are cheering every wise, virtuous decision you make.

Today our journey together comes to an end. Perhaps, in addition to the support you found on the pages of this book, you also had the privilege of traveling through this study with a group of women in your church or community. Soon, that, too, will end. And in a real sense, this is when your true journey begins.

Will you be able to press on toward becoming the woman God has called you to be? You can if you exert the power of your will. Character is the ability to do what should be done, when and how it should be done, whether or not you feel like doing it, whether or not you get an instant reward, whether or not anyone stands up to cheer you on. It's the ability to say no to your natural inclinations and yes to your responsibilities.

Much of life consists of the mundane, the tedious, and the downright difficult. Frankly, the problem with life is that it's just so *daily*. It's a matter of obediently putting one foot in front of the other, just because that's what it takes to run the race. Several years ago, God directed me to run a marathon. That's 26.2 miles. As I trained with a team of people, week after week, I had all kinds of grand illusions about what an amazing experience the marathon would be. I envisioned myself being transformed into one of the women on the cover of *Runner's World* magazine. I fantasized about how thin my thighs would look as I triumphantly crossed the finish line, where dozens of family members, friends, and Christian leaders would be waiting to celebrate my great accomplishment.

It wasn't like that at all.

I arrived at the starting line almost ten pounds heavier than the day I began my training. *No, it wasn't muscle.* When you run long distances, your body stores fat. And it had stored every ounce of it on my hips and thighs. I'm embarrassed to admit how many tears I cried over that totally unjust metabolic phenomenon.

When the gun went off, I had a few training buddies alongside of me, but they soon left me in the dust. Around the halfway point, I realized the bottom of both feet were covered in blisters. From that moment forward, every step was painful. People were passing me like I was standing still. Around the twenty-mile mark, I hit the famous wall. My legs felt like lead. You know, the legs that didn't look anything whatsoever like the women on the cover of sports magazines. My physical body literally had nothing left to give. The only thing that could possibly keep me going was the power of my will.

I knew that God had asked me to run a marathon, and I was determined that, even if I had to crawl, I was going to cross the finish line. And I did. There wasn't a big crowd of adoring friends or fans, just my husband, his best friend, and my two children. When my daughters saw the agony on my face, and I saw the look of love and admiration in their eyes, we all cried.

That's what it's all about, sisters. Rugged determination. Steadfast obedience. Life doesn't always turn out the way we hope it will. We don't always get the results we're dreaming of or the applause we're hoping for. But God has called us to run with perseverance the race marked out for us, fixing our eyes on Jesus because he's the one who wrote our life story and promises to help us across the finish line.

So what if no one "extols" you for devoting yourself to the day-after-day, one-foot-in-front-of-the-other race toward becoming the woman God has called you to be? It doesn't matter. You are not here on earth to be extolled; you are here to *extol* the Lord, to praise him no matter what, to remain obedient no matter how difficult.

I know you can do it. Just put one foot in front of the other today, and tomorrow, and every day after that, until Jesus comes back or calls you home. Your reward is waiting and it's a whole lot better than a silly medal.

Affirmation: I'm running my race with perseverance.

Practical

Do at least one thing today that you don't feel like doing. Note what it is:

_____

Day 89

Final Checkup

Cumulative Scripture Review

A wife of noble character who can find?
    She is worth far more than rubies.
Her husband has full confidence in her
    and lacks nothing of value.
She brings him good, not harm,
    all the days of her life.
She selects wool and flax
    and works with eager hands.
She is like the merchant ships,
    bringing her food from afar.
She gets up while it is still dark;
    she provides food for her family
    and portions for her servant girls.
She considers a field and buys it;
    out of her earnings she plants a vineyard.
She sets about her work vigorously;
    her arms are strong for her tasks.
She sees that her trading is profitable,
    and her lamp does not go out at night.
In her hand she holds the distaff
    and grasps the spindles with her fingers.
She opens her arms to the poor

and extends her hands to the needy.
When it snows, she has no fear for her household;
    for all of them are clothed in scarlet.
She makes coverings for her bed;
    she is clothed in fine linen and purple.
Her husband is respected at the city gate,
    where he takes his seat among the elders of the land.
She makes linen garments and sells them,
    and supplies the merchants with sashes.
She is clothed with strength and dignity;
    she can laugh at the days to come.
She speaks with wisdom,
    and faithful instruction is on her tongue.
She watches over the affairs of her household
    and does not eat the bread of idleness.
Her children arise and call her blessed;
    her husband also, and he praises her:
"Many women do noble things,
    but you surpass them all."
Charm is deceptive, and beauty is fleeting;
    but a woman who fears the LORD is to be praised.
Give her the reward she has earned,
    and let her works bring her praise at the city gate.

Proverbs 31:10–31

Using the verses that have become the most meaningful to you, write your own Scripture-based prayer:

_____

_____

_____

_____

_____

Practical

Review and catch up on any unfinished items. Check to confirm that you have completed the following one-time tasks:

- ☐ I have committed myself to healthy aging and am taking practical steps in that direction.
- ☐ I have prayed, asking God to grant me a Caleb heart.
- ☐ I am reading the biography of a great Christian who lived a long, productive life for the kingdom of God.
- ☐ I identified resources that will enable me to encourage and strengthen myself.
- ☐ I am committed to continuing to run the race well, even when this 90-Day Jumpstart is complete.
- ☐ I did one thing I didn't feel like doing.

Check to confirm you are routinely incorporating the following positive changes into your daily routine:

- ☐ I'm using my Personal Notebook.
- ☐ I'm regularly reviewing my Personal Vision Statement.
- ☐ I'm spending time in my prayer place, enjoying TAG.
- ☐ I'm dealing proactively with my secret sins.
- ☐ I'm completing this study every day, practicing the memory verse, and reciting affirmations daily.
- ☐ I'm becoming consciously selective about how I dress and how I use my time and resources.
- ☐ I'm becoming a more serious student of the Bible.
- ☐ I'm practicing the presence of God, being watchful, thankful, and prayerful.
- ☐ I'm following my EVENING ROUTINE and going to bed on time.
- ☐ I'm inviting God to awaken me each morning, saying no to the snooze button, and following a MORNING ROUTINE.
- ☐ I'm exercising control over my eating habits and limiting sugar intake.
- ☐ I'm using smaller plates and controlling food portions.
- ☐ I'm planning ahead for healthier eating.
- ☐ I'm prayer walking three to five days per week.

- ☐ I begin each day with a cleansing drink and consume sixty-four ounces of water every day.
- ☐ I stop eating several hours before bed.
- ☐ I'm using a rebounder to fight gravity and cellulite.
- ☐ I routinely take cleansing baths.
- ☐ I'm using my DAILY PAGE and applying the 80/20 rule.
- ☐ I routinely give away everything I can.
- ☐ I'm tackling items on my TACKLE LIST.
- ☐ I'm tithing.
- ☐ I'm clearing out the rubble of debt and paying with cash.
- ☐ I have my savings and investments on autopilot.
- ☐ I'm wearing fashionable yet modest, correct-color clothing that actually fits and flatters me.
- ☐ I'm developing multiple streams of income through home enterprise.
- ☐ My family is maintaining our home using the shared servanthood strategy.
- ☐ I'm focusing on being a better wife, mother, and general family member.
- ☐ My family is developing "we always" traditions, including honoring the Sabbath.
- ☐ As far as it depends on me, I am at peace with all people.
- ☐ I'm taking every opportunity to share meals with my family, beginning with breakfast each morning.
- ☐ I'm practicing hospitality, opening my home to the workers and the work of the Lord.
- ☐ I live within my means.
- ☐ I sow financial seed in good soil; I don't throw good money after bad.
- ☐ I'm keeping my VITAL INFORMATION folder up to date.
- ☐ I'm living every day with longevity in view.
- ☐ I listen to good Bible teaching daily.

Day 90

Final Evaluation

Fill in the remainder of Proverbs 31:10–31 from memory:

A _____ __ _____ _____ who can find?
   She is worth ____ _____ _____ _____.
Her husband ____ ____ _____ __ ___
   and lacks _____ __ _____.
She brings him _____, ____ _____,
   all the _____ __ ____ _____.
She selects _____ ____ _____
   and works _____ _____ _____.
She is like _____ _____ _____,
   bringing her _____ _____ _____.
She gets up _____ __ __ _____ _____;
   she provides _____ ____ ____ _____
   and portions ____ ____ _____ _____.
She considers _ _____ ____ _____ ___;
   out of her earnings ____ _____ __ _____.
She sets about ____ _____ _____;
   her arms ____ _____ ____ ____ _____.
She sees that ____ _____ __ _____,
   and her _____ _____ ____ __ ____ __ _____.
In her hand ____ _____ ____ _____
   and grasps ____ _____ _____ ____ _____.
She opens ____ _____ __ ___ _____
   and extends ____ _____ __ ___ _____.
When it _____, she ____ ___ _____ ____ ___
   _____;

for all ___ _____ ____ _____ ___ _____.

She makes _____ ____ ____ ____;

   she is _____ ___ _____ _____ ____ _____.

Her husband ___ _____ __ ___ _____ _____,

   where he takes ____ _____ _____ ____ _____ __

   _____ _____.

She makes _____ _____ ____ _____ _____,

   and supplies ____ _____ _____ _____.

She is clothed _____ _____ ____ _____;

   she can _____ __ ____ _____ ___ _____.

She speaks _____ _____,

   and faithful _____ ___ ___ ____ _____.

She watches _____ ____ _____ ___ ___ _____

   and does not ____ ____ _____ __ _____.

Her children _____ ____ _____ ____ _____;

   her husband _____, and ___ _____ ____:

"Many women ___ _____ _____,

   but you _____ ____ ___."

Charm is _____, and _____ ___ _____;

   but a woman ____ _____ ____ _____ ___ __ __

   _____.

Give her ____ _____ ____ ____ _____,

   and let her _____ _____ ____ _____ ___ ____

   _____ _____.

Evaluation of the Last Ninety Days

1. Am I listening for and hearing God's voice? What is he saying to me?

_____

_____

2. Am I increasingly manifesting the fruit of the Spirit: love, joy, peace, patience, kindness, goodness, faithfulness, gentleness, and self-control (Gal. 5:22–23)? What areas look encouraging? What needs prayer?

_____

_____

3. What did God teach me during my TAG?

_____

_____

4. Which priorities did I live by? Which goals did I pursue?

_____

_____

5. Which priorities or goals did I neglect?

_____

_____

6. What new thing did I learn—about life, God, my family, and the people around me?

_____

_____

7. What are my specific priorities/goals for the next ninety days?

_____

_____

Final Thoughts

Congratulations! You have made it through a very challenging ninety-day program designed with one goal in mind: to help you move closer to becoming the woman God wants you to be. I pray you've experienced some dramatic changes in many different areas of your life, from your physical health and daily routine to your finances and spiritual maturity. But your journey will continue tomorrow and every day for the rest of your life. When you stop learning and growing, you stop truly living. Jesus died that we might have life, so make the most of the one he's given you.

I invite you to join me online or at a future event so we can continue learning and growing together. If your church or organization would like to learn more about hosting a Becoming the Woman God Wants Me to Be event, let's talk! Visit www.donnapartow.com for details.

Godspeed!

Blessings,
Donna Partow

Bible Study Worksheet

All Scripture is God-breathed and is useful for teaching, rebuking, correcting and training in righteousness, so that the man of God may be thoroughly equipped for every good work.

2 Timothy 3:16–17

Date: _____

Passage: _____

1. Summarize in a few sentences what the passage is about:

2. Is there an example for me to follow?

3. Is there an error I need to avoid?

4. Is there a command for me to obey?

5. Is there a sin I need to forsake?

6. What application of this passage can I make today?

Menu Planner/Grocery List

	Sun.	Mon.	Tue.	Wed.	Thurs.	Fri.	Sat.
Breakfast							
Lunch							
Dinner							
Misc.							

Produce

_____

_____

_____

_____

_____

_____

Breads/Cereals

_____

_____

_____

_____

_____

Meats

_____

_____

_____

_____

_____

Dairy

_____

_____

_____

_____

Household Items

_____

_____

_____

_____

_____

Drinks

_____

_____

_____

_____

_____

Frozen

_____

_____

_____

_____

Snacks/Misc.

_____

_____

_____

_____

_____

Daily Page

Daily Page for _____

Appointments

Time	Purpose/Place	Contact/Info
_____	_____	_____
_____	_____	_____
_____	_____	_____
_____	_____	_____

☐ Spiritual: _____

☐ Physical: _____

☐ Relational: _____

☐ Personal: _____

☐ Ministry: _____

☐ Financial: _____

To Do/Tackle:

1. _____   6. _____

2. _____   7. _____

3. _____   8. _____

4. _____   9. _____

5. _____   10. _____

List five things you are grateful for today: List two things you want to pray about today:

1. _____   1. _____

2. _____   2. _____

3. _____

4. _____

5. _____

Assets and Liabilities Worksheet

Get a handle on your complete financial picture. I recommend you purchase Quicken or Microsoft Money. However, you can use the following to create your own balance sheet.

Assets

Mutual funds _____

Stocks _____

Bonds _____

Notes _____

Savings accounts _____

Money market accounts _____

Real estate _____

Intellectual property _____

Other _____

Liabilities

Mortgage _____

Car loan _____

Other loans _____

Credit card debt _____

Other _____

Debt Reduction Strategy

Pull out your credit card statements. List your debt from smallest to largest:

Credit Card	Total due	Monthly Payment
_____	_____	_____
_____	_____	_____
_____	_____	_____
_____	_____	_____
_____	_____	_____
_____	_____	_____
_____	_____	_____
_____	_____	_____
_____	_____	_____
_____	_____	_____

Focus on paying down the first (smallest) debt first. Then apply the monthly payment from the first debt toward paying down the second debt, and so on. Use pencil (or put this on your computer) to make it easier to update each month.

Memory Verse Cards

A wife of noble character who
can find?
She is worth far more than
rubies.
Her husband has full
confidence in her and
lacks nothing of value.

Proverbs 31:10–11

A wife of noble character who
can find?
She is worth far more than
rubies
Her husband has full
confidence in her and
lacks nothing of value.
She brings him good, not harm,
all the days of her life.

Proverbs 31:10–12

She brings him good, not harm,
all the days of her life.
She selects wool and flax
and works with eager hands.

Proverbs 31:12–13

She is like the merchant ships,
bringing her food from afar.
She gets up while it is still dark;
she provides food for her
family
and portions for her
servant girls.

Proverbs 31:14–15

She considers a field and buys it;
out of her earnings she plants
a vineyard.
She sets about her work
vigorously;
her arms are strong for her
tasks.

Proverbs 31:16–17

She sees that her trading is
profitable,
and her lamp does not go out
at night.
In her hand she holds the distaff
and grasps the spindles with
her fingers.

Proverbs 31:18–19

She opens her hands to the poor
and extends her hands to the
needy.
When it snows, she has no fear
for her household;
for all of them are clothed
in scarlet.

Proverbs 31:20–21

She makes coverings for her bed;
she is clothed in fine linen
and purple.
Her husband is respected at the
city gate,
where he takes his seat among
the elders of the land.

Proverbs 31:22–23

She makes linen garments and
sells them,
and supplies the merchants
with sashes.
She is clothed with strength
and dignity;
she can laugh at the days to
come.

Proverbs 31:24–25

She speaks with wisdom,
and faithful instruction is on
her tongue.
She watches over the affairs of
her household
and does not eat the bread
of idleness.

Proverbs 31:26–27

Her children arise and call her
blessed;
her husband also, and he
praises her:
"Many women do noble things,
but you surpass them all."

Proverbs 31:28–29

Charm is deceptive and beauty
is fleeting;
but a woman who fears the
LORD
is to be praised.

Proverbs 31:30

Give her the reward she has
earned,
and let her works bring her
praise at the city gate.

Proverbs 31:31

Notes

Introduction

1. If you have already completed the 90-Day Renewal or read *Becoming the Woman I Want to Be*, some of the early foundational material will be a review for you. But as the weeks progress, we will be covering many subjects and establishing habits that go far beyond the 90-Day Renewal. Be patient and enjoy the reminders!

Week One: Faith Foundations

1. **Day 1:** Jack Canfield with Janet Switzer, *The Success Principles: How to Get from Where You Are to Where You Want to Be* (New York: HarperCollins, 2005), 23.

2. **Day 2:** Henri J. M. Nouwen, *From Fear to Love: Lenten Reflections on the Prodigal Son* (Creative Communications for the Parish, Fenton, MO, 1998), 11.

3. **Day 2:** Bruce Wilkinson, *Secrets of the Vine: Breaking Through to Abundance* (Sisters, OR: Multnomah, 2001), 107.

4. **Day 5:** "Humor, Laughter & Health," HelpGuide.org. http://helpguide.org/life/humor_laughter_health.htm.

5. **Day 5:** George Vaillant, *Aging Well: Surprising Guideposts to a Happier Life from the Landmark Harvard Study of Adult Development* (New York: Little, Brown & Co., 2002).

6. **Day 5:** As of this writing, January 2008.

Week Three: Healthy Eating

1. **Day 16:** I'm not saying you need to become a vegetarian for life. This is a ten-day experiment. However, you can make a permanent move away from foods with ingredients you cannot pronounce!

2. **Day 16:** Check with your physician first if you have any chronic health issues. If you are concerned about a strict vegetarian diet, use flax oil as a salad dressing with tofu, nuts, and seeds to add some protein.

3. **Day 17:** http://www.drbob4health.com/FoodsToAvoid/Sugar.htm.

4. **Day 18:** http://www.mercola.com/2006/sep/16/portion_distortion_larger_servings_lead_to_larger_waistlines.htm.

5. **Day 18:** Vaillant, *Aging Well*.

Week Four: Strengthening Your Body

1. **Day 22:** A study by a Boston hospital, published in the *New England Journal of Medicine*, cited in Janet Holm McHenry, *PrayerWalk* (Colorado Springs: Waterbrook, 2001), 41.

2. **Day 22:** Ibid., 42.

3. **Day 22:** Ibid.

4. **Day 23:** Cheryl Townsley, *Food Smart* (Colorado Springs: Pinon Press, 1994), 173.

5. **Day 23:** Nalgene is a brand of reusable polycarbonate containers that are extremely well made so they are durable and virtually unbreakable. Best of all, they are easy to wash; won't pick up odors; won't leech chemicals, as plastic bottles do; and are better for the environment. Nalgene bottles are available at outdoor and sporting goods stores.

6. **Day 25:** Albert E. Carter, "The Most Efficient, Effective Form of Exercise Yet Devised by Man," American Institute of Reboundology, audio CD recording. Used with permission.

7. **Day 25:** Ibid.

8. **Day 26:** Donna Partow, *Becoming the Woman I Want to Be* (Minneapolis: Bethany House, 2004), 189.

9. **Day 26:** For information on the protein powder I recommend, visit www.donnapartow.com.

10. **Day 27:** If you live in an area with severe weather, pick up a treadmill at a local yard sale!

Week Six: Financial Planning

1. **Day 37:** According to research conducted by Steve Moore of Crown Financial Ministries, per phone interview, January 2005.

2. **Day 37:** Dave Ramsey, *The Total Money Makeover* (Nashville, Thomas Nelson, 2003), 93.

3. **Day 37:** Robert Kiyosaki, *Rich Dad, Poor Dad* (New York: Warner Business Books, 1997), 35.

4. **Day 37:** Ibid., 58.

5. **Day 37:** Ibid., 61.

6. **Day 38:** Ramsey, *Total Money Makeover*, 109–32.

7. **Day 39:** Credit counseling statistics, creditcounselingbiz.com/credit_counsel ing_statistics.htm.

8. **Day 39:** Robert Allen, *Multiple Streams of Income* (New York: John Wiley & Sons, Inc., 2000), 25.

9. **Day 39:** Ramsey, *Total Money Makeover*, 41.

10. **Day 40:** "Why Money Is the Leading Cause of Divorce," November 11, 1996, www.highbeam.com/doc/1G1-18930297.html.

11. **Day 40:** Allen, *Multiple Streams of Income*, 26.

12. **Day 40:** www.usatoday.com/money/economy/2006–03–04–americans-savings_ x.htm.

13. **Day 40:** David Bach, *The Automatic Millionaire* (New York: Broadway Books, 2004), 57–78.

14. **Day 40:** Ibid., 112.

15. **Day 40:** Allen, *Multiple Streams of Income*, 54.

16. **Day 40:** "Warren Buffet on Index Funds," December 26, 2007, http://socialize.morningstar.com/NewSocialize/forums/1/2469214/showthread.aspx?MRR=1198707666.

Week Seven: Personal Appearance

1. **Day 44:** http://www.consumer.gov/weightloss/bmi.htm.

2. **Day 46:** Trinny Woodall and Susannah Constantine, *What Not to Wear* (New York: Riverhead Books, 2002).

Week Eight: Home Enterprises

1. **Day 50:** According to Nielsen BookScan, 93 percent of books sold fewer than 1,000 units in 2004, reported on www.thebookstandard.com.

2. **Day 50:** Janet Switzer, *Instant Income* (New York: McGraw-Hill, 2007), 1.

3. **Day 51:** Mark Victor Hansen and Robert G. Allen, *The One Minute Millionaire* (New York: Harmony Books, 2002).

4. **Day 51:** Donald J. Trump and Robert T. Kiyosaki, *Why We Want You to Be Rich* (Scottsdale, AZ: Rich Press, 2006).

5. **Day 54:** Linda Rosencrance, www.computerworld.com article, May 24, 2006.

Week Nine: Household Management

1. **Day 59:** Dr. Joyce M. Woods, "Create a Safe and Healthy Home," www.toxicfree moms.com/CSHH.htm.

2. **Day 60:** Mark Brandenburg, "Giving Kids Chores," Keepkidshealthy.com, http://www.keepkidshealthy.com/experts/mbb/giving_kids_chores.html.

Week Ten: Family Relationships

1. **Day 65:** Ruth Tucker, *From Jerusalem to Irian Jaya* (Grand Rapids: Zondervan, 1983).

2. **Day 65:** "Christian Education Program," September 11, 2007. www.obiweb.org/prod03.htm.

Week Eleven: The Ministry of the Home

1. **Day 71:** Laurie Tarkan, "Benefits of the Dinner Table Ritual," *New York Times*, May 3, 2005, http://www.nytimes.com/2005/05/03/health/nutrition/03dinn.html.

2. **Day 71:** Dianne Neumack-Sztainec, PhD, "Family Meals and Disordered Eating in Adolescents," January 2008, http://archpedi.ama-assn.org/cgi/content/full/162/1/17.

3. **Day 71:** Tarkan, "Benefits of the Dinner Table Ritual."

4. **Day 71:** "Busy Families Rediscover the Pleasure of the Dinner Hour" at prweb.com, July 6, 2005.

5. **Day 71:** The Bureau of Labor Statistics, cited in "Busy Families Rediscover the Pleasure of the Family Dinner Hour."

Week Twelve: Retirement Planning

1. **Day 78:** Miranda Hitti, "New Record for U.S. Life Expectancy," www.webmd.com/news/20060419/Record-us-life-expectancy.

2. **Day 78:** Jeanne Wei, MD, PhD, and Sue Levkoff, ScD, *Aging Well: The Complete Guide to Physical and Emotional Health* (New York: John Wiley, 2000), vii–viii.

3. **Day 78:** Kim Kiyosaki, *Rich Woman* (Scottsdale, AZ: Rich Press, 2006).

4. **Day 78:** Ibid.

5. **Day 78:** "Born Again Christians Just as Likely to Divorce as Are Non-Christians," September 8, 2004, www.barna.org/FlexPage.aspx?Page=BarnaUpdate&BarnaUpdateID=170.

6. **Day 79:** David Bach, *The Automatic Millionaire Homeowner* (New York: Broadway Books, 2005).

Week Thirteen: Finish Strong

1. **Day 85:** Adapted from the book I coauthored with Cameron Partow, *Families That Play Together Stay Together* (Minneapolis: Bethany House, 1996), which is now out of print.

2. **Day 85:** Sally Beare, *50 Secrets to the World's Longest Living People* (New York: Marlowe & Company, 2005).

Donna Partow is a bestselling author and Christian communicator with a compelling testimony of God's transforming power. Her previous books, including *Becoming a Vessel God Can Use* and *Becoming the Woman I Want to Be*, have sold almost a million copies on all seven continents and have been translated into numerous languages.

Donna's unique message cuts across social, cultural, and denominational barriers. She toured with Women of Virtue for three years and now travels worldwide, sharing her faith at church conferences, on crowded street corners, in prisons, caves, jungles, and anywhere else people need to experience God's love. She has been featured on hundreds of radio and television programs.

To learn more about Donna's ministry, or if your church or organization would like to invite her to speak, visit www.donnapartow.com. Her popular website is filled with practical tools to help you transform your life so God can transform the world through you.

"If you're stuck in a rut in your personal Bible study . . . or you long for God to use you in fresh new ways . . . or you and your small group are tired of pat answers . . . this book is for you!"

—SUSAN ALEXANDER YATES, author of
A House Full of Friends and *And Then I Had Kids*

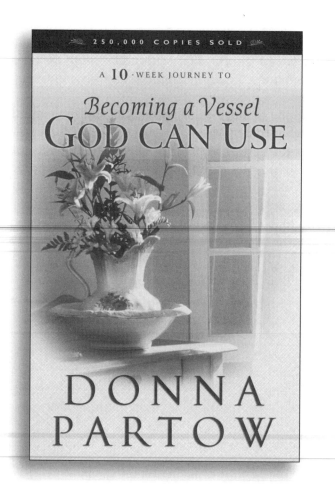

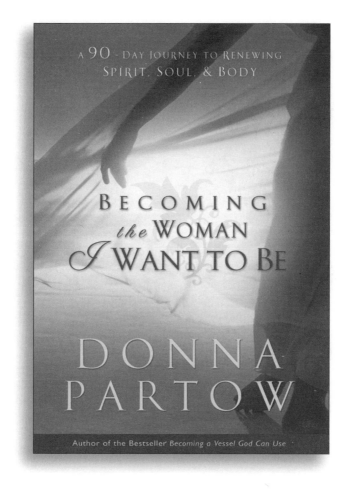 

Are you READY to discover a better way of LIFE?

A 10-Week Journey to Hope and Healing

this isn't the life I signed up for

Author of the Bestselling
Becoming a Vessel God Can Use

DONNA PARTOW